Catholic Girl

The Life and Times of Mabel Normand

By

Sean Crose

BearManor Media.com

Catholic Girl: The Life and Times of Mabel Normand

Disclaimer: All content presented under this title was gained from common and reputable sources in both print and online. If any details within this title are found to be incorrect, the author apologizes and will be happy to make corrections in the next edition.

Credit the TMNFE Collection.

Typesetting and layout by PKJ Passion Global

Published in the USA by
BearManor Media
1317 Edgewater Dr #110
Orlando FL 32804
www.BearManorMedia.com

Softcover Edition
ISBN-10:
ISBN-13: 979-8-88771-473-8

Published in the USA by Bear Manor Media

Dedication: As always, to Jen

Thank yous: Special thanks go to Mary Sharnick, Stephen Normand, Stephanie Dionne, Wayne Sharnick, Heather Nanni, Ben Ohmart, and Sarah Christopher, all of whom provided much needed guidance and support.

Contents

Prologue 9
Staten Island 10
Max Linder 14
From Sweatshop to Studio 17
Flickering Images on A Screen 21
A Face to Be Found Everywhere 25
D.W. Griffith 28
"Great Big Brown Eyes, And Eyelashes Two Inches Long" 31
Mack Sennett 35
Starting From Scratch 38
John Bunny 41
"Troublesome Secretaries" 44
Fred Mace 48
"A Determined and Unrepentant Comedienne" 51
Ford Sterling 54
"The Diving Girl" 57
Thomas Edison 61
California 64
Roscoe Arbuckle 69
A Comedy of Irreverence 72
Barney Oldfield 75
Insanity Can Be Fun 78
Minta Durfee 82
Moving Behind The Camera 85
Charlie Chaplin 90

Also Known as Muriel Fortescue	94
Marie Dressler	98
The First Feature Length Comedy	102
Franz Ferdinand	106
"Queen Of the Movies"	109
Mae Busch	113
Beyond The Breaking Point	117
Vincent Chiappa	120
Mabel Normand Studio	123
Minnie Devereaux	127
"Mickey"	130
Samuel Goldwyn	136
A Thousand Dollars A Week	139
Edith Wilson	142
"Dark, Windy Days and Chocolate Cake"	145
Alexei Nikolaevich Romanov	149
Hollywood Pioneer	152
F. Richard Jones	156
Back To Mack (Professionally)	159
Virginia Rappe	163
Molly O'	166
William Desmond Taylor	170
"Under A Terrible Nervous Strain"	173
William Randolph Hearst	177
Media Assault	180
William H. Hays	185
Europe	188
Edna Purviance	192
The Extra Girl	195

Courtland Dines	198
Another Shooting	201
Asa Keyes	205
Rumors Thrive	208
Mary Pickford	212
The Performance Of A Lifetime	215
Al Woods	218
“The Little Mouse”	221
Hal Roach	226
After The Tempest	229
Stan Laurel And Oliver Hardy	232
The Final Films	235
Lew Cody	238
Marriage	241
Sid Sutherland	244
The Long Fight	247
Frances Pottenger	253
Those Going About Their Everyday Lives	256
Epilogue	261
Notes	262

Prologue

She's in a fashionable bathing suit on a dock which leads to a rough patch of water, perhaps Long Island Sound. The waves are choppy and menacing on this day. With her swimming cap and bright smile, it looks as if this attractive young woman is going to throw risk aside and jump right into the tumultuous sea water. Whether she does or doesn't, however, remains a mystery, for the black and white footage stops before we can learn what happens. No matter what actually does or doesn't transpire we will always see her at the edge, just about to jump, yet forever remaining on just this side of safety.

Staten Island

Hollywood pioneer Mabel Normand was born on November 9th, 1892, in the town of New Brighton on Staten Island in New York. Her mother Mary was from Rhode Island and was of Irish stock while her father Claude was a Canadian immigrant who worked as a carpenter for nearby Snug Harbor, a retirement community for ex-sailors. No one in the future star's family was particularly focused on show business, much less the burgeoning motion picture industry at the time of Mabel's birth, though it was said Claude would arrange shows at Snug Harbor and was proficient at the piano, a skill he would reportedly pass on to his daughter.

There is some debate concerning what the year of Mabel's birth truly was. Her tomb at Cavalry Cemetery in Hollywood states she was born in 1905 while the 1900 census has Mabel being born in 1893. There is, however, reason not only for the confusion but for why 1892 should be recognized as the year of Mabel's birth. The Mabel Normand Estate, which is controlled and operated by Mabel's great nephew Stephen Normand, provides adequate insight not only into Mabel's birth, but into the stressful circumstances which surrounded it.

Amabel Ethelreid Normand was born prematurely, so prematurely that it seemed as if the infant was literally about to go from womb to tomb in a very short period of time. What's more, after giving birth to her first daughter, Mary was profoundly ill herself. To make matters even more unsettling, baby Mabel was born with a caul, a membrane which covers the head of an infant. With the infant mortality rate at the time being at least ten percent, and the mortality rate for mothers of newborns being not far behind, the Normand family had good reason to fear for both Mary's and Mabel's lives.

Being a devoutly Catholic household – something that would have an enormous impact on Mabel throughout her life – the Normand's summoned a priest immediately to baptize the newborn and to tend to the spiritual needs of the Normand clan. Fortunately, both mother and daughter went on to survive their illnesses. Yet the chaos surrounding the birth of Mabel and the near death of both her and her mother naturally led to a misunderstanding as to the where's and when's of Mabel's entrance into the world. Records for both births and Catholic baptisms at the time generally tended to be accessible and/or accurate, at least in the United States. The tempest surrounding Mabel's first days on earth, however, did not offer family, civic, or religious officials the luxury of performing up to their usual standards.

As for her childhood, young Mabel certainly witnessed firsthand how difficult life could be. There were, however, enormously positive aspects to her Staten Island upbringing. North Brighton being right on the Staten Island shoreline, Mabel was able to become an excellent swimmer and diver. She also clearly came from a loving home, with two brothers, Ralph and Claude Jr., and a younger sister Gladys, all of whom she adored throughout her life. Indeed, the Normand's were so close that Mabel made sure never to cease being an active member of the family, even while living in high style a continent away, traveling the world, or simply being one of the most recognizable faces on earth.

Still, there were extremely serious challenges facing the young Mabel while growing up. "Up to the time I left school there was nothing eventful or particularly interesting in my life," Mable was to say long after she had become one of the world's biggest celebrities. This, however, simply wasn't true. Although Mabel's upbringing may not have been as searing as those of future peers Charlie Chaplin and Roscoe "Fatty" Arbuckle, there's no doubt that her youth was a grueling one. First of all, her oldest brother, Claude Jr, died from tuberculosis at the exceedingly young age of 16 – a brutal loss for any child. To make matters worse, Mabel contracted tuberculosis herself, which, at the turn of the last century, immediately ended any chance of her having a conventional childhood.

With her daughter's symptoms known to range from fevers to coughing up blood, Mary wisely kept Mabel out of school, lest Mabel inadvertently spread the contagious disease to her peers or teachers. Not only then was Mabel unable to be educated past grammar school, she was also largely kept away from socializing and spending time with people her own age outside of her siblings. Such circumstances can obviously have a horrible effect physically, emotionally, and socially on someone who has not yet entered into adulthood.

"Mabel," wrote journalist and close friend Sidney Sutherland years later, "recalls that she was quite lonely then; that while she knew all about the neighborhood children and divined what they were thinking about, they never really knew her or had any idea what was taking place in the unexplored jungle of her thoughts... this manifestly set the child apart from childish associations, just as in maturity it raised a barrier few adults ever were permitted to scale."

Indeed, one can picture a young Mabel standing alone, away from those she might accidentally harm, on the shore of the Hudson, watching the river slowly work its way towards the Atlantic, realizing what a great world there was beyond the horizon, one she would most likely never fully partake in. Mabel, however, was – in a very positive way - an oddity, someone who would go on to seemingly rule the world that she had once largely been a victim of. Her journey from a sickly child of humble beginnings to a famous, extraordinarily wealthy, groundbreaking star, director, and producer of motion pictures would prove to be nothing short of jaw dropping.

How, though, did this obscure girl from working class Staten Island manage to defy the odds in such a profound way, especially in a world where women weren't even allowed to vote? The truth is that being raised in a Catholic home meant Mabel was brought up to have hope, even with the passing of a brother, even with her father earning humble pay. Indeed, hope was and is seen by Roman Catholics as being a virtue. A sense of hope can also lead to an openness to life's opportunities and possibilities. Mable never proved to be a person to say, "Oh, why bother?" Rather, she spent her life and career grasping at opportunities as if they were gifts. It was a practice that would serve her well. A lonely working-class upbringing near a retirement home for sailors in an unfashionable shoreline community might not have been impressive to most – but it gave a young Mabel Normand a solid platform from which to spring.

Max Linder

Behold the dapper Frenchman.

The gruesome murder-suicide (Or is it double suicide?) that claimed the life of both him and his young wife remains decades away. Now the top hatted, mustachioed gentleman is in his prime, oozing confidence, too much confidence perhaps, as he is about to flop about a frozen Parisian pond called the Lac Daumesnil in the middle of winter for the sole purpose of making people laugh. The year is 1906. The gentleman's name is Max Linder and he's working to show the world that black and white images of silent characters on a motion picture screen can amuse untold numbers of people without the actors having to utter a single audible word.

The motion picture was called "The Skater's Debut," and it introduced the world to Linder's alter ego – known simply as "Max." A snazzy, sharply dressed member of the cosmopolitan upper class, Max, contrary to his dapper appearance, simply cannot help but get himself into trouble, be it crashing repeatedly on hard ice, screwing up a meeting with his future in-laws, or even making his way through traffic on foot. His background may have been more impressive than that of the average French theater goer, but Max's comical disasters made him relatable. It was a brilliant stroke of creativity, actually – having the role of jester played by a member of the elite.

In truth, Linder was arguably from the same class as his alter ego. Born Gabriel-Maximilien Leuvielle (close to a decade before Mabel was born) in the town of Girande, France, Linder came from a well to do family which owned and operated a vineyard. Linder himself was expected to get into the vineyard business, but the young man had other ideas – mainly becoming involved in the theater. Although his family didn't truly understand their son's creative leanings, Linder had been a pro thespian since at least the dawn of the 20th century when he fumbled comically before a camera on the frozen pond that cold Parisian day. To say the young man would go on to attain incredible success would be an understatement.

In large part, that success arrived courtesy of the Pathé Brothers Company, which soon enough made the bold decision to promote Linder himself as well as the films he starred in. This particular strategy proved to be a game changer. For up until that moment, studios were known for being in the motion picture business, not the celebrity business. Linder's "Max" character, however, became a known and highly sought-after commodity. Linder, at least as much as the films he starred in, was the selling point. People who paid to see Linder's films knew what they were getting – sophisticated clownery that was sharply funny.

In the 21st century, such a strategy became known as branding. In the first decade of the 1900's, however, it was thoroughly unheard of – at least as far as the motion picture industry was concerned. So successful did Linder become, however, that his works were shown internationally. No longer a French brand, Max Linder morphed into a global brand. Linder, simply put, became the world's first movie star. Suffice it to say, motion picture studios in America took note soon enough. Stories and scenarios were still important, of course, but star power was about to reign as king of the motion picture business.

Naturally, there were pitfalls to the new star centered film industry, namely that the actors themselves ended up having more power than perhaps even the studios. Suffice to say, there was a reason why actors in films remained relatively anonymous up until this point. Anonymity equaled lack of power for an actor. Once the public found a name to put with a face, however, the actor behind that name and face often became the financial bread and butter of an entire studio. Such things were worrying to studio heads – but Linder proved that the pros outweighed the cons in enormous ways.

And so, Linder, fumbling on the ice in Paris, his screams and gasps soon to be inaudible to motion picture audiences, stood – or, rather, poorly skated – on the cusp of a level of success he himself might not even have believed imaginable. Ultimately, changing times, a world war, and mental illness destroyed the popular Linder. The wheel had already begun to turn, however, and the man's impact on the film world survived and prospered for decade after decade. In fact, the world outside of France and Europe, indeed, outside of the west itself, embraced numerous movie stars within the next ten years. A massive cultural trend started, as did a massive social trend, for the impact of these stars extended far beyond movie theaters.

Advertising, activism, and even politics was soon to be part of the terrain for those who made a living acting in relatively short, black and white motion pictures. Companies wanted the images of stars in their newspaper ads. Powerful government officials wanted to use these stars to promote their pet causes. Children emulated them. And massive sums of money were earned by those who helped these stars along the journey of celebrity. Starting with Linder, big names became big business. The motion picture studios soon did all they could to keep their stars happy while perpetually being on the hunt for new stars to make money off. It was a cruel business, really, but for those who benefited from it, the star centered motion picture industry proved to be the source of monumental sums of money, popularity, and influence.

In the meantime, Linder stumbled along on the frozen pond, fortunate not to break a leg or get a concussion. At the same time, close to four thousand miles away, young Mabel witnessed firsthand the underside of the American experiment. The Staten Island teenager had absolutely no idea the kind of future that awaited her, nor how far removed she would one day be from where she started. Were Mabel to somehow see into the future, those she would tell of it would have found her insane. And perhaps with good reason. Those people, however, would be wrong.

From Sweatshop to Studio

As a teenager, Mabel took the Staten Island Ferry into lower Manhattan in order to work. Tuberculosis may have kept her from a good education, but those who made money off what was essentially child labor weren't troubled by such matters as who did or didn't attend school. And so there Mabel sat, riding one of the five spacious boats that made up the Ferry service– each one named after one the five boroughs of New York City – as the vessel slowly worked its way through the waves towards the expansive Manhattan skyline. In truth, Staten Island itself had become part of New York City shortly after Mabel was born. Technically Mabel was merely traveling from one part of the city to another. The truth, however, was that Mabel may as well have been going back and forth between distant worlds.

While New Brighton might not have been considered a quaint hamlet, it was a community of residents who essentially went about their daily lives without much notice or fanfare. Manhattan, on the other hand, had an entire personality of its own, an outsized personality teeming with commerce, immigration, pedestrians, vehicles, criminals, and towering structures.

Indeed, one of those structures reached even higher into the sky than those around it. In fact, the Butterick Building stood prominently on Spring Street and, at fifteen stories in height, stood imposingly over a large portion of the city. Butterick's business was the publication of sewing patterns, and it dominated the industry. Through its magazines, particularly *The Delineator*, those sewing patterns allowed Butterick to unquestionably reign as one of the biggest publishers on earth.

And it showed.

The inside of Butterick's massive headquarters had been designed by Tiffany. Due to the enormous number of periodicals published within its walls – between thirty-five and forty – the building contained eighty-six printing presses. According to *Village Preservation*: "With such a large floor area the building accommodated a large range of activities, from seamstresses making sample garments to workers printing and shipping sewing pattern envelopes." Mabel's job at Butterick, according to Stephan Normand, was to cut out the many fashionable designs that were to make their way to publication. The Butterick Building may have had a Tiffany interior, but it's clear that Mabel and her immediate coworkers toiled in a sweat shop.

One could only imagine a fourteen-year-old Mabel arriving on Manhattan Island off the ferry, then making her way through the noisy streets towards the towering Butterick headquarters, where work men loaded carriages with product to be delivered by horse to merchants and customers. The sights, sounds and utter HUGENESS of it all must have been overwhelming to the girl from New Brighton. Small in stature, Mabel must have looked like she was being swallowed whole as she entered the enormous building.

Still, what today is considered underage labor was a common practice of the time. "With so many avenues available for employment," states the *US Bureau of Labor Statistics*, "children were seen as a resource, rather than a drain, to many parents who were struggling financially." And the Normand's were certainly struggling. A carpenter at a retirement community couldn't bring down a great deal of money in the very early 1900s. What's more, Claude Normand had five mouths to feed. As was the practice of the time, the children who were of age – including those who were barely teenagers – would be expected to work. Hence poor, uneducated Mabel's sad regular trek to lower Manhattan to toil as an anonymous young cog of a crushingly enormous and overbearing wheel. Objectively, it would appear her future was quite bleak – yet Mabel had two distinct things going for her.

First, the young girl from New Brighton was pretty. Standing no more than 5'1, the diminutive Staten Islander had large brown eyes and very – some might say extremely – long eyelashes. Coupled

After all, if a character's words or exposition were very much needed, a small card appeared on the screen with clear writing. As for soundtracks, theaters would provide their own to go with the action on the screen. As time went on, entire orchestras played in synch along with the moving images before them. Motion pictures may not have been entirely lifelike, but the experience was enthralling to audiences nonetheless – just as it remains enthralling in the 21st century.

Perhaps surprising to some, the motion picture industry in the United States got its start in New York. It made sense too, as New York at the time was, as it remains in the 21st century, the hub of the American economy as well as American culture. New York was the city for money and motion pictures were big money indeed. Plus, there were unseen numbers of people who loved nothing more than to appear as images on the screen. Transporting copies of films nationwide? What better place to have the hub of distribution be than New York City itself? Indeed, the reasons seem obvious. Boats and trains could easily deliver motion pictures across the country at a relatively fast pace. Plus, there were so many people in the city, both entertainers and specialists, that there was an enormous pool of potential employees to choose from.

Of course, New York City was crowded, and it took room to film motion pictures, often lots of room. Thomas Edison, the father of motion pictures, had opened a studio in New Jersey. And to be sure, the area in and around nearby Union Country was both inexpensive and easily accessible for motion picture locations. It also had a plethora of wonderful natural spots that could fill in for all variety of settings. The west may not have been calling, but just across the river from New York City, New Jersey appeared to be a prime place for motion pictures to be filmed.

And so, for the moment, at least, studios like Biograph, Vitograph, and Kalem called New York City home. There appeared to be plenty of business for everyone involved, because business – frankly – was booming. And the industry was always looking for people with special skills, talent, good looks, or a combination of the three. The competition, however, was fierce. Only those with the combination of boldness, looks, and unique skills could truly succeed. Many people wanted to make it big in the motion picture industry. The vast majority wouldn't. There were, however, always a few that would rise above the others.

A Face to Be Found Everywhere

"I attended school, the last few years, at North Westport, Mass., near Martha's Vineyard. Once a month I went home, in charge of a stewardess on the Fall River Line, but I stayed at school, during the summer, studying hard and trying to skip a class and get ahead faster."

It's impossible to write about Mabel honestly without mentioning the fact that she was, or became, a world class exaggerator and fibber after she attained stardom. There is no evidence of an education near Martha's Vineyard. Nor is there evidence of once-a-month trips to Staten Island in the care of a stewardess. These fabrications may as well have come from the imaginings of a press agent – which perhaps they did.

Even fabricated stories contain elements of truth, however. In that same *L.A. Examiner* article, Mabel spoke of her time as an artists' model in New York. The fact that Mabel worked as a model while a teenager can be verified by, among other examples, the numerous likenesses of her that could be found in advertisements of the time, a considerable amount of which are still in existence. There may not be evidence of a boarding school education, but there is an abundance of evidence to prove Mabel knew what she was talking about when it came to working as a model for some of the top artists of her day.

To be sure, Mabel's promotion from floor worker to artist's muse changed her outlook on life. Modeling was not, however, something Mabel's personality was inclined to partake in wholeheartedly. "Most of the work I did was to pose for heads for magazine covers," she said. "And I didn't like it. I hated to stand still. I hated to be simply a means by which someone else was creating something. I wanted to do it myself, but I couldn't. I had only the longing, without the ability."

According to Sutherland, Butterick art department head Kleinschmidt told Mabel "that when he couldn't use her, other artists, to whom he would give her a note of introduction, would employ her; that additional money was to be made posing for lantern slides with which popular songs of that era were illustrated, and in working for the commercial photographers." This not only offered Mabel more money, but it also allowed her to get out of Butterick and into the bustling New York world. As Mablel told the *L.A. Examiner*, she went on to pose for the likes of artists such as James Montgomery Flagg, who went on to create the iconic image of Uncle Sam, and Charles Dana Gibson, whose models - including Mabel – became known as "Gibson Girls."

"I made money, too," Mabel would recall, "at the commercial photographers. posing for newspaper and magazine advertisements. There was tremendous variety in this: hats, cold cream, hairbrushes, shoes, stockings, combs, hair tonics, hair nets, veils, gloves, satchels, lingerie, umbrellas, necklaces, frocks, evening wraps, furs, bracelets -- everything the world at large pauses to glance at in that shop window of life known as advertising."

It wasn't easy, but Mabel was unafraid to hustle in order to earn money. "I received $1.50 in the morning," Mabel said, "and the same amount in the afternoon for posing. Thirty cents of that went for carfare and ferry fare and I had to spend a little money for lunch. Sometimes, however, I didn't get any lunch. I used my lunch hour instead to pose for a commercial photographer. Wearing a hat or a dress that he wanted to photograph, we models would stand around in front of the camera during the noon hour and he would sell the pictures to trade journals." Perhaps more than anything else, modeling honed Mabel's ambition. All those wonderful and expensive outfits she posed in had to be returned when the painting was done or the required photographs were taken. Then, later on in the day, it was back to Staten Island and her struggling family. Mabel later made it clear that she wanted better, and not just for herself.

"I wondered," she said, "what it would be like to have a wardrobe that would permit giving away clothes like those I was wearing and I used to visualize the parties at which they had been worn, giving myself all the airs and graces that I felt I would have put on and smiling condescendingly at multitudes of suitors in evening clothes with ribbons across their shirt fronts. Very distinguished were all the men of my dream parties, with iron gray hair and manners that included bowing from the waist and much courtly kissing of the hand."

Such youthful fantasies have an impact in shaping lives. The daydreams of high-end parties may have faded into the background of Mabel's psyche, but the desire to have what those higher up the Edwardian ladder of her time had most distinctly did not. Nor did the desire to engage in generous behavior. Mabel was a Catholic girl, after all – something she would never stop being – and Catholic girls were to think beyond themselves. Sure enough, as she became more and more successful, Mabel's charitable actions – often done in secret - became hallmarks of her personality among those who were to know her best.

At the moment, though, Mabel was a busy working model who nonetheless was still looking for more. The question was, what? Here was a young woman looking for a chance to attain financial security and what in the 21st century would be known as "job satisfaction." Fortunately for Mabel, there was no questioning the fact that she was in the right place to satisfy her employment desires. There were all variety of opportunities in New York for all variety of occupations.

Yet there was also a great amount of competition to be found in New York. Still, Mabel was self-assured. Not only had she climbed to the level of top model, but she had also experienced a bit of what one can achieve if one were daring enough to try. Besides, modeling may not have paid enormous sums of money, but it allowed Mabel to, at least to some degree, become known. Newspapers, magazines, Coca Cola advertisements – hers was a face to be found everywhere.

D.W. Griffith

His father had been a soldier in the Civil War known as Thunder Jake, who was said to have been an owner of five slaves. After the war, Thunder Jake returned to Kentucky, having been physically wounded and most likely psychologically wounded fighting for the Confederacy. After fathering a total of seven children, Jacob Griffith, "Thunder Jake" himself, passed away, leaving his family and a pile of debts behind him. The entire experience was no doubt jarring for the Griffith family, but seems to have been particularly acute for Thunder Jake's youngest son, David. "Young David had adored and idolized his father," Kenneth S Lynn was to write in the pages of "American Scholar" over a hundred years later. "Yet he never felt able to count on his love."

Perhaps young David, who came to be known as D.W. Griffith, was right in feeling his father's love couldn't be counted on. Neither of Griffith's parents appear to have been keen on sharing their feelings. Out of this less than nurturing environment emerged a man who was intent on making his mark on the world. And the venue through which D.W. Griffith chose to make that mark was the world of motion pictures. Enhancing such previously employed tools such as camera pans, close-ups and still shots, Griffith went on to become one of the most renowned directors of the early 20th century motion picture industry.

Yet Griffith would also earn a large degree of notoriety. In 1915, he made "Birth of a Nation," an epic, highly successful film that nonetheless painted the Ku Klux Klan in the role of heroes against armed Black Freemen in the south. Not only is the film controversial by 21st century standards, some people at the time of its release complained about overt racism being present, as well. Griffith took the charges of racism to heart and made the progressive minded "Intolerance" in response. Wherever Griffith's heart was, there was no denying he remained in the collective memory, both as an artist and as someone who, at the very least, had racist leanings.

By the time he made "Birth of a Nation," however, Griffith had spent the better part of a decade making far less hot button material (though there was to be no denying the casual racism to be found in seemingly endless aspects of American life at the time, such as in the United States Armed forces, where personal were separated by skin color). Starting in 1908, Griffith was directing motion pictures, mostly short in nature, for Biograph Studios in New York. He had begun at Biograph as an actor as well as a writer, earning five dollars a day. Through a series of mishaps, however, the southern gentleman found himself as the studio's head director.

Known officially as the American Mutoscope and Biograph Company, Biograph was headquartered in a brownstone at 11 East Fourteenth Street by Union Square in Manhattan. It employed the latest in technology, primarily Cooper Hewitt lamps, which made it possible to film indoors twenty-four hours a day. When a director needed to film an afternoon scene after the sun had gone down, the new Cooper Hewitt lights made that afternoon scene possible. This development gave Biograph a leg up on its competition, namely Thomas Edison, who had his own studio in New Jersey. Being in an environment like the one at Biograph, which stood at the forefront of the contemporary motion picture industry, likely matched Griffith's personality, and artistic ambitions, well.

Not that the man was always happy. In her memoir "When The Movies Were Young," Griffith's first wife, Linda Arvidson, wrote of a man sometimes weighed down by his profession, even to the point of lashing out. "We were always conscious of the fact that we were in this messy business," she stated, "because everything else had failed—because nobody had seemed to want us, and we just hadn't been able to hang on any longer." Still, Arvidson claimed her husband made it a point to succeed behind the camera regardless. "It was his job," she stated, "and he would dignify it." Besides, it wasn't as if the movie business was stifling Griffith's ambitions. To the contrary.

One of the things Griffith did to satisfy those ambitions was to snatch a talented young actress named Flora Lawrence away from the competing Vitagraph company. Offering the young woman twenty-five dollars a week allowed Griffith not only to find a leading actress who suited his tastes, but also allowed him to help create the first American movie star. Known as "Biograph Betty," Lawrence became so popular with the public that she went beyond being an employee of her studio and became a brand of and to herself. Realizing how popular she was, Lawrence went on to make demands of Biograph, demands which the company finally ended up having enough of, leading to her eventual firing in 1910. By that time, however, Griffith had another individual well situated to become his lead actress, one who would soon be a mentor to Mabel.

Like Mabel, Mary Pickford, was born in 1892. While Mabel was born on the eastern seaboard of the United States, Mary was born in Montreal, Canada. With her father having died young Mary, much like young Mabel, found herself having to help provide for the family. Whereas Mabel found employment in a sweatshop, however, Mary took to working in the theater. While a theater life appeared on the surface to have been better than a life toiling at Butterick, the grind that went with being a traveling stage actress proved to be quite grueling for Mary. It wasn't school, and it certainly wasn't play. It was work which required perfectionism and which by its very nature made no one particular place truly be home.

Yet, like Mabel and Griffith, Mary was incredibly ambitious. That ambition, along with talent, led her to Broadway, which then led her to Griffith, who knew a potential asset when he saw one. Still, the son of Thunder Jake needed someone to play opposite his Canadian leaning lady, someone preferably different in looks and perhaps even temperament. That someone was far closer in vicinity to the Biograph studios on 11 East Fourteenth Street than he might have imagined.

"Great Big Brown Eyes, And Eyelashes Two Inches Long"

Mabel may not have been crazy about posing for cameramen when not modeling for artists, but it was while posing for the camera that she found her connection to the future. "I was posing at the studios of Mr. Gibson and Mr. Flagg, and augmenting my slender wages by parading during the noon hour before a fashion camera," she said. "It was there that I met Alice Joyce, and it was to her that I owed my first chance in motion pictures." According to Mabel, she saw Alice on the street one day after not having spotted her fellow model for some time. Alice told Mabel she was now acting in movies for the Kalem Company at its Manhattan studio and suggested Mabel stop by.

Mabel dutifully showed up at the studio after work that evening and was subsequently asked by "the assistant director" if she would like to be an extra in one of Kalem's films. "I told him I would like to try it," she said. "I was directed to be there at 8 o'clock the next morning to start for Fort Lee, New Jersey. I worked three days in that picture, and I never shall forget it." The job called for Mabel and other extras to run up and down a hill dressed as Puritans in the freezing cold while being chased by actors dressed as Indians. "At first it was all very interesting," Mabel said, "and I was filled with shivering enthusiasm. But after a while all the enthusiasm froze up and I concluded that motion pictures would be a wonderful career for an Eskimo lady but wasn't quite suited for me."

Mabel returned to modeling, but when Gibson informed her he would be away from his business for a while due to "litigation," Mabel took the advice of an actor she knew and had bumped into on the street named Frank Lanning. Lanning told Mabel he was working at the Biograph Studio and offered to introduce her to the casting director. "If Mr. Gibson had not suspended work that day," Mabel said. "I probably would have told Mr. Lanning that it was very nice of him to suggest it, but that I thought I'd better stick to posing." Gibson, however, was not working at his studio that day, which meant Mabel had time to do what she pleased.

"But I took the great plunge one day," she was to recall. "I got on a streetcar after I left Mr. Gibson's office and alighted in Union Square. I asked the first man I met at Eleven East Fourteenth St. for a job." Mary Pickford one day vividly recalled the first time she laid eyes on Mabel at the Biograph Building. "I was the first one to get a peek at her," Pickford remembered in 1916, "as she sat in the office waiting to see him." Mary immediately went to fetch Griffith, informing him there was a young woman waiting who he really should speak with. Right away Griffith asked if Mabel was blonde. Although Mabel was certainly not blonde, Mary convinced Griffith to give the diminutive model a look anyway.

"She has jet black, shiny hair," Mary told the director, "great big brown eyes, and eyelashes two inches long." Griffith decided to speak to Mabel, and – if Mary is to be believed – hired her on the spot. Mabel's lashes may not have been a full two inches long, but they were certainly long enough to be quite notable. "It was only ten minutes after the interview," Mary claimed, "that Miss Normand was engaged to play leads and heavies in the Biograph studio." And so, Mabel was back in the movie business.

She may not have physically been Griffith's "type" to cast, but there was no doubt the girl from Staten Island was attractive and personable enough to take a chance on. "I shall never forget Mr. Griffith," she would one day inform the readers of the *L.A. Examiner*. "Already he was one of the most important men in motion pictures, but he was as kind and simple in his talk with me as a man could possibly be. His voice charmed me, particularly. It had a timbre and a gentleness that encouraged me." There is, however, a discrepancy between Mabel's version of events and Mary's: According to Mabel she wasn't put in as a lead right away but was put to work right then and there as an extra.

Mabel claimed to have played a page in that first screen appearance – one of six. She was uncomfortable with what she felt was the immodesty of her costume. Still, Mabel worked late with the rest of the production and received ten dollars for her efforts rather than the usual five. Arriving home from the ferry that night, however, teenaged Mabel realized she had other problems to deal with besides her costume, for her mother was less than thrilled with her tardiness. "I got a scolding that made me realize how I had worried her," Mabel recollected. "And it put an end to motion picture work, for me, for a considerable time. Without bothering to telephone the Biograph studio that I was not coming back, I just quit, and went back to posing for Mr. Flagg, Mr. Gibson and several other artists."

This time, however, it wasn't so easy to walk off into the sunset. According to Mabel, she was confronted at the 42nd Street Subway Station sometime later by three Biograph employees who happened to bump into her. First, they wanted to know where she had been, as she was supposed to have returned after that first night to finish her job playing a page. Then, seeing how uncomfortable the girl was, they lightened up a bit and asked if she might be willing to give the movies another shot.

"We stood there quite a while talking. And they bought me a malted milk shake, with an egg in it," Mabel recollected. "I remember that because I had been contemplating such a purchase myself, but I couldn't afford the egg." Milk shake or not, it was time for Mabel to make a serious decision. These men were willing to stick their necks out so Griffith would agree to take her back on. Agreeing to go back to Biograph now dictated the course her life would take from then on. Modeling became a thing of the past. Throwing herself into motion pictures was nothing if not a risky proposition…but Mabel decided to be daring.

"Anyhow," she said, "the upshot of the conversation was that they enthused me all over again with motion picture work. They said they would explain it to Mr. Griffith and told me to ask my mother if I couldn't come back to the studio.... I did and she consented finally."

Mack Sennett

One of the men who confronted Mabel that day at the 42nd Street Station was a big Canadian gentleman of Irish descent named Mack Sennett. He may have seemed like an anonymous individual that day to passerby in Manhattan, but he became the single most influential person in Mabel's life, a man she loved, was tested by, left, and worked with for years on end. Theirs was one of the most remarkable relationships in Hollywood, a town and industry overflowing with relationships of note.

"Where in the world do you live, young lady?" Mabel remembered Mack asking her that day at the 42nd Street Station. "We telephoned all over Brooklyn and Staten Island trying to locate you." This is not the kind of question one expected a future suitor to ask the girl he would one day become engaged to. Yet, even though Mack's version of that afternoon encounter was slightly different from Mabel's (he had it taking place on Fifth Avenue, for instance) there is no denying that – although their relationship became remarkable - it was quite strange, as well.

For starters, Mack was close to thirteen years older than Mabel. What's more, he was reportedly boorish and didn't always practice the best hygiene. This is at least somewhat asserted by Sennet himself in his autobiography when he wrote about staying at the Alexandria Hotel during his first journey to California. "I could not really afford the comforts of the Alexandria," he wrote, "but it was about this time that I discovered what a joy it was to take a bath." Although he bathed while growing up in Canada, it was only on Saturdays. What's more, a bath at the time consisted of hot water being poured into a small tub in the family kitchen.

California was a long way away from Canada, but before arriving in the land that became known as the Golden State, Sennett had previously moved with his family to the northeastern United

States (where he claimed he developed a friendship with future President Calvin Coolidge) before finally settling in New York to make his career as a showman, eventually landing at the Biograph Building on 11 East Fourteenth Street.

As for Mack's personality, Arvidson left a less than flattering recollection of the man's early days working at the studio. "One of our regular 'extra' people was Mack Sennett," she wrote. "He quietly dubbed along like the rest, only he grouched. He never approved whole-heartedly of anything we did, nor how we did it, nor who did it. There was something wrong about all of us—even Mary Pickford!" There must have been something to the odd Canadian, however, otherwise Biograph surely wouldn't have kept Sennett around. "Beneath all this discontent," wrote Arvidson, "was the feeling that he wasn't being given a fair chance, which, along with a smoldering ambition, was the reason for the grouch."

Sennett got his chance soon enough, and when he did, he would run with it. Despite whatever flaws he may have had, Sennett became a groundbreaking force in motion picture comedy, showing a real flair for the zany and the surreal which perfectly aligned with the tastes of untold numbers of people across the world. Yet Sennett, like everyone else at Biograph, had to pay his dues before reaching the top of Olympus. He had to push himself. But push himself Sennett did, first by acting and writing out scenarios, then – finally – as a director. As Arvidson said: "Mack Sennett grouched himself into success."

Sennett, though, was more than a simple crudely behaved rube. Hard though some might have found it to believe, the man developed a very clear vision, for himself, for the films he was to make, and for the studio he was to eventually run. As much businessman as showman – if not more – Sennett proved stubborn and ruthless. While still learning the trade, however, he was persistent more than anything else. Arvidson wrote of Sennett walking alongside her husband as Griffith walked home from work, always trying to get the director's undivided attention. And whether the action was in New

York, Fort Lee, New Jersey, or on the coast of the Pacific Ocean, Sennet made sure he was present, to see and to be seen, to involve himself in whatever project was in motion in order to get ahead. The stocky Canadian was nothing if not bold.

That boldness may have brought with it success, but Sennett was eventually to learn that success isn't always a permanent thing. What's more, his driving ambition, over time, led to some serious regrets. Although he was successful enough to warrant an autobiography, he wrote that autobiography under a keen sense of failure. Although it may have been self-serving, Sennett's book, "King of Comedy" was also a study of genuine regret. Whatever the man's sins, it's hard not to feel sympathy for Sennett while reading certain portions of his first-person narrative.

"If you should take a pencil and make notes," he wrote. "or sit alone late at night and try to think about what you have amounted to, and why, and what became of your true dreams, you will probably agree with me about this: whatever your center ring was like and no matter what kind of show went on there, this is not where the most important things in your life happened."

Yet "The King of Comedy" was published in 1955, many years after he hounded D.W. Griffith along the streets of New York City. The passing of time can change perspective, offer clarity, and even provide wisdom. The more reflective version of Sennett present in "The King of Comedy" appears to have been largely absent during Sennett's formative years in show business. He might not have known what true fulfillment was, but the Mack Sennet who could be found at the Biograph Building during his apprentice years was on a clear mission to satiate his ambitions, nonetheless.

Starting From Scratch

"My first parts were all in tragedies," Mabel told the *Los Angeles Examiner*. "Mr. Griffith never could see me as a comedienne." This statement comes across as odd, of course, as Mabel did become famous as a groundbreaking comedienne. It may not be as odd as it at first appears, however. Griffith, after all, was never famous for his comedies. Perhaps he knew that comedy simply wasn't his strong suit, or where his talents lay. Whatever the reason, Griffith simply may not have had any indication that Mabel was a born comedienne. Either way, the director clearly saw the wide-eyed Staten Islander as having enough screen value to benefit his films.

Mabel herself didn't seem to mind the situation too terribly. Indeed, she referred to her early period at Biograph as "my happiest days in pictures." She also believed that her time in New York led her to grow into the renowned comedienne she became. Perhaps that's why she referred to "the invaluable training we received at the hands of Mr. Griffith" years later. "With the exception of Mary Pickford," she explained, "we were shifted around, from lead to extra, and back again to lead, so that we became capable of meeting any situation, playing any part."

There's more to this statement than simple fondness for a time that has passed. One of the impressive and lasting aspects of Mabel's later film work was her ability to underplay at times. Unlike many comedians who overplayed, Mabel had the confidence to let the likes of Ford Sterling, Roscoe Arbuckle or Charlie Chaplin shine. Mabel moved on from Biograph to break through comedic and celebrity barriers for women in part because she understood that comedy, good comedy, even if it seemed quite broad, required a degree of subtlety. And her time working for Griffith may well have taught Mabel the value of nuance.

Appearing before Griffith's cameras also showed Mabel the importance of teamwork. Being part of a rotating cast of Mary Pickford co-stars undoubtedly instilled in Mabel the love of seeing coworkers as a team. This team mentality carried through for years. In the late 30s, former Mabel co-star Ford Sterling fondly reminisced about the *we're all in this together* era of filmmaking. In "the old days," according to Sterling, it was the belief that "everyone should help everyone else." Motion picture making changed as time went on, improvements were made, and synchronized sound became a vital part of industry. The camaraderie of old, however, was deeply missed.

Yet, while Mabel may have enjoyed the company of her peers, her behavior at Biograph raised some eyebrows. Having decided on what course her life would take, Mabel clearly felt free to be herself in the workplace. And, while she was pretty, charming, and funny, Mabel was also obnoxious. The fact that she was one of the more popular figures at the studio might not have helped matters, either. "On the set there were always people around her," Sennett would later write. "She would tell stories, wisecrack, and tell practical jokes by the hour."

It's understandable that Mabel let loose at the time. She was deprived a socially healthy upbringing, after all. Tuberculosis saw to that. Then, when the disease went into enough remission for her to socialize, Mabel found herself working in a sweat shop in Brooklyn. Now she actually had an opportunity to be herself. The problem was that Mabel was hyperactive and possibly disruptive. Unlike many of the girls her age at Biograph, Mabel wasn't a product of the theater. And, unlike Mary Pickford, Mabel wasn't steeped in the ins and outs of acting culture. As far as film making went, Mabel was starting from scratch.

Be that as it may, Varvidson writes that many of the young women at Biograph wanted to emulate Mabel. Much to the chagrin of their parents and chaperones, they admired her worldly ways, as well as her foul mouth and her rebellious attitude towards the studio culture. Mabel was attractive and unique and, with her history of factory work – in gritty Brooklyn, of all places – fascinating to those under the thumb of stage mothers. All on her own in the big city, Mabel seems to have had what in later years would be referred to as the "cool factor." Needless to say, Sennet felt Mabel's manner and antics kept Griffith from ever taking her seriously.

Then again, Sennett in hindsight felt he himself may have harmed Mabel in the eyes of Griffith, too.

"I was courting Mabel Normand," he would write, "in a mild sort of way at the time." While most of the women around Biograph appeared to have been far less than thrilled with Sennett, Mabel seems to have been the exception to the rule. According to Stephen Normand, "Mack and Mabel had an immediate chemistry." Perhaps Mabel saw a charm in Sennett that others didn't. Or perhaps she related to his Catholic background. Or to his Irish heritage. Perhaps even having been a lone child on an enormous work floor in an enormous building in an enormous and menacing city had something to do with Mabel's attraction to the older man. Whatever it was, young, charming, pretty Mabel found herself getting close with the older, not particularly charming, Mack Sennett.

No matter how it all may be viewed as a whole, those early Biograph days in their entirety were thrilling for Mabel…yet her first real foray into film making was about to end. "We were going to Los Angeles," wrote Arvidson of Biograph, "to take moving pictures." Mabel was stuck behind without having truly made her mark on the moviegoing public. "It was Griffith's practice to escape the leaden winter skies of Manhattan by taking the company to Hollywood from Christmas until May," she said. "He told me he would not want me and suggested I ask Vitagraph for a job over in the Flatbush studios." No doubt Mabel was stung by Griffith's rejection. There was no turning back now, however. There were other studios in New York, after all. She had already dared to enter the motion picture business. Now Mabel would dare to take her talents somewhere else. The experience would prove to be a valuable one.

John Bunny

John Bunny was born during the American Civil War and died during the First World War. A product of New York City, Bunny made his living as an actor, starting in minstrel shows before moving on to more legitimate theater where he performed roles in Shakespearean plays and other high-end affairs. Although perhaps not the most famous stage presence of his era, Bunny was successful nonetheless, which in and of itself was a bit strange. Bunny didn't look like a theater star, after all. Overweight and far from handsome, the man looked more like a shop owner than a man of the stage. Looks, however, can be deceiving. They can also prove to be quite valuable when used properly.

Unlike many in his profession, Bunny saw a future in the blooming motion picture industry. Where others of his ilk found the practice of acting before a camera low class and embarrassing, Bunny saw it as a chance to lead a more successful life. So sure was Bunny of the promise motion pictures represented that he offered to take a pay cut in order to be a screen performer. It was a decision that would lead the man to enormous popularity, wealth, and global recognition. For Bunny's man on the street looks endeared him to movie audiences, as did his comedic ability. Indeed, it was in comedies where Bunny was to make his mark. He may have performed Shakespeare on the stage, but onscreen he became known playing for laughs.

One of the more ironic facts about Bunny was that, like Mabel, he brought subtlety to film comedy. This was surprising due to his stage background. The stage, after all, called for exaggerated speech and exaggerated movement. Yet Bunny knew, perhaps intuitively, that the camera didn't call for an over-the-top performance. All one had to do was deliver the goods effectively...and effective screen acting required a degree of subtlety. Bunny may have been well into his forties when he started his movie career, but the nuance he brought to comedic films helped him move the craft of screen acting in new directions.

It's worth noting that Bunny didn't just become a star in America. He became an international star, one who was seemingly recognized and praised everywhere he went around the world. Max Linder was the first true movie star. Florence Lawrence was the first true North American movie star. John Bunny, however, was the cinema's first true American comedic star – and his fame became phenomenal, his works appreciated from New York to Paris to London. Bunny's influence did more than give the film world a new perspective on comedy, it gave the entire film industry a degree of respectability that it desperately needed. Bunny, after all, had been a legitimate stage actor. If movies were good enough for him, why weren't they good enough for other thespians of note? Bunny not only made it okay to act in films – he made it okay to ENJOY films, as well.

Of course, the man had practical reasons for his jump from stage to screen. Indeed, Bunny was quite open about the fact that he liked acting in motion pictures because they paid better than the theater and because the work was easier. A theater role had to be performed day in and day out, all over the country and even the world. A film role only had to be played once. What's more, it often was played in the same studio instead of a seemingly endless variety of locations. Bunny's choices may not have ultimately been proven to be artful, but they were exceedingly lucrative. By the end of his career, he was said to have earned as much money yearly as the President of the United States.

Yet Bunny didn't succeed as explosively as he did on his own. The married father of two had a family who undoubtedly supported him, after all. He also had a motion picture powerhouse behind him, as the Brooklyn based Vitagraph Studios were not only highly respected, they also had at their Brooklyn headquarters the best technology, the best high quality sets, and the even the best costumes to be found in the industry. Lastly, Bunny often had Flora Finch beside him on screen. Although Finch wasn't his co-star in every picture, the tall, thin actress essentially became his screen partner, playing everything from his wife to his foil (sometimes simultaneously).

They were an odd pairing, Bunny and Finch, which was part – a big part – of why they proved to be such a successful team. Bunny, short and stocky, and Finch, tall and lean, were practically physical opposites. Yet it wasn't just the comical differences in build that led the two to work effectively onscreen (off-screen was reportedly another story). For both presented the world with the kind of home and family centered comedy that dominated American television screens later in the century. Rather than presenting over the top scenarios, the works of Bunny and Finch often centered on middle or working class issues that audiences could relate to. The humor wasn't so much found in jokes and gags as it was in the characters and the situations they inevitably found themselves in. It was easygoing stuff, to be sure, the kind of entertainment audiences could be comfortable with.

Yet there was always need for fresh faces. Bunny and Finch couldn't be the only ones in their films, after all. People were needed to play friends, family, and co-workers. There was, in short, a need for talent, unique talent that could blend well with the chemistry already established onscreen. Vitagraph was the place that talent could develop, could grow and learn from established stars like Finch and Bunny. That talent, should it prove worthy, could also potentially be seen by countless numbers of people the world over. Bunny would always be the main attraction, of course, but his films were so popular they proved beneficial to those who worked alongside him. Those individuals didn't have to be established to work with Bunny, they simply had to have what it took to pull it off.

There was, of course, one young actress out on Staten Island who would be just who Bunny, Finch and Vitagraph were looking for.

"Troublesome Secretaries"

With the gang at Biograph headed across the country, Mabel's chances to prove herself onscreen had dimmed substantially. She wasn't an established talent, after all. Indeed, she hadn't done anything of note on the screen save perhaps for appearing in the Mary Pickford vehicle *Willful Peggy*. Yet Mabel's family still needed money. Of course, she could probably go back to posing for painters and photographers. She wasn't even twenty, which meant she was still young enough to find plenty of employment. Mabel, however, had made her decision to be a film actress, and she was going to stick with that decision.

With that in mind, it makes sense then that Mabel took Griffith's advice and went to Biograph rival Vitagraph to find work. The situation was indeed precarious. Not only might Mabel, who didn't have much work of note to reference, not get a chance to act for Vitagraph, she might find only minor work that would keep her where she was at the moment, which was arguably nowhere. Furthermore, Griffith didn't appear to be impressed with her antics at the studio. Would Vitagraph see her the same way Griffith did?

High energy Mabel was probably able to push her fears aside once she actually found that Vitagraph wanted to hire her "on steady at thirty dollars a week." Perhaps even she was surprised when she was chosen to work in major parts alongside Bunny. She shouldn't have been. After proving herself in several Vitagraph motion pictures, Mabel rapidly ended up being a co-star in *Troublesome Secretaries*. Perhaps Mabel's first prominent surviving film, it starred Bunny, along with Alec B. Francis. Viewing *Troublesome Secretaries* over a hundred years after its 1911 release, it's clear Mabel was already showing herself as an attractive, energetic, and appealing screen presence. Bunny's works were rather polished and the girl from working class Staten Island found a way to seem perfectly at home in the thoroughly middle-class setting. While on screen, Mabel naturally attracted the eye through her warm smile and easy movements.

Mabel plays Bunny's attractive daughter in the motion picture. After Bunny's male secretary, who has eyes for Mabel, gets fired, Bunny finds himself dealing with inept replacements. Mabel's character then comes up with a plan, where the original secretary disguises himself as an elderly man in order to once again work for her father. Bunny, of course, discovers what's going on, but changes his attitude so that Mabel and the original secretary end up together. It's a quaintly funny piece, one which Mabel's talents add to considerably.

An appealing character, after all, has to be played by an appealing performer. And Mabel is nothing if not appealing in *Troublesome Secretaries*. Not only is she pretty to look at, especially with her wide smile, but she moves with a quickness that betrays a high level of confidence in what she's doing before the camera. If she isn't right at home acting alongside the great John Bunny, she's certainly doing a wonderful job pretending. Watching *Troublesome Secretaries*, there's no denying Mabel has dared to match her talent alongside one of the world's most famous individuals, and that the risk has paid off.

Mabel went on to make a total of roughly 11 motion pictures with Vitagraph. Indeed, only one appears to have survived, that one being *Troublesome Secretaries*. Works like *Betty Becomes A Maid*, however, show that Vitagraph recognized her as star material. There was reason, after all, for Mabel to act again with Bunny in *The Subduing of Mrs. Nag*, a comedy which also included Flora Finch. Yet, impressive as it was to appear in Vitagraph films – alongside Bunny and Finch no less! – it took some time for Mabel to find her true footing as a daring and influential comedienne.

In the meantime, Mabel was just starting off on a journey which eventually led her to trouble in life down the road. "I attended my first party, as they are now called," she said, "while working for

Vitagraph. Some celebrated artist had done Lillian Walker in a full-length oil painting, and Dimples, as we called her, invited us over to take a look…I told mother I was working late that night and borrowed the extra pay from Constance Talmadge who, in her deceiving turn, told Peg, as she and Norma call their darling mother, that my mother was sick and needed a loan."

It was all largely innocuous underhandedness, of course, the sort of thing that one could expect from teenagers in the big city. Yet the more she matured, the more and more Mabel got a taste, not so much for the party life, but for what was consumed at the party. "When I think now how diabolical we girls felt that night," she said, "with the case of iced beer somebody brought and the sandwiches Dimples provided, I have to laugh at our youth and genuine innocence and ignorance of what the future was to hold for all of us."

Indeed.

Though her time at Vitagraph was successful, Mabel had reasons aside from her career to want to try to go back to Biograph at 11 East Fourteenth Street. Sennett wrote that, before heading west with the Biograph crew, he escorted Mabel back to her family home on Staten Island one evening. While the Ferry continued its trek west from Manhattan, Sennett presented Mabel with a ring he had purchased. "As I don't have to tell you," he would write, "it was a cheap ring. It cost two dollars and a half but it had a lot of *shine* to it and I had to save up to buy it. Mabel knew that." Surprisingly, Mabel at first handled the situation awkwardly, without being able to say much. After some popcorn and kisses, however, she appears to have regained her footing.

"You put the ring on my finger," Sennett recalled her saying. "It's the most beautifullest ring in all the world." For once, Mabel, the gritty, smart alecky product of working class Staten Island and Brooklyn child labor, appeared to have been serious. When she called it "the most beautifullest ring in the world" in her distinct New York accent, she meant it. Yet Mabel still showed she could throw a curve ball. After listening to Sennett go on to essentially promise her the moon and the stars, Mabel set the record straight before the ferry reached Staten Island.

"I don't know whether you are a man to fall in love with or not," she told him, "and I haven't said I *have* fallen for you." Clearly, this was not a young woman who could be easily swept off her feet. She may have come from a humble background, but Mabel was making it clear she had plenty of confidence and self-esteem. "That is sort of how it was with Mabel and me," Sennett wrote, "all the way through." Although there may have been some truth to this statement, there was far more to their complex relationship than that. Stephen Normand, who has Mabel's diary and firsthand family accounts to gather information from, makes it clear the couple was certainly "in love" over time.

Indeed, after leaving for California Sennett expressed his feelings for Mabel in writing. He also sent along a poem he had written for her. "She wrote me very sweetly," he was to say, "and said the poem was beautiful and showed I was a much more romantic fellow than she thought I was. She signed the letter, 'Your girl, Mabel,' and she was exactly that from then on." Little wonder Mabel was happy upon learning she'd be able to return to Biograph, the home of her ambitious now-boyfriend, once the company returned to New York in the spring.

Fred Mace

It was learned that the man had resided at 7700 Hollywood Boulevard with his father, mother and the wife who he had married a few years previously. The most important facts for the New York City authorities at that moment, however, were that comedian and film star Fred Mace had suddenly died of a stroke while exercising at midtown's hotel Astor. Mace was only 38 years old at the time of his demise. According to friends, the man had lost a large amount of weight in a very brief period of time – about fifty pounds in six weeks. Such trauma to Mace's body proved to be too much. While trying to get healthy, Mace inadvertently gave himself a stroke that, in a case of tragic irony, cost him his life.

While he had arguably been past his prime as a comedic film star at the time of his death, there was no arguing that Mace had been a trailblazer. Those who knew the man or who had watched his films before his untimely 1917 passing could attest that Mace was a versatile, courageous, and indeed funny comedian. Having gotten his start performing musical comedy on the stage, Mace became, as the "Los Angeles Evening Express" put it, "one of the first to desert the stage for the silent drama."

Like John Bunny, Mace didn't have motion picture star looks. Stocky and with thinning hair, he could have been anyone. Mace's strong suit, however, was the willingness, and even eagerness, to present himself in a variety of comical guises. While actors like Charlie Chaplin and Laurel and Hardy played a single character ad infinitum to great success, Mace appeared before the camera in any number of guises. Mace was also aware of the distinct differences between theater acting and screen acting.

"When I first started acting up before the camera," he said, "I realized that in place of dialogue and effects, worked by the drummer in the orchestra, which I had been used to on the speaking stage, I

had to depend on comedy and facial expressions." Mace was also quite open about how difficult it was to make the transition from the stage to the screen. "To the uninitiated," he said, "let me say it is the hardest thing in the world to make a camera laugh." Performing comedy on camera, Mace made clear, was a difficult task which required a large degree of courage.

Like Mabel, Mace was a risk taker driven by a willingness to dare – as opposed to possessing a sense of daring. Not only did Mace make the jump from stage to screen, but he had previously jumped from medicine to the stage. Perhaps surprising, the heavyset comedic star had abandoned a career in dentistry. Indeed, Mace had gotten his degree at Philadelphia's Hahnemann College and practiced in Erie Pennsylvania. The thrill of the theater, however, made the respectable Mace wish to pursue bigger things. It was a decision he might have soon regretted. In fact, the odds were that he WOULD regret the decision. Mace didn't regret his career change, however. In fact, after making his move to the theater, he never looked back. Not only did Mace have an acute case of the acting bug, but the money he made on stage proved to be more than he had made in his dentist office.

An excellent example of how well the risks Mace took paid off came from an article that appeared in the "New York Times" in March of 1907. While gambling in Denver the actor, who was then starring in "The Umpire," got cleaned out while playing Roulette and Faro. Borrowing 10 dollars from an agent from famed actress Lillian Russel's company, the down on his luck Mace went on to win big – eleven thousand dollars to be exact, almost three hundred fifty thousand 21st century dollars.

Mace's winning streak extended itself enormously when he became one of the most popular motion picture comedians in the world. Not just satisfied with that, however, the ambitious Mace went on to become the President of the Photoplayers, an early actor's organization. What's more, he became a director, and even went to Cuba to cover the historic heavyweight title fight between

Jack Johnson and Jess Willard. No winning streak lasts forever, however, and Mace's tank of success eventually began to drain. For starters, he decided to go on his own as a motion picture maker, which led to failure. He returned to being simply an actor rather than a studio head, but his popularity by then was waning. Even the coverage of the Johnson-Willard fight had proved a disappointment as Mace couldn't show it in America (Johnson, the world's first black heavyweight champion, was a victim of racism in his native United States).

Mace died while attempting to make a comeback, both physically and mentally. Whether or not he would have succeeded is clearly something no one can tell. Sadly, his contributions to the film industry are nearly completely forgotten. Fortunately, many of his films are still accessible and easy to watch. Although his fortunes took a turn for the worse – as it has for many in the film industry over the decades – there is no doubt that Mace found huge success on the screen. Mace simply wouldn't have reached the heights he did, after all, if he hadn't had the unique ability to make audiences laugh.

Mace also wouldn't have succeeded had he not had the personal ability to work with all variety of individuals – one of those individuals being Mabel. For the older man was there right when the still struggling actress was first making her mark on the industry. Sure enough, Mace went on to perform in some of Mabel's earliest and most memorable comedies such as "The Diving Girl" and *"A Dash Through the Clouds." He may not be viewed as legendary through 21st century eyes, but the man made an impact, particularly with the young woman who was soon known as "Madcap Mabel."*

"A Determined and Unrepentant Comedienne"

Although there's no doubt Griffith overlooked or outright didn't notice Mabel's true strength as a performer there's also no doubt that he featured her in some quality films. Although Mabel may have been afraid of going back to being more or less a second-rate member of the Griffith universe, a moment has to be taken to credit not just Griffith for casting Mabel in some quality films, but to credit Mabel herself for performing quite well in those dramatic productions.

In 1911's *Saved from Himself,* for instance, Mabel isn't only attractive to look at, she also shows that, at this early stage of her career, she can successfully navigate the treacherous waters between expressive and naturalistic acting. What's more, although *Saved from Himself* is a morality tale about an honest woman keeping her boyfriend on the straight and narrow, there's a surprising touch of sexuality to Mabel's performance. Although she worked with John Bunny, from whom she undoubtedly learned, it seems obvious that Mabel's naturalism – as well as her onscreen sexuality – were organic rather than willed into existence. Mabel didn't come from a stage background, after all, which meant – as she herself admitted – she had no foundation to base her acting upon. Plus, being a devout Catholic in the early 20th century, Mabel was an unlikely candidate for aspiring motion picture vixen.

Mabel's natural screen qualities can also be found in 1912's *The Eternal Mother.* Although she only has a small part in this film as the antagonist, Mabel's expressive eyes once again highlight her performance in a Griffith morality tale. In the later portion of *The Eternal Mother,* as her character dies while being cared for by the woman she wronged, Mabel looks completely natural, as if she hadn't been prepped for the shoot, which she most certainly would have been.

Perhaps the most notable of Mabel's surviving films with Griffith, however, is 1911's *A Squaw's Love*. Mabel once again appears young and surprisingly sensuous in this very early action drama, about a young Native American girl who saves her fiancé and another couple. Ions before CGI and the ubiquitous employment of stunt performers, *A Squaw's Love* showcases Mabel's physical skills as she jumps from jagged stones into water, and does quite a bit of swimming, including under a canoe. While certainly not the high-end stunt work audiences grew accustomed to over time, there's no arguing that Mabel is doing some risky things on screen. It's likely no 21st century actor of note would be asked to do such things on account of insurance liability.

Whether she even realized it or not, the naturally physical Mabel here was separating from her peers by virtue of merely being herself – someone who loves the water and who isn't afraid of physical challenges. It's difficult to imagine Mary Pickford or Flora Finch in such a role. Ironically, however, Mabel later claimed she was still determined at the time to succeed as a dramatic actress. "I had an ambition to become a g-r-r-reat tragedienne," she said.

It was not meant to be – which, also ironically enough, proved to be a fortunate thing for Mabel. She employed dramatic acting and scenarios later, but they were always combined with comedy, making her a pioneer of hybrid motion picture making. Although Mabel alone can't confidently be credited with creating the romantic comedy, the comedy drama, or the action comedy, she was certainly at the forefront of the wagon train, making her a true Hollywood pioneer. That development, however, was still some ways down the road.

"My chance in comedy really came as an accident," Mabel said. "There was nothing for me to do, one week, and Mr. Griffith sent me down to Huntington, L. I., where the Biograph comedy unit was making a funny picture." To Mabel's dismay, she learned there was nothing for her to do with the comedy being filmed at Huntington beach, either. So, having grown up swimming on the shores of Staten Island, Mabel decided to spend some time in the water. "And," Mabel continued, "as I was diving and swimming around, it occurred to Mr. Powell (the director) that it would make a good scene for the comedy if one of the characters watched me through a pair of binoculars. So they 'shot' him as he peered through the glasses and then they came down to the pier and turned the camera on me for a dive or two."

Then, it seems, Powell and company – being comedic film makers - asked Mabel "to do a few comedy stunts." There would be no turning back. "They appeared to like me in the role," Mabel said, "so they asked Mr. Griffith, in the next picture, if they could borrow me again." Griffith wasn't crazy about the idea at first, not seeing Mabel as a comedienne, but eventually relented. Mabel, needless to say, was none too happy. "I was furious," she said. "I thought it was terrible of Mr. Griffith to farm me out to the comedy company. Gone were all my dreams of tragedy, of stalking across the set, with the spectators sighing and shuddering at my art."

Mabel's negative attitude proved to be short lived. "I didn't know my luck," she later admitted. "Opportunity was knocking and I was totally deaf to her insistence." Mabel was healed of her deafness quickly enough, for she soon became, in her own words, "a determined and unrepentant comedienne." And Mack Sennett was there, by then leading the way for Mabel and a handful of others with his own off the wall style of comedy which, combined with a guerilla film making style, proved to be a gut shot to the motion picture business. There had been nothing like the surreal, zany and irreverent form of comedy that was on its way to cinema screens. Suffice to say diminutive Mabel landed at the head of the pack, eager to leave her mark.

Ford Sterling

When it comes to stars from the past there are those who are remembered, those who are forgotten, those who should be remembered, and those who ***really*** *should be remembered. Ford Stitch Jr, better known as Ford Sterling, was a star from the past who really should be remembered. Chaplin was a genius, Arbuckle oozed likeability, Buster Keaton and Harold Lloyd epitomized physical courage and foresight – but Sterling was just plain funny. Although his kinetic, quirky, over the top brand of humor might take some getting used to for modern viewers, once Sterling breaks through the barrier of modernity, the man's wild genius is able to step to the forefront.*

Born to a fairly well to do family, Sterling grew up in Chicago. He attended Notre Dame in Indiana as a young man, but left after his father died. He had developed an addiction to acting while in school, however, and so set out to be an actor. A daring young man, Sterling made his way around the theater circuit before joining a circus. He actually went on to become a trapeze artist, which shouldn't be all that much of a surprise when one notices how fluidly the man moves on film. Yet Sterling was more than a performer. He also played professional baseball for several seasons. A legitimately unique individual, Sterling ended up acting before the camera at Biograph. Teaming with Sennett, the former circus clown skyrocketed to success as a screen comedian.

For a 21st century viewer, Sterling is initially a striking, nearly off putting presence, at least that's the case when he's "in character" as his "Dutch" persona. Wearing a beat up top hat, rimless glasses, a goatee, and donning an endless array of weird expressions, Sterling rants and raves, while engaged in what can only be described as high speed, insane movement. Indeed, it's strange to see, so unreal and unlike the modern world it all is. Yet, after a certain point, the 21'st century viewer reacts as one does when faced with a situation so absurd it's hard to believe it's real – that is, he or she with reacts with inexplicable, but genuine, amusement. And then it becomes clear why Sterling was so popular in his own time - because his routine was carefully crafted theater of the absurd.

Yet this, too, should probably come as no surprise. Sterling was an educated man, after all. What's more, he had performed Shakespeare, and in his spare time was an award-winning photographer. The man even had his own show at the Louvre. How surprising should it be that his wacky screen antics had far more to them than at first meets the eye?

Of course, Sterling isn't completely forgotten. People still speak of the "Keystone Cops" of the silent era. In fact, the term "Keystone Cop" remains in common usage when referring to instances of bumbling law enforcement. Playing Chief Tehiezel, the leader of the inept Cops, Sterling firmly planted himself in the ground of motion picture history. It's also well worth wondering what kind of overall impact the man had on American comedy in general. Warner Bros.' "Looney Tunes" (especially the character of Daffy Duck) have a very distinct Sterlingesque quality about them.

Sure enough, Sterling once brought back the character of Chief Tehiezal for a Warner Bros.' short film in the 1930's, one where he actually spoke. What's more, Warner Bros was so happy with the results that it wanted Sterling to return to playing the character regularly again, though ultimately the money could unfortunately not be agreed upon. Likewise, comedians ranging from Groucho Marx to Jerry Lewis to Robin Williams to Jim Carrey can all be seen performing, to some degree or other, in a Sterling-like manner.

Influence or lack thereof aside, there is no denying Sterling's enormous popularity in the 1910's. Furthermore, Sterling was wise enough to know that the tastes of the times were changing as the Roaring 20s neared. He subsequently toned down his act and became a popular character actor. Unlike many silent stars, Sterling was able to make the transition to talking pictures once sound was widely able to be effectively synched with motion pictures in the 1920s. Suffice to say, the man did quite well for himself financially.

Unfortunately for Sterling, things took a turn for the worse near the end of his life. He lost his money, as so many did, during the years of the Great Depression. Still, he remained humorous. "I'm down to the bare beginning of my second million," Sterling said good naturedly after the loss of his money. "I've heard there was a depression."

Even more seriously, however, Sterling became quite sick with thrombosis and had to have his leg amputated. He ended up dying of a heart attack in 1939, largely an afterthought, at the young age of fifty-five. One of the few bright spots of what ultimately became a tragic story is that Sterling reconciled with this wife Teddy Sampson in the early 1930s after a thirteen-year separation. For a woman deemed crazy, Sampson went on to stick with Sterling to the bitter end, even after his fame and fortune had expired.

On top of that, a team of silent film lovers found the unmarked grave where Sterling's remains were buried in Hollywood Forever Cemetery and in 2009 gathered up enough money to give the great comedian his own crypt in the cemetery's mausoleum, along with a fitting memorial plaque. Ironically enough, it was reported that, at the time of his death, Sterling didn't recognize the tragedy of his situation – either that or he refused to focus on it. Success even in failure.

Although he may be most remembered as Chief Tehiezal, there is another image of Sterling that has lodged itself in the collective memory. It's a still shot of Sterling playing a dastardly comedic villain, replete with handlebar moustache and a ridiculously oversized mallet. He and two goons have tied a woman to railroad tracks. The image, which has even been used as an album cover, is sometimes confused with being from a poorly done drama. It's actually from a comedy called "Barney Oldfield's Race for a Life." And the desperate looking young woman tied to the tracks? Sterling's frequent co-star, Mabel Normand.

"The Diving Girl"

Perhaps coming as a surprise even to him, Mack Sennett, in 1911, found himself in the role of director. "I got the chance to direct," he said, "because of the illness of Frank Powell, the No. 2 behind D. W. Griffith, and because I was on hand, very much available, and begging for a chance." Suffice it to say, Sennett was off and running, making film after film for Biograph. And being a comedian by nature – one who wanted to show his girlfriend exactly how successful he could be – Sennett soon arranged to direct Mabel in his movies.

Their first known film together as director and star was 1911's *The Diving Girl.* Whether or not this is the movie Mabel said was being filmed when she first did comedy for Biograph is up for debate. She didn't mention Sennett in her version of events, but she did mention the fact that her scenes were filmed at Huntington Beach, where *The Diving Girl* was filmed. The truth is that *The Diving Girl* is most likely different from the swimming film Mabel spoke of in detail. For *The Diving Girl* focuses on Mabel's character, which means she likely wouldn't have been a quick addition to the cast, as she indicated she had been when she was first asked to do comedy before the camera.

No matter what the exact scenario was around the filming of *The Diving Girl,* the brief, six minute motion picture introduced Mabel to the world. Mabel had done numerous other films before, of course, but it was *The Diving Girl* that showcased the Mabel who would become a household name. In the film, Fred Mace's character takes his niece, played by Mabel, to the shore. There, in a stylish swimsuit, Mabel engages in daring dives and other impressive displays of water acumen. Needless to say, the uncle is shocked and horrified, opening the door for hijinks to ensue.

Mabel, of course, does her own stunts in the movie, which is what makes her stand out. Here is a pretty girl, briming with confidence (wearing a bathing suit onscreen in 1911, no less!), diving as if she's in a competition. To be sure, Mabel's diving is impressive, coming from a considerable height. It's obvious this actress knows what she's doing. Again, Mabel's performance is the sort of thing that viewers take note of. Even in the 21st century, it's hard to imagine an actor performing as Mabel does in *The Diving Girl*. Perhaps most impressive of all, Mabel is clearly *happy* in the water. She's obviously *enjoying* the silliness of the narrative. Her magnetism is contagious. Combined with the risks presented on the screen, the world saw a new kind of film actress. Truly, there was no one else like the bold, smiling young woman in the water. And while there were still Griffith films of note to come out featuring Mabel, including the well regarded *Her Awakening*, Mabel was now well on her way to becoming the first genuine female comedic star.

"I had nobody to tell me what to do," Mabel recalled. "Dramatic actresses had the stage to fall back on, the sure-fire hits of theatrical history in pose and facial expression; but I had to do something that nobody had ever done before…I had no precedent, nothing to imitate, for Flora Finch's art, based as it was on her angularity and candidly exploited homeliness, never would have fitted me. Other comediennes with equal frankness got their laughs with their fat bodies or their somewhat ghastly grotesquery of gesture."

Surprising frankness aside, Mabel would rightfully see herself as the comedic pioneer she was. "Since all previous laughs had been achieved through the spoken word and, in our early days, through slapstick hokey," she said, "I had to cleave a new path to laughter through the wilderness of the industry's ignorance and inexperience. I created my own standard of fun, simply letting spontaneity and my inborn sense of what is mirth-provoking guide me, for no director ever taught me a thing."

Yet Mabel wasn't merely a new kind of film actress, or even a new kind of comedienne. Although some may find the statement hyperbolic, Mabel without doubt presented the public with a new kind of woman. Indeed, even years after Mabel came into her own, there remained an edge, evident in her words, about how women were treated. "I wasn't satisfied with merely being kicked, though," she said. "I've been kicked oftener and more heartily than any woman who ever lived. But while I was getting kicked or bowled over, it was because somebody else wanted to get a laugh and got it at my expense…well, I didn't mind; there were enough laughs to go around -- and nobody ever stole a picture from me! And most of the kickers are in oblivion."

As for Sennett, new responsibilities meant more money. "That inspired me to be Great Man," he wrote of his finally becoming a director. "I took Mabel to expensive restaurants and tried to wear better clothes." This undoubtedly thrilled Mabel. As time would go on, no matter how wealthy and famous she became, a part of her would always be the poor young model who had dreamed of owning the fashionable, expensive attire that painters and photographers had her pose in.

Yet, despite how she might come across at times, Mabel was ultimately a serious person. And a serious person needs more than clothes, jewels and high-end restaurants. She had gotten a ring from Mack, now Catholic Mabel would want more – as would Mack's mother. When asked by Mrs. Sennett at one point why she wasn't married to Mack, Mabel responded that he had never asked her. Mack, it seems, was too busy making a name for himself. Mabel was great to have around, but ambition was his true love. According to Stephen Normand, Mabel and Mack did indeed at some point become engaged. Furthermore, a wedding was planned. At the moment, though, Mack had other things on his mind besides marriage, yet they too involved Mabel, the girl he felt too busy to wed.

"I wasn't too busy to realize," he said, "that Mabel Normand could become a major motion-picture star and I wasn't too frightened to ask her to leave D.W. Griffith and Biograph – where she would most certainly have become a celebrity – and join the new bookmaker-backed Keystone Company." Indeed, Sennett was leaving Biograph to join up with the New York Motion Picture Company. Under the backing of organization heads Charles Baumann and Adam Kessel, he was being allowed to run his own operation, called Keystone, which he had named himself when he saw the word Keystone painted on a train. Whether he succeeded or failed, two things were certain: First, Mack would finally be a man in charge. Secondly, others would succeed or fail with him, Mabel especially.

"Late in the spring of 1912," Mabel said, "Mack Sennett took me to Luchow's cafe on Fourteenth Street for luncheon." Suffice to say, Mack didn't just take Mabel out for a meal. "He explained," Mabel continued, "in great detail that he signed a contract with Bauman and Kessel, who ran the New York Motion Picture Company, and was to make comedies for them in Hollywood. He said he wanted me to sign up with them."

It was perhaps the turning point of Mabel's life. Even more than when she had quietly made her way to Biograph not long before, Mabel was now about to make a decision that definitively determined how her future would play out. All of the possible consequences that might emerge from that decision might well have been unfathomable at the time. Some potential consequences were certainly fathomable enough to scare some people off, however. Yet Mabel simply wasn't built like such people.

She decided to leave Biograph to work with Mack at Keystone.

"Mabel was so naïve," Mack would later write, "that she left D.W. Griffith to join a motion-picture company that had no money to speak of, no studio, no list of players under contract, no stories, and no camera." While he may have been right about the slim chances Mabel had of actually succeeding, Mack was wrong about her being naïve. Once again, Mabel did what few others probably would have – she decided to risk it all. Once again, it was a dare that paid off handsomely.

Thomas Edison

He was in his sixties by the time Mabel had entered the motion picture business, an aging American titan if ever there had been one. Not only had he famously made improvements to the light bulb some time earlier, Thomas Edison was also one of the creators of motion pictures. Although it was argued he had no idea how big motion pictures would become or what road their development would take, Edison had nonetheless received U.S. patents for his motion picture cameras. "Companies that wanted to make pictures," Mack would write, "were forced to rent cameras from him." Suffice it to say, it was not an optimal way to operate in the motion picture business if your name wasn't Thomas Edison. Yet, although Edison may have been known as one of the founding fathers of motion pictures, his company – the Thomas Edison Company (of course) – eventually ended up falling behind its competitors. "Despite its arrangement with the Motion Picture Patents Company," wrote the Library of Congress, "Edison films could not keep pace with the quality of competitors' films in terms of the advances made in narration."

He may have helped usher the world into the 20th century, but Edison couldn't hold on to the motion picture business forever. People liked entertaining films before all else, after all, and Edison, though many things, was no entertainer. Nor, it seems, were those who worked for him entertainers. At least they weren't particularly strong entertainers. "The Edison Company," the Library of Congress stated, eventually "tried to improve its image through several initiatives. Imitating its competitors, Edison developed a stock company of actors in 1910." Against the likes of Keystone, it stood no chance.

Edison was unquestionably a visionary, perhaps one of the greatest in all history. He was not, however, a creative visionary along the lines of Sennett. While there's no denying Edison improved life as people knew it with his inventions, the far smaller matter of entertainment, of comedy more specifically, belonged to those like Sennett and his oddball team of Mabel, Ford Sterling, and Fred Mace, all of whom had decided to hitch their wagons to Sennett's Keystone star. Under Sennett's guidance they stuck their thumb in the sense of order that had seeped through the Victorian age into the Edwardian age. Their unique brand of comedy would become a no holds barred variety.

Still, it was Edison who had the patent for his equipment, and so motion picture company heads were forced to have to line the inventor's pockets if they wished to ply their trade. Unless, of course, they were like Mack. To Mack, the new head of Keystone, patents "merely meant that we had to become bootleggers, like many another small outfit." Illegally using someone else's equipment, however, could prove to be a dangerous game. "Any time we were shooting," he wrote, "the Patents Company might break us up and take our camera away. We posted guards." For Mack, however, it was all worth the risk. As he was starting off with Keystone, he claimed, "we found a camera which Thomas A. Edison did not know about."

Of course, Edison wasn't solely obsessed with motion pictures. He was always a man of varied interests and endeavors. Still, he had created patents for cameras and projectors and had taken to charging theaters to run the movies made from his materials and the projectors used to show them. On top of everything else, Edison's equipment wasn't particularly easy to operate in the early days.

Motion picture cameras had to be hand cranked, after all, which meant the person manning the camera had to make sure not to crank too fast or too slow in order for the pictures to be seen effectively at a rate of about six shots a second. Such work could be tedious and nerve wracking. It also required real skill. In short, the motion picture industry in America at the time was largely held hostage by Edison and his Motion Picture Patents Company. Fortunately for those who made motion pictures, like Mack and others, the government finally stepped in.

With the support of major studios, the Motion Picture Patents Company found itself under assault by the government for running a trust in 1915. By 1917, the trust was broken up and the studios essentially came out from under Edison's thumb. Truth be told, his studio had been in decline for a while by that time. Again, motion picture making, and entertainment were far from the aging Edison's only priorities. They were the top priorities of people like Mack, Mabel, and others, however, so it worked out well that Edison's monopoly was eventually broken.

It must be stated, however, that Mack didn't just make do with what he had early on. He employed a renegade strategy when it came to stories, locations, and even extras. In a sense, Mack was a guerilla film maker who often flew by the seat of his pants. In short, the man knew how to do a lot with a little. He also had considerable talent supporting him, not least of whom was Mabel, his girlfriend and eventual fiancée. She would have as much to do with Keystone's success as any of Thomas Edison's equipment would.

California

"Look," Mack remembered telling his investors after first basing the Keystone Company on the east coast, "we have no studio here and the light and the weather is always bad in New York. Let me take our people to California. It will be cheaper." According to Mack, the investors behind Keystone were more than happy to send him and his small team out to California. If Mack is to be believed, he was starting to get on the nerves of those with the purse strings on the east coast. In other words, the investors were happy to see him and his rag tag band of comedians head west. Aside from Sennett himself there would primarily be Fred Mace, Ford Sterling, and, of course, Mabel.

It was no doubt hard for Mabel to leave her family, friends, and home. Very hard. Yet, Mabel had made up her mind to stand by Mack and that was it. The whole thing was, of course, incredibly risky, but by this point Mabel's sense of daring was beginning to define her. Besides, she would be making more money now – money that could help her family. Still, at the beginning of 1912, Mabel found herself on a train with three older men, making her way across the endlessly vast United States on her way to California, where she would eventually live and work on her own. Mack was her beau, no doubt, but they weren't married, and Catholic Mabel wouldn't embarrass her family by living with a man outside of marriage. She must have seemed a sympathetic figure to those who spotted her on the train during that long trip.

Mabel, however, was ready to pounce as a comedienne. Perhaps the move out to California had an impact on her psyche. While she played it serious in some of her upcoming films, that seriousness merely served as a contrast to the on-screen madness that was going on around her. Like a student dropped off at college for the first time, she was free from the constraints of family and former authority figures. Mabel, who had always been unique due to her sickly childhood and quirky personality, was now completely free to be herself.

"There weren't many of us, and only a few were known to the public at all, and we didn't know what the future held for us out on those faraway, sun-kissed slopes," she recalled. "But we didn't care. We were a jolly outfit of friendly comedians, and we were going to make the world laugh, and I was to get $125 a week and be a star. Oh, the gay years when I went tripping down the road in the crystal sunshine! I often think a marvelous story could be written about the early days of the baby industry out here in California."

Upon arriving at the Santa Fe station in Los Angeles, Mabel and the others stepped out into the warm California climate...and, if Mack is to be believed, immediately got to work. A parade of Shriners was making its way down Main Street, and, noticing the notable event, the Keystone gang, who had essentially just gotten off the train, sprang into motion. "A gorgeous welcome it is to you indeed, O Maestro Mack Napoleon Sennett!" Mabel cracked before a plan was hatched. After several moments, camera and cast were discreetly inserted into the crowd.

With a shawl and a doll taken from the very limited collection of props available, Mabel then ran smack into the middle of the procession, pretending to be a desperate young mother looking for the lout who had fathered the child in her arms. The embarrassed and shocked Shriners had no idea what to do, yet Mabel kept up her routine while the camera rolled, "pleading, stumbling, holding out her baby," remembered Mack. As he put it, "Mabel Normand could throw herself into any part instantly, even into a part that didn't exist." One kind soul stepped out of the march to help Mabel, only to be suddenly confronted by Sterling, who began screaming incoherently at the poor man. The Shriner, along with everyone else at the parade, must have felt the world had suddenly gone mad.

It was at that point that law enforcement got involved. "The police moved in on Ford and Mabel," said Mack. "Ford fled, leaping, insulting the police, and they – God bless the police! – they chased him." The Keystone gang had officially introduced itself to the southern Californian populace. It was only the start. "We enjoyed it," Mabel saidof the guerilla filmmaking style Keystone would regularly engage in. "It was great fun. 'Stealing' our stuff was lots more exciting than just 'shooting' it on our own. Mr. Sterling and I became quite adept at it." The strategy, it seems, was simple: just embed within in a group or gathering and be persistent.

"I remember a baby show that was held on the roof of a big department store," Mabel recalled fondly. "The camera man would get a lot of people around him to conceal the camera until the right minute, then they would step aside and I would leap off the platform where the babies were being judged and rush madly toward the camera with Ford in close pursuit." The Keystone crew was also not shy about swiping other people's material, as fellow motion picture maker Thomas Ince could attest. "Ince would get all set for one of his mammoth panorama pictures with cameras mounted everywhere," Mabel would recall. "Long companies of pioneer families would pass in wagons from the mesa down the ravines and along the beach, and Indians would attack and cavalry come dashing up to save them."

Never one to pass up an opportunity, Mack situated his team nearby. "Sennett would have us waiting, and at the most spectacular climax of the great panorama he'd give a signal and we'd dash out and do our stuff against that mighty background. There'd be no connection between our comedy and the drama, but that made no difference. Ince would see us and come running, screaming through his megaphone: 'Mack, you damned thief! Get those infernal clowns off my set!'…we'd beat it, of course, but we had our scenes. Tom and Mack wouldn't speak for a couple of days, but of course they were devoted friends and laughed about it afterward." Such heady times clearly coincided well with Mabel's youth. She was not yet 20, and the great thrill of life must have been accentuated tenfold by the off the wall actions of herself, Mack, Sterling, Mace and the others who were subsequently hired to make up the Keystone Company.

Southern California was still essentially virgin territory at the time, more of an outpost than a center of civilization. In fact, it was Mabel and those like her from the film making east who helped turn the sun-drenched area into the famed, bustling destination it would become. To Keystone, and to Mabel in particular, the entire area must have seemed like a playground. "We were a feverish, guessing, suddenly enriched throng of youthful people who didn›t know what to do while we were working and didn›t know or care what we did while we were playing," she remembered.

Indeed, Mabel was keen and intelligent enough to view the situation objectively. "Remember," she said, "the camera is an insatiable Minotaur demanding youth and beauty. That is all it requires. Brains can be supplied by scenario writers and dialogists and directors if they have any. And youth and beauty seldom are escorted through life by common sense or stability of character, since the law of compensation declines to shower on one individual all the qualities with which the myths endowed the ancient gods."

Looking back on the film industry's early days in Southern California, Mabel was able to view the past critically – something a number of her peers were unable to. "So, you may be sure," she said, "the inevitable happened -- lovely girls and handsome lads, both young and often uneducated, suddenly were deluged with gold, and a lot of us flung prudence and conservatism and thrift and restraint to the soft breezes of the Pacific Ocean and frolicked madly through the early days of our careers…it got some of us, and some of us died notoriously; others it dropped swiftly out of the pictures; and a few of us finally got our feet back on firm ground and survived."

Mabel was able to say those words, however, in hindsight. As a teenager in the fresh faced motion picture community, Mabel was able to luxuriate in her good fortune. In fact, it took years for Mabel to even settle down enough to purchase a home in Southern California. At first, she lived at the Ambassador Hotel's opulent cottages on Wilshire Boulevard. She then moved to a variety of addresses until finally purchasing a Beverley Hills Mansion in 1924.

The Keystone Company, however, had a home of its own in Southern California far sooner, "a small studio in Edendale, just east of Los Angeles, and almost in Glendale," said Mack, describing the studio as "exactly what I needed and where I had pined to make pictures when I first saw Southern California along with D.W. Giffith."

Roscoe Arbuckle

It was said his father had named him after the notoriously corrupt U.S. Senator Roscoe Conklin. So wretched was William Arbuckle's behavior towards his family that the man made the failings of Conklin seem quaint by comparison. William's son, Roscoe Arbuckle, who became famous as "Fatty Arbuckle," was most distinctly not the product of good parenting. His mother, though she most likely didn't approve of her husband's drinking, disappearances, and physical abuse of Roscoe, appears to have been a classic enabler. As for William, Stuart Oderman wrote that he alternated from beating his son to apologizing profusely. Suffice it to say, the man never became of Father of the Year.

After Roscoe's mother died, Roscoe, the youngest child, went to live with relatives. After a point, however, he was sent to live with his father and brother, who promptly stood him up, literally leaving the boy an orphan. Fortunately, the kindness of a stranger changed the young Kansan's life. Being sent to a hotel, Arbuckle was allowed to stay while working at small tasks. Performing at a local talent show one evening, the heavyset Roscoe proved to be a hit with those in attendance.

"When the hook came out to pull him offstage during one of his performances, to allow another amateur to go on," Oderman writes, "he did a surprise summersault into the orchestra pit. The audience loved it." What Arbuckle was able to do at a young age, despite the obstacles he faced, was to be aware of what worked for him. He could, for instance, sing quite well. He also had a sense of daring – as evidenced by that tumble into the orchestra pit – and a keen insight into the fact that seemingly negative attributes can actually prove to be positive ones. For instance, he used his weight to his advantage. People could laugh about that weight – so long as they

laughed with and not at the entertainer. Laugh along with him they did.

Arbuckle clearly had gotten the itch to perform and so he grew up to take on the hardscrabble life of vaudeville entertainer, travelling constantly, perfecting his combination of physical humor, role playing and singing. By the 1910's, however, a now adult Arbuckle, along with his wife Minta Durfee, had decided on the film business. He may have weighed close to three hundred pounds, but Arbuckle was a perfect fit for the motion picture business. For one thing the man was incredibly agile for his size. It was as if the overweight Arbuckle was actually athletic, which in a sense he was. What's more, whether he was playing the nice guy, the underdog, the husband with a wandering eye or an exasperated straight man, Arbuckle knew how to perform on camera. Again, he used his size, along with some effective mugging and considerable nuance, to give memorable comedic performances.

Although he could play many types of characters, it was the role of goofy nice guy that audiences of the time seemed to appreciate the most. Perhaps this had something to do with an America that was moving too fast, with technology and international strife changing not only the look of the globe but also the entire way Americans lived their lives. Arbuckle on screen was largely pleasant, innocuous. He offered audiences a break from the world outside the theater. That, most likely more than anything else, was the source of the man's incredible popularity.

Just how popular was Arbuckle in his prime? Popular enough to be the first actor ever to sign a million-dollar contract in the early 1920s. Aside from Charlie Chaplin, Arbuckle was unquestionably the most popular motion picture comedian of the time. The man did not, however, get to enjoy his enormous success for long. On Labor Day Weekend, 1921, the famous entertainer threw a party at a San Francisco hotel, a party which ended in the death of a young woman. Arbuckle got arrested on account of the woman's death and one of the biggest court cases – actually three court cases – in American history transpired for what mainly appeared to be public consumption (the initial tragedy, as well as its subsequent trials, will be thoroughly examined in another chapter).

As newspaper tycoon William Randolph Hearst was to reportedly claim, the Arbuckle scandal sold a lot of newspapers. In short, Arbuckle's' fall was the media's gain. Although eventually acquitted for manslaughter after two hung juries, the once beloved Arbuckle was nonetheless seen as a pariah. What's more, he was made to be the scapegoat for any and all bad behavior that had emerged from the southern California motion picture industry in previous years. William Hays of the Motion Picture Producers and Distributers of America banned the actor from making motion pictures even though Arbuckle had been officially ruled not guilty of any wrongdoing. Arbuckle, in short, was ruined.

The man eventually made a comeback in the early thirties, but it proved to be too little too late, as the 46 year old former star ended up dying of a heart attack while in bed next to his third wife in 1933. The man's name sadly lived on, not as a symbol of success, but as a symbol of scandal and media hysterics. Sure enough, after the Arbuckle scandal, the Hollywood community was never seen the same way again. American society forever viewed the motion picture industry with as much suspicion as it did wonder. People liked the product, and they certainly liked particular stars. They did not, however, trust the motion picture community as a whole. Nor would they as time moved on.

The Arbuckle scandal didn't simply shake the foundations of the motion picture industry as a whole, it played havoc with the lives of the individuals who existed in it as well. What should have been an obvious truth – that the people seen on the screen acted differently in their private lives than they did in their motion pictures – came as a stark surprise to the public, one that caused them to turn on some of the industries' biggest stars, especially when some of those stars were in much need of public support. This certainly proved true in the case of Arbuckle's' friend and former partner Mabel, who one day suffered through scandals and torments of her own.

A Comedy of Irreverence

"Anything on film made money," Mack was to write of the early days in southern California in his biography. Across the country and beyond, audiences wanted motion pictures. And Mack had just the kind of motion pictures many desired. There were no comedies of manners to be found in his directorial offerings. A Sennett short was, more often than not, a slapstick comedy, one where physical hijinks and absurdity were the order of the day. Some found Mack's unique brand of comedy low class, and in fact, some critics and historians still do. What these people are missing is one simple fact – Mack's works practice a comedy of irreverence. Not irreverence to God or country, but to the kind of everyday behaviors and norms people are expected not only to engage in, but also to have presented to them in their entertainment as well.

Take 1912s *The Brave Hunter*. Modern viewers can see here why Mabel got so popular. She acts with a bear in this film. A trained bear, sure, but a bear – for a decent amount of time. The story itself, of a "brave" boastful hunter who is terrified of a bear Mabel ends up befriending, is genuinely funny. Any 1912 theater goer who expected to see the story of a great courageous hunter saving an innocent young woman from a ferocious grizzly was in for a surprise. The great hunter, played by Mack, ends up being a complete coward in the film.

This sort of plot just wasn't to be expected. Nor was a young girl supposed to be spending time with a live bear outside of a circus. The short film is daring, not only for turning expectations on their heads, but also for Mabel's performance. Actors get hurt with live animals. That fact was as true in 1912 as it is in the 21st century. Not only does Mabel clearly spend a considerable amount of screen time with the bear, however – she actually comes across as genuinely enjoying the experience. In *The Brave Hunter*, Mabel and Sennet let the viewer know that Mabel is no run of the mill leading lady. She's something entirely unique.

Likewise, Mabel's starring part in *The Tragedy of a Dress Suit*, which was released that same year, showcases Mabel's ability to mock the melodrama of the Victorian and Edwardian dramas audiences had come to know so well. In the short, a rogue steals his landlord's suit to impress wealthy Mable, all to disastrous results. A fair woman fainting from the drama of her experience was common in such a part. Yet Mabel went ahead and fainted not once, but twice in *The Tragedy of a Dress Suit*, taking the stereotype of a frail woman and using it as fodder for satire. By engaging in excessive fainting, the actress sent up the already melodramatic trope of weak-willed women passing out. Again, Mabel was something different, unexpected.

Mabel and Mack truly decided to test the boundaries of what was considered acceptable entertainment when, that same year, Mabel starred in *Mabel's Strategem*. Not only did the film allow Mabel to be known by audiences by her own name (no small thing) the film also showcased a switching of gender roles. Mabel in the film dresses as a man to get her job back after her boss' jealous wife has her fired...only to have the wife hit on her thinking she's a man. This sort of thing might play as commonplace and even quaint in the 21st century. The same can most certainly not be said for 1912, the year of *Mabel's Strategem's* making and release.

Yet it was another of Mabel's films that year that truly showed she represented a new kind of female comedienne, one whose characters simply had no concern for the niceties of the contemporary world, who went ahead and did things men were literally afraid to do. *A Dash Through The Clouds* shows Mabel flying in the crudest airplane this side of Kitty Hawk. Just how crude is the flying contraption? Mabel and the pilot both have to seat themselves on the wings. What's more *A Dash Through the Clouds* engages in unconventional storytelling which actually makes this short piece even more unique.

Already annoyed by her boyfriend, Mabel's character hops on a plane after learning her boyfriend is in the clutches of a deadly gang in Mexico. Swooping down from the sky Mabel fires at the gang with a pistol. Then, having saved her boyfriend, she turns, gets back on the plane wing and flies off with the pilot, leaving the boyfriend to make it back to the United States on his own.

The end.

Not only does *A Dash Through the Clouds* showcase the latest technology America has to offer at the time of its making, it presents a tale that's downright surreal. Some may argue that the story doesn't really exist, that the motion picture is simply a chance to showcase a flying machine. After all the work that went into getting a plane, however, why would Sennett and company pass on the opportunity to offer the audience a conventional ending where Mabel remains with her boyfriend after saving him from the gang?

The truth is that 1912 was a defining year for Mabel. It was, to put it plainly, the year Mabel became the Mabel the world would know or would think it knew. There she was on screen, literally putting her life at risk, her characters partaking in wildly inappropriate behavior (in *Tomboy Bessie*, for instance, Mabel literally plays a hyperactive, nearly psychotic child who is endlessly amused annoying her sister and sister's suitor), and being appealing all at the same time. On top of being a pioneering actress and comedienne in 1912, Mabel was also extremely busy. By year's end she was only twenty years of age, yet with forty-eight movies to her record for that year alone.

All the work paid off but being daring could be a risky business indeed. As Stephen Normand says, Mabel had a tendency to overwork. What's more, Phillip Orin Parmelee, the pilot in *A Dash Through the Clouds*, was dead before the film was released, having died in a plane crash shortly after filming. That event didn't keep Mabel from wanting to learn to fly on her own, nor did the fact that five of her instructors reportedly ended up crashing to their deaths, as well. Mabel took the term "Fearless Performer" and essentially redefined it.

Barney Oldfield

"The rear wheels slid sideways for a distance of 50 feet, throwing up a huge cloud of dirt. Men were white-faced and breathless, while women covered their eyes and sank back, overcome by the recklessness of it all." So wrote a magazine called "The Automobile" in 1903 as it described star race driver Barney Oldfield pushing 999, a car designed by Henry Ford and powered by gas, to the point where it went over a mile a minute over a dirt track in Yonkers – successfully breaking the speed record he had set a few weeks earlier. The speed reached by Oldfield that day may seem quaint by 21st century standards, but it was legitimately impressive – and dangerous - at the time.

"It was Barney Oldfield," Michael Kernan wrote in "Smithsonian Magazine" close to a century later, "who made Ford a household word." Although he had driven 999 himself, Ford decided that Oldfield, a young man who had previously raced bikes, should be the one behind the wheel. Yet Oldfield made more than just Ford famous. "Soon," wrote Kernan, "every small boy in the country was copying Oldfield's swagger and round goggles." Although the cars Oldfield drove, including the 999, were awe inspiring and forward looking for their time, Oldfield made sure that he was as big an attraction as the automobiles he drove were.

In a sense, Oldfield was nothing if not a man of his time and place. With his cigar and gritty looks, he appeared nothing like a dashing portrait of adventure. Oldfield didn't come from money or from a family of note. He wasn't a tycoon, and he certainly wasn't royalty. Oldfield, simply put, looked like the man on the street. In an era where the old order of life was starting to be questioned in the western world, such things mattered. What's more, America was on the rise while class-centered Europe was on the road to mass destruction. Like America itself, Oldfield came across as a gritty, determined underdog who wasn't afraid to find out how successful he could be.

And so, the product of Wauseon, Wisconsin continued on, earning fame, bringing in an enormous amount of money and breaking record after record. By 1910, Oldfied had driven a Blitzen Benz automobile at speeds of over one hundred thirty miles an hour. In an era where cars were most distinctly not made for safety and comfort, the feat is impressive even by 21st century standards. Oldfield was more than a personality. He was someone who could back up his reputation with eyebrow raising accomplishments. And people loved him for it.

What's more, Oldfield loved the success. "He often sported thousands of dollars' worth of jewelry," Kernan would write, "including a four-carat diamond pinky ring, and he handed out $5 tips when a dime would do. Once in San Francisco, greeted at the station by a brass band, he invited all 65 musicians to dinner at the Palace Hotel and paid a tab of $845, two years' income for many Americans at the time." As if that all weren't enough, Oldfield took his show on the road, visiting various towns and even having his own show on Broadway. Naturally, he appeared in – and offered advice on – motion pictures.

Retiring at 40, Oldfield opened the Oldfield Tire and Rubber Company. With the wear and tear of racing, drinking, brawling, and numerous marriages having taken their toll on him, Oldfield moved to Beverly Hills where, as Kernan puts it, he "watched for years while others broke his records." The man was 68 years old when he passed in 1946. Many probably had expected the gritty Oldfield to die earlier. Indeed, it must have seemed a bit strange that the man who got an automobile to ride at one mile a minute had lived to see the atomic age. Still, Oldfield played a small role – but still a significant role – in the technological wave that ended up sweeping the United States to its dominant global position.

After all, it was Henry Ford who transformed the automobile from a plaything for the rich to an integral part of all aspects of

American and, ultimately global, society. And it was Oldfield who put Ford on the map, speeding along, kicking up massive amounts of dust in his wake, chomping on his cigar, oil splattering onto his face and the goggles that protected his eyes. Oldfield was in a sense America – or perhaps how America wanted to see itself at the time - racing forward, fearless, undaunted by seemingly impossible odds and life-threatening dangers. Here was a man and a country that made it clear it was okay to get dirty, to be grimy and exhausted at the end of the day so long as the end goal – that which heretofore had seemed unattainable – was met.

Of course, Oldfield's races and performances could hardly be seen as highbrow entertainment. That, however, was the point. Ford was looking to sell his product to everyday Americans. That, he knew, was where the real money would be for him. And Oldfield appealed to the market Ford was trying to entice. It made a lot of sense for both men to promote each other. Oldfield didn't only drive Fords, of course, but it was he and Ford who essentially introduced one another to the public at large. The unusual partnership paid off handsomely for each man.

Like racing, motion pictures such as the kind Keystone produced were most certainly not regarded as high-end affairs. Perhaps it's only fitting, then, that Oldfield found himself in a short motion picture from Keystone that would go on to become a classic, one that even (shrewdly) had his name in the title: "Barney Oldfield's Race for A Life." Racing to save Mabel from a dastardly Ford Sterling, Oldfield helped send up the style of melodrama that motion pictures and theatergoers of the time had been accustomed to. There was, however, more to it than that. "Barney Oldfield's Race for A Life" proved that Keystone films could have layers to them, racing celebrities and all.

Insanity Can Be Fun

"Papa and his darling," the card on the screen reads. The film is *The Speed Kings* and it stars Mabel and Sterling. Although they play a father and daughter in this short motion picture, the title card is meant to be humorous – for both father and daughter are clearly insane. While Sterling's father character is clearly the more insane of the two, Mabel's daughter character is certainly quite daffy herself. The plot is simple: Father wants daughter to marry race car driver Earl Cooper while daughter wants to marry race car driver Teddy Tetzlaff. Like Oldfield, each man is a real-life professional race driver. And, like Oldfield, each man is playing himself in the film.

Father tries to sabotage Tetzlaff's car before Tetzlaff enters a big race, one which Cooper will also be racing in. The plot, however, is about as pointless as the character's actions in the film. The authentic footage of car races which stand in for the fictional race onscreen are fascinating for their historic value, but the action – who is winning or losing – is hard to follow.... because it's not meant to be followed. It's Mabel and Sterling who are the focus here and they put on quite the performance. Sterling, decked out in his classic beat-up top hat, and goatee mugs, yells, and motions wildly while Mabel acts thrilled and the extras behind them try to keep from laughing.

At one point, Mabel jumps up and runs down to the track itself to cheer on the action. None other than Arbuckle is there, playing a racing official. Seeing Mabel waving away crazily, he roughly grabs her by the shoulders, only to have defensive dad Sterling race up to him. Mabel slaps Arbuckle, then runs back off while Sterling jumps atop Arbuckle and starts biting his ear, only to turn and wildly chase Mabel back up the bleachers. Finally, at the supposed end of the race, Mabel slaps Sterling, and runs off, with Sterling in hot pursuit. Ultimately, Mabel rides off with Cooper while Sterling and

Arbuckle's characters beat the tar out of each other on someone's lawn.

The end.

The point of it all? That insanity – provided it appear harmlessly on a screen – is fun. That and the fact that Mabel and Sterling are a truly great comic duo, one sinfully underappreciated over the decades. Sterling is best remembered as the chief of the Keystone Cops while Mabel is largely remembered for who she would go on to share the screen with. Puzzlingly, the terrific chemistry between Mabel and Sterling is largely unnoted by contemporary film scholars. With Mabel and Sterling there is nothing but wild behavior, with Mabel often playing the role of straight man, her reactions to Sterling's insanity accentuating the humor. The result is first rate comedy which can still be appreciated over a hundred years after its production.

A Muddy Romance, released in 1913, was another film starring the pair that would become a classic of slapstick comedy. If *The Speed Kings* showcases the crazy antics of the Mabel-Sterling pairing, *A Muddy Romance* takes those antics and runs with them. The plot is again rather simple. Sterling and Mabel (or, rather, their characters) are going to get married. A troublesome second suitor shows up and chaos ensues. Sterling accidentally lodges a pie at Mabel's face. Furious, Mabel tosses bricks at Sterling, as does the second suiter, who Mabel inexplicably now decides to marry. The odd couple grabs a preacher and heads off to the woods – but a gun wielding Sterling is in hot pursuit.

Mabel, her new fiancé, and the preacher get onto a boat and paddle to the middle of Echo Lake…but Sterling, after firing round after round from his gun, decides to drain the lake. And drain the lake he does by twisting a stand-up crank, grimacing, and mugging all the while. The police arrive, then the water police arrive. By this point the lake is completely drained and Mabel and the others must be dragged through the mud to shore by the hapless cops in order to be saved. And what does Sterling do after everyone is safely ashore?

Fakes his suicide, of course! After everyone has turned in horror at the sound of his gunshot, Sterling, perfectly unharmed, takes the opportunity to run away to safety. Upon turning back around, the crowd is shocked to see that Sterling has disappeared. Mabel, covered head to toe in mud, promptly passes out from shock.

The end.

Senseless? Completely. Senseless, but funny. And also telling. Mabel once again shows that it pays to dare. First off, she dares to allow herself to play second fiddle in the film to her frequent partner Sterling – but she also dares to allow herself to be literally dragged through the mud for a laugh. One can think of few movie stars, both then and in the 21st century, willing to take such a risk. Again, however, the risk paid off for Mabel, as films like *A Muddy Romance* helped establish her as one of the bigger stars of her era. Yet Mabel also shows in *A Muddy Romance* what a subtle actor she can be, as well. Early on, for instance, she can be spotted by the careful eye discreetly tugging her mother's blouse uneasily after the second suitor arrives. The real Mabel is ultimately interested in more here than just playing the damsel in distress…though she successfully plays into that type, too, in 1913's *Barney Oldfield's Race for a Life.*

Mabel shows in *Barney Oldfield's Race for a Life* that she can play the victim as good as anyone. She gives Sterling room to shine here, her character brushing off his crude character's advances as he struts about with a handlebar moustache, looking more like bareknuckle fighter John L Sullivan than a leading man. Needless to say, Sterling plays comically psychotic this time around. Gathering his henchmen, he chains poor Mabel to nearby railroad tracks, true Victorian villain style. With an oncoming train approaching, the situation is as perilous for Mabel as it is familiar to viewers.

Yet, with death racing towards poor Mabel, in comes the one and only Barney Oldfield, racing along behind the wheel of his car in order to beat the train, loyal Mack Sennet in tow. What makes this short motion picture rather odd is the fact that it's strangely thrilling. The editing and compositions are sharp, making it something of a nail biter. The viewer KNOWS Mabel is going to be saved, but still isn't completely sold on the idea.

Suffice to say, upon Mabel's being rescued, the villainous Sterling proceeds to shoot his henchmen as well as the cops who are after him, making this an oddly dark Keystone movie – if only for a moment. After having run out of bullets, the sneering Sterling decides to commit suicide by chocking himself, crashing in high vaudeville fashion onto the tracks. Barney Oldfield has indeed saved the day.

The end.

What's fascinating about these three films, all made in 1913, is that they not only showcase Sterling's manic brand of comedy, but also show Mabel willing to step to the back – if need be – in order to make a better product. While she more than holds her own with Sterling in *The Speed Kings* and wildly tosses bricks at him in *A Muddy Romance,* Mabel is able to also play the helpless victim in a sendup of Victorian melodrama. A strange aside – some have taken to seeing the famous still photo of Mabel being chained to the tracks by the mustachioed Sterling and his goons as being from a genuine drama. In truth, it's from a comedy, and an effective one at that.

Looking at Mabel's entire body of work as a whole, her starring roles alongside Sterling are certainly a high point. In brief, the two were a zany team. Each star went solo, however, or teamed up with others, often to excellent results. Indeed, 1913 proved to be a watershed year for Mabel, a twelve-month period which saw her truly come into her own. For in 1913 Mabel started to become as big as the films she performed in, a legitimate star by any standard.

In a very definitive way, Mabel was letting the world know women too could succeed, whether they were Gibson Girls, or unfortunate brides caught up in the most unlikely of circumstances.

Minta Durfee

"Oh, she was so beautiful! So beautiful. And do you know, she was so cute, she would try to cuddle up a little to you, you know what I mean, in her little ways of expression, and she was a great tease, a little imp, a minx, I guess that is the better word." So Minta Durfee told Stephen Normand and Don Schneider *in 1974. The former actress, most famous for being the first wife of Arbuckle, was the picture of loyalty. Not only did she support her then ex-husband through Arbuckle's trials, Durfee proved herself to be a longtime defender of her friend Mabel as well.*

Young Minta reportedly met her future husband while she and Arbuckle were on a train. She was eighteen at the time. "Please don't touch my suitcase," she said to him after he offered his assistance. "I don't know you, and I'll manage it myself. Another thing, I don't like blonds or fat men!" Needless to say, the Kansas native's charms ended up winning the young Californian over.

Like Arbuckle, Minta was involved in the theater, and had been for the previous two years. After a brief courtship, the two were married at the Byde-A-Wyle Theater in Long Beach, California. From there the two continued living the vaudeville life. As the second decade of the 20th century approached, Arbuckle began making movies. It wasn't until 1913, however, that the man became an actual film comedian. And he became one under none other than Mack Sennett. What's more, Minta entered the film business, as well, becoming a notable herself in the Keystone Universe.

Starting with "A Quiet Little Wedding," which she starred in alongside her husband in 1913, all the way until the 1970s, Minta appeared on screen – first in films, then in films and television. Strangely enough, the last movie Minta appeared in was a 1972 film version of John Updike's "Portnoy's Complaint". Hers was undoubtedly a long and storied career, one which sadly remained in the shadow of her famous husband, even after their marriage had ended, even after Arbuckle's death.

Still, Minta played alongside some of the biggest names of the 1910s. Aside from her husband, she could be seen as Sterling's leading lady. Or Chaplin's. She often acted alongside Mabel. Sure enough, it's Minta's blouse Mabel nervously tugs at in "A Muddy Romance," as it's Minta who in the wacky comedy plays Mabel's poor, put upon mother. Throughout both of their respective careers, the women worked together at least ten to fifteen times. Not only did they have good working relations, Mabel and both Arbuckle's became quite close.

"She and Roscoe would SWIM and DIVE hours upon end," Durfee would say decades later, referring to the downtime she and Roscoe spent with Mabel on the Pacific shore, "they just loved to play in the water." Indeed, beach time with the Arbuckle's appears to have been a regular event. "Mabel of course, she would come down, but she had always rented an apartment, but she came down every Sunday and she and Roscoe would SWIM in front of our house, to the Venice pier and back again, at eleven o'clock every Sunday morning." It all appeared quite idyllic. In just a few short years, however, Durfee put her own reputation on the line in defense of her then ex-husband Arbuckle.

Although it might be difficult to ascertain through her upbeat words, Mina's marriage was not as wonderful as it may have appeared. In truth, the couple grew apart over the years. Whether or not this had anything to do with Arbuckle's growing career might be difficult to ascertain. The fact remains, however, that Minta and Arbuckle had been separated for half a decade before Arbuckle's trials for murder and manslaughter. Still, Durfee made it a point to stand by Arbuckle both physically and figuratively until the man was eventually acquitted.

Suffice it to say, her presence was noted. As was her mother's, and Arbuckle's brother, Arthur. Whether she was wearing a colorful hat to court or laughing at the fact that she had gone from less than one hundred pounds at the time of her marriage to potentially being called "Mrs. Fatty," Durfee was clearly helpful to her husband and his defense team. And, in truth, it's likely she absolutely couldn't imagine Arbuckle committing murder, manslaughter, or any other number of heinous crimes. Objectively speaking, the teams of jurors assigned to Arbuckle's trials ultimately couldn't imagine it either.

Still, after Arbuckle was finally acquitted in 1922, the vindicated but ruined couple was unable, or uninterested, in saving their marriage. Hoping for a French divorce, Minta went to Paris where none other than famed international comedian, Max Linder, the world's first movie star himself, asked her to be his co-star. Things went from bad to worse, however, when Linder and his wife committed suicide shortly thereafter (though many believe Linder actually killed them both). Minta finally got her divorce on the last day of 1923, and even then, she was treated snarkily. The "Pomona Progress Bulletin" ran the story under the title "Minta Arbuckle Forgets Vow To 'Stick By' Fatty."

Mina continued appearing in films, however, for the next five decades. And even after Arbuckle died in a New York City hotel room with this third wife in 1933, Mina fought for his reputation. Although her interviews had a melodramatic quality to them, Minta proved to be a treasure trove into a past that was quickly being forgotten. She always appeared willing to set the record straight. That was particularly true in the case of Mabel, her former friend and costar. Of course, by the 70s there were likely others still alive to defend Mabel's memory. Few did so as passionately as Minta, however. She may have been a lifelong actor and entertainer, but perhaps above all else, Minta Arbuckle was an energetic chronicler of a time that had long since passed. Ultimately, her recollections proved to be invaluable.

Moving Behind The Camera

As the year 1913 wound to a close Mabel could rest assured she was finding enormous success in the film industry. Not only did she star in such popular motion pictures as *Barney Oldfield's Race for a Life*, she also appeared in other notable shorts such as *Bangville Police,* which introduced the world to the Keystone Cops, and *Mabel's Dramatic Career*, which featured a movie within a movie. What's more, Mabel became a legitimate celebrity as the movie industry grew by leaps and bounds. She hosted the Photoplayer's Inaugural Ball that year with Fred Mace, finding herself in a position of prominence. "Fred Mace," wrote the *Los Angeles Times*, "president of the ceremony of the Photoplayer's Club, and Miss Mabel Normand, leading lady of the Keystone Company, led the grand march, in which eighthly-four couples, all prominent members of the local photoplay colony, participated."

The age of celebrity was arising, and Mabel was leading the march, both literally and figuratively. "Nearly 10,000 tickets were sold," the *Times* wrote of the event, "and more than half that number of persons attended the event. Even before the grand march, virtually every seat was occupied. The scene was one of brilliant color. Beautiful women more familiar to the onlookers in the guiro of western heroines, picturesquely attired in rough-and-ready garments known to the plains in pioneer days were there in gorgeous gowns of Parisian make, but they were recognized just the same."

Motion picture stars were clearly now becoming a part of everyday life in American and international culture. The following summer, Mabel played a large part in San Francisco's Exhibitor's Ball. "The excitement began at 9:30 in the morning," wrote the *The Moving Picture World,* "with the arrival of Mabel Normand of the Keystone Company, Carlyle Blackwell of the Kalem Company, and

Miss Anne Schaeffer and George C. Stanley of the Western Vitagraph Company. The players were met by State Secretary, W. A. Cory, and representatives of the Golden Gate and General Film Exchange, who took the players to their hotel, where they made ready for the pageant, which started at noon at Van Ness Avenue and Market Street."

Mabel was clearly treated as if she were royalty, or even a conquering hero, which in a sense, she perhaps was. "Mabel Normand," *The Moving Picture World* continued, "having been voted the most popular player in California was chosen queen of the occasion and occupied the first automobile with Carlyle Blackwell and W. A. Cory and wife." Mabel had come a long way from her lonely childhood on the Staten Island shore. And here she was, a mere twenty-two years of age. Hers was the most unlikely of success stories.

"I am getting to be some speech maker," she wrote to a friend. "I have been making impromptu speeches at all of the picture houses in Southern California and feel very proud of myself." She then let on as to which direction her political leanings went. "I really think when woman's suffrage invades California I shall run for mayor of Los Angeles on the suffrage ticket." She might have been kidding, but there was no doubt that, in a land where women couldn't vote, Mabel was showing the public how influential and essential a woman could actually be. No doubt her sympathies lie with the suffragettes, who pushed for the right of women to cast their ballots on election days.

At the very least, Mabel was showing how successful a woman could be in America, as was evidenced by a December article in *The Motion Picture World.* "Mabel Normand, leading woman of the Keystone Co since its inception, is in the future to direct every picture she acts in," the article claimed. "This will undoubtedly make Keystone more popular than ever, and this will give Miss Normand the opportunity of injecting some of her comedy, which she has never had an opportunity to put over before."

While Mabel may have still loved to horse around and to play pranks, the young woman was nothing if not serious about the movie business. Stephen Normand speaks of his aunt's tending to be overworked and there are stories of Mabel going to see the motion pictures of others after a shooting day to see what others were up to with the still young art form. There are even reports of Mabel discussing screen characterization at length with a novice Chaplin in order to help the stage comedian better make the move to film. It's perhaps no surprise, then, that Mabel eventually made the jump from star to director.

There was no denying the fact Mabel was engaging in work that women were generally considered to be innately unqualified for. This was a period of history, after all, when women weren't even considered worthy of voting. What's more, this was an era where fewer than one in four women worked any kind of paying job at all. Mabel was not only working; she was now on her way to directing. And the work she was directing – the making of popular motion pictures – was no small endeavor.

"While Mabel was by far not the first female director or producer (Alice Guy Blache is probably the first)," wrote Mabel's Estate, "she was one of the first female directors and producers. While stars like Pickford were quiet about producing or directing less it detract from their image (Pickford likely directed a small percentage of her films on her own, but never took credit. A few early films she was credited where due), Mabel appears to have always been credited for any contribution she made."

The now fully functional Keystone Studios was located on a small hillside in the town of Edendale, just outside of Los Angeles proper, at 1712 Allesandro Street. As Brent E. Walker writes, "the studio featured naturally-lit stages with translucent roofs, and diffuser walls erected to make the best use of the sun's rays to light the shots while avoiding harsh shadows." Here and in the area outside the studio is where Mabel directed nine films in the year 1914…a considerable achievement especially considering that Mabel starred or co-starred in each of these films, as well.

The job of the director consisted, among other things, of arranging shots, guiding the actors along, and orchestrating the film crew. After the film was shot, it was then to be edited and set up to play in theaters as a cohesive whole rather than a series of shots and cards. Finally, the finished film was sent to New York to be introduced to the world. It was an enormous undertaking, and one would understand why a new director would simply want to get used to the process before trying anything the least bit out of the norm.

Mabel, of course, was different. In 2010, a lost film that Mabel starred in and directed was discovered in New Zealand. Called *Won in A Cupboard*, this completely absurd short comedy involved wildly physical, almost surreal, performances from virtually the entire cast. What starts off as a goofy romance between Mabel and Charles Avery ends up as a case of mistaken identity involving Charles Inslee and Alice Davenport, who find themselves stuffed in a closet while the town accosts them with a fire hose. The abrupt end in particular is very funny. Mabel is very much into classic panic-stricken Mabel mode throughout much of this.

What makes this film stand out, however, aside from it's being discovered, is a single, intentionally ridiculous shot involving Mabel and Avery. As two yahoos who fall in love at first sight, the pretty but goofy looking Mabel, and the even goofier looking Avery slowly move towards each other via split screen, finally settling into a single shot. This may not have been the first time split screen and dissolves were used in a film, but in a comedy featuring two bumpkins coming together in a single comedic shot? Such decisions take daring.

This one brief moment of cinematic history is indicative for two things. First, it shows that Mabel isn't afraid to go beyond the very simple Keystone filming style, where actors were literally apt to perform against the wind blowing in the trees behind them. Secondly, it shows Mabel has the desire to go beyond the standard Keystone fare. Whether or not Mabel had to fight Mack for this unusual, but effective, cinematic moment or not, the finished scene gives a hint of the artistic ambitions Mabel one day developed and refined.

Charlie Chaplin

There he stands, alone and anxious in the middle of the dance floor of a packed establishment. Turning to the young, beautiful girl standing the wings, the short, mustachioed man indicates he's lost the lyrics he's about to sing. The girl, forever loyal, informs him to make it up as he goes along. And so the man does, singing in utter gibberish as the crowd laughs and he performs dance moves that literally foreshadow Michael Jackson's famous moonwalk. It's a completely marvelous piece of film making and performance art, combined. In fact, this one scene, from 1936's "Modern Times," may well be the crowning achievement of Charlie Chaplin's legendary career.

Even the biggest of legends, however, can have humble beginnings. And Chaplin's background was humble indeed. Born in 1889, most likely in London, Chaplin was the product of show business parents. While his mother and father may have been talented performers, they were most distinctly not effective parents. Chaplin's alcoholic father died before his son was thirteen and his mother subsequently found herself in institutions due to emotional issues. That left Chaplin and his half-brother Sydney to fend for themselves in the massive and unforgiving city of London. Fortunately, both Chaplin and his sibling were talented, as their mother had been.

By the time he was an adult, Chaplin had impressively worked his way up to being a full-fledged comedic star on the traveling circuit. So popular was Chaplin and his company that they went to the United States, where they continued to be warmly accepted. Indeed, Mack himself got wind of Chaplin and, after watching him perform, signed him to Keystone, where the soon to be famous star got his start in film acting. After something of a rough beginning, Chaplin soon found himself hugely popular with the moviegoing public. By 1915, Chaplin was offered a fortune by the Essanay company and subsequently left Keystone.

Thanks to his iconic character, "The Tramp," a mustachioed, odd walking, cane twirling, derby wearing lovable/somewhat amoral oddball, Chaplin was an all-out phenomenon, with everything from product placement to look alike contests being attributed to him. With the dawn of "talkie films" however, Chaplin was left with a brutal decision: Try to take up speaking on camera or remain a silent relic of the past. Perhaps surprisingly, the man stuck with what he was good at. And as was often the case with Mabel, Chaplin found that his daring paid off. Chaplin continued making silent films well into the era of "talkies" that were successful by both financial and critical standards.

Life wasn't particularly charmed for the London native, however. First, there were the affairs with younger women. Indeed, by 21st century standards, it's hard to imagine Chaplin not having been completely ruined by his peccadilloes, such as the affair he had at the age of thirty five with fifteen year old co-star Lita Grey. Then there were the critics back home who argued he should have made his way to the front of the First World War, where untold thousands of his British countrymen were being slaughtered wholesale. Lastly, and perhaps most damaging, there went on to be Cold War criticism of Chaplin being a communist, a charge that Chaplin (most likely in honesty) denied. "These days, he said, "if you step off the curb with your left foot, they accuse you being a communist."

Chaplin's strange behavior did him no favors, either. His fellow Englishman Stan Laurel, of Laurel and Hardy fame, stated he thought Chaplin was completely insane. Marlon Brando, the great American method actor, later accused Chaplin of being a mean and overbearing parent (Brando, Sophia Loren, and Tippi Hedren worked with Chaplin's son Sydney on the forgotten 1967 comedy, "A Countess From Hong Kong," which Chaplin himself directed). A brutal divorce and the fact Chaplin went on to marry iconic playwright Eugene O'Neil's eighteen year old daughter at the age of fifty-four only added to the man's reputation of being amoral, eccentric to a fault, and perhaps even treasonous.

By the 1950s, then, Chaplin had become a target of the US government for all variety of reasons. Packing up his large family, the famous screen star went into bitter exile in Austria, which remained his home until his death in 1977 at the age of 88. On a bright note, Chaplin returned to Hollywood a conquering hero to accept an honorary Oscar at the 1972 Academy Awards. He received a full twelve-minute applause. Whatever the man's numerous flaws, Chaplin's contribution to both the arts of comedy and cinema were literally exceptional.

Indeed, Chaplin's greatness rests on three distinct features. The first is the man's amazing physicality on screen. It took a lot of work and perfectionism to get those strange and seemingly flawless movements of his down. Indeed, a Chaplin-directed film was reportedly a grueling experience to be a part of. The second distinct feature of Chaplin's was his decision to stick with silent cinema – or at least with silent acting – as the world transitioned to the "talkies." His contrariness struck a surprisingly strong chord which still plays to this day.

The third distinct feature of the man's career? His ability to make socially conscious films that were actually entertaining and of high quality. Anyone can make a film with an agenda. Making a GOOD film with an agenda is exceedingly hard, however, sometimes no doubt impossible. With films such as "City Lights," "Modern Times," "The Kid," and "The Great Dictator," Chaplin was able to pull the rare feat of combining entertainment and messaging off over and over again. Impressive to say the least.

Of course, it's hard to refer to Chaplin in any meaningful way without bringing up Mabel. It was she, after all, who first directed him as "The Tramp," just as it was she who also directed and/or co-starred with him in early films. Although younger than Chaplin, she acted as a mentor – something he resented, much as he may have admired her. While it would be wrong, as some have, to claim

Mabel "made" Chaplin or that Chaplin somehow took credit for Mabel's achievements, it would be blatantly untrue to argue the young woman from a Brooklyn sweatshop didn't provide the young man from the rougher part of London with essential guidance and discipline during his climb to Olympian heights.

"Nappy turned him over to me," said Mabel, "and I directed several of his pictures, in some of which I also played. And while it would be folly and untrue for me to say I am responsible for very much of his present standing as the screen artist beyond compare, yet I'm proud to say that he held my hand while he found his way through the swamp of learning the game."

Also Known as Muriel Fortescue

The year 1914 found Mabel to be ubiquitous, both in motion picture houses as well as in newspapers across the United States and beyond. There was now no questioning the woman's stardom and vast popularity. *They Marysville Appeal* described Mabel as the "only woman director in the world." The assertion may have been untrue, though in all likelihood, Mabel may well have been the most famous woman director in the world at that time. Likewise, the *Lyon's Daily News* presented a very favorable article on Mabel's film *The Sea Nymph* along with an ad that had its own positive writeup – one which discreetly mentioned that Mabel could be found wearing a bathing suit and swimming in the picture.

Yet when Mabel wasn't off entering race driver Lou Serrel in a fifty-mile contest in Bakersfield or attending the Picture Player's Cameramen's Ball, she was busy acting in, as well as directing, motion pictures. This of course was a job in and of itself. Being a celebrity, however, meant that Mabel now had other obligations aside from those before and behind the camera. Like Max Linder and Florence Lawrence a few years earlier, Mabel herself was the reason people were coming to see her works.

It was not only Mabel's job then to simply produce and sell a product, she also had to be available for public consumption in other ways, often through newspapers and film magazines. So popular was Mabel at this time that Australia's *Perth Sunday Times* published a poem by a "Mr. A. W. Stewart of the Railway Department," in honor of Muriel Fortescue, the name Mabel sometimes went by outside the United States. *The Sunday Oregonian* published a full two-page article on Mabel under the title: "MOVIE ACTTRESS, 20 YEARS OLD, IS HER OWN MANAGER: Miss. Mabel Normand Dares Death Cheerfully and Often in Order to Provide Thrills for Patrons on Film Dramatic Productions."

The article was typical of pieces to be found throughout Mabel's career in that it was a blend of truth and fiction. Although some parts of *The Sunday Oregonian* piece– such as Mabel's age – were unverified, the article's subsequent stories of Mabel risking her wellbeing, perhaps even her life, in the service of her line of work provided genuine insight into what separated Mabel from her peers. And, in fairness to many of the publications that wrote about Mabel, the truth was sometimes impossible or, at the very least quite difficult, to come by at the time.

As for her motion pictures, Mabel continued to provide the kind of material her audiences expected. *Mabel's Blunder* showcases Mabel at her cutest in a comedy of errors. *Those Country Kids* has Arbuckle and Mabel get together, then, after many hijinks, marrying against her father's wishes. Suffice to say, *Those Country Kids* once again presents the kind of wild material offered by Keystone at the time: bricks are thrown, guns are fired, fighting breaks out, and there's an abundance of people falling. Sure enough, Mabel and Arbuckle were now starting down the road that led to them becoming one of the most popular pairings in cinema.

Yet two motion pictures Mabel directed in 1914 have drawn more attention over time than all the others she acted and/or starred in that year. Both co-star the newly arrived Keystone player, Chaplin. It's hard to get stories straight when it comes to Mabel and Chaplin, though Stephen Normand might have hit on something when he suggested Chaplin may have been a bit jealous of the young woman who became his director and mentor. "I could not take it," Chaplin admitted years later in his autobiography of the fact he had to take orders from Mabel. "And from such a pretty girl."

A forward minded man Chaplin was not.

Still, if Chaplin wanted to make it at Keystone he at first had to abide by the way things were done. And things were often done with Mabel starring both before and behind the camera. Not that she didn't give Chaplin opportunity to grow. Sure enough, it was Mabel who first directed Chaplin as "The Tramp." The motion picture was called *Mabel's Strange Predicament* and it was a situation comedy where Mabel gets locked out of her hotel room while being simultaneously hassled by Chaplin's Tramp. Although it's his first time playing his most iconic character, Chaplin is somewhat menacing here. Indeed, there's something about the Tramp in *Mabel's Strange Predicament* that is, if not outright dangerous, then drunkenly belligerent.

Without doubt, Chaplin is memorable, but Mabel is apt to draw more attention, not only because she's the main character, but because she comes across as particularly appealing, especially when she is seen in the film playing with her dog in her hotel room. Whereas Chaplin seems more like a genuine alcoholic vagrant than the character he eventually developed, Mabel's love of her four-legged friend on screen seems genuine in its own right. She's not so much playing a role as she is simply playing with a dog. All in all, *Mabel's Strange Predicament* is a well-made, memorable Keystone endeavor. The relationship between director and actor took a bad turn, however, during the filming of *Mabel at the Wheel.*

Chaplin plays the outright villain of this particular film, who, after trying to win Mabel over with his motorcycle, decides to wreak havoc, kidnapping Mabel's racecar boyfriend before a big race, leading Mabel to race the car herself – and subsequently win. Mabel, who during *Mabel at the Wheel* is actually seen riding the car around the track, is clearly comfortable behind the wheel of a vehicle designed to go close to one hundred miles an hour. The smile on her face during these recorded moments is beaming. Again, she was a young woman unique to her profession.

As for Chaplin, he's clearly abandoned – or been told to abandon – the Tramp for the time being in *Mabel at the Wheel.* Here, he's doing his best Ford Sterling imitation, right down to the hammy expressions and top hat. There's a distinction between the two men's styles, however. Sterling had the rare gift of playing a menacing character without coming across as menacing to an audience. Chaplin, brave as he was, would either come across as trying too hard or genuinely appearing menacing himself when playing a Keystone "villain." At this early stage in his film career, it simply wasn't Chaplin's strong suit.

Still, none of this kept Chaplin from writing of an incident in his autobiography where, during the filming of *Mabel at the Wheel*, he walked off the set because Mabel wouldn't take his advice. Chaplin suggested the move, made at the dawn of his film career, led him to becoming a director. If true, it would appear there would be more to the story than first meets the eye. Mabel was known for being generous, after all, both as an actor – she regularly let Sterling take center stage – and as a director – she arguably gave Chaplin too much screen time on *Mabel's Strange Predicament.* It's hard then to imagine her rejecting valuable input unless it simply wasn't possible at the moment to accept it (motion pictures at the time, much like today, were timely, costly affairs to bring to life).

Either way, it's difficult to believe someone as good natured as Mabel was known to be, giving an actor good reason to leave the set. If the story is true, she and the rest of the crew probably found Chaplin to be acting childishly. Which, again, if the story is true, he certainly was. Fortunately, the film ended up being completed to audiences' satisfaction.

Marie Dressler

Later in her career, when she acted in the film "Dinner at Eight," Marie Dressler showed just how comfortably she had made the transition from the stage to the silent screen, to "the talkies." Seeing her perform alongside Lionel Barrymore in the film, it's clear that this is an actor in full control of her words, body and mind as she performs. It might come across as dated by the standards of the 21st century – indeed, the entire film might – but there's no denying that Dressler's performance is a completely disciplined affair. Little wonder she had won a Best Actress Academy Award for her work in "Min and Bill" a few years earlier. "Of all the scene stealers I've ever watched," famous gossip columnist Hedda Hopper wrote all the way in 1953, "Marie Dressler was tops."

According to Dressler biographer Barbara Garrick, among the high points for Dressler – aside from that Academy Award – was the fact she became "at one time, the highest paid star in the movie industry, earning more than Greta Garbo or Mickey Mouse." Dressler also made the cover of "Time Magazine" in 1933. "At an age when most stars are long forgotten by Hollywood producers," writes Garrick, "Dressler reached the pinnacle of her career."

What perhaps was most surprising was the fact Dressler proved to be successful at all. In an industry that even then worshipped beauty, Dressler certainly didn't look like an individual one would expect to be a major film star. Aging, tall, and heavyset, Canadian native Dressler nonetheless made her mark in numerous ways. Taking up the theater at fourteen, the young girl found herself drawn to comedy. Success came eventually, but it certainly didn't come easily. Ultimately, however, Dressler's determination, coupled with her skill, paid off. "By 1892 (the year Mabel was born), she was on Broadway," writes Tony Fontana of the Internet Movie

Database, "and she later became a star comedienne on the vaudeville circuit."

By 1910, Dressler was starring in "Tillie's Nightmare," a quite popular play which ran for almost eight months and eighty-five performances on Broadway. Her performance caught the attention of Mack, who offered her a hefty thirty-five thousand dollars - over a million 21st century dollars - to make a movie for Keystone. Dressler accepted the offer and starred in "Tillie's Punctured Romance," which was based on "Tillie's Nightmare." It was unquestionably a success. Unfortunately for Dressler, however, her motion picture debut didn't lead to bigger and better things.

Rather than reaching Olympian heights, Dressler was on her way to some very difficult times. As Fortuna writes, after "Tillie's Punctured Romance's" success "her film career never took off and by 1918, she was out of films and out of work. Her role in the chorus girls' strike of 1917 had her blacklisted from the theaters." Things became so bad for Dressler, Fortuna claims, that by "the late 1920s she had been largely forgotten and reduced to near-poverty." Not good for a woman roughly sixty years of age.

Yet Dressler was to discover she had a guardian angel on earth.

Irving Thalberg was in many ways nothing like Dressler. A product of the mean streets of New York City, Thalberg went west and made himself an emperor of sorts. Whereas some studio honchos enjoyed being administrators, Thalberg's interest was in the films themselves. So memorable was the man to those who knew him that F Scott Fitzgerald based his last hero, Monroe Stahr, on Thalberg in his unfinished final novel, "The Last Tycoon." Obsessive, controlling and always overworked, Thalberg was nothing short of a movie studio perfectionist. Things like cost overrides didn't matter to Thalberg. What mattered was the final product...the movies themselves.

And Thalberg believed the seemingly washed-up Dressler could be a major factor in creating excellent films for him. "By the time we hit fifty," Dressler would say, "we have learned our hardest lessons. We have found out that only a few things are really important. We have learned to take life seriously, but never ourselves." If this was representative of Dressler's true outlook it was one that ended up working exceedingly well for her. Still, with or without the support of Thalberg, Dressler needed to firm her resolve to go from has-been to Oscar winner. "Like an old Model-T Ford," she claimed of working on "Min and Bill," the film which won her an Academy Award, "I had to be cranked up. I was scared stiff." Suffice to say, Dressler, the former silent screen comedienne, ended up rising to the occasion. As Fontana succinctly stated: "it was sound that made her a star again."

Passing of cancer in 1934, Dressler, had been able to work until her sickness got the better of her, dying a beloved and vindicated figure. Surprisingly enough, the man who had saved her career did not survive much longer than Dressler. Thalberg, who was also beloved by those who knew him best, was too low key to allow himself to have become a celebrity. Still, his death at the way too young age of 37 had a profound impact on Hollywood. Here was a man who had indeed altered the way movies were made. And he certainly altered the course of Dressler's fortunes.

Although she had gone on to achieve incredible success belatedly in the film industry, Dressler is still perhaps best known today for her initial movie – Keystone's "Tillie's Punctured Romance." For this was a groundbreaking motion picture in numerous ways. It is also the one that has withstood the test of time as the decades have come and gone. As much as she stands out in the role of Tillie, however, the enduring popularity of "Tillie's Punctured Romance" has a lot to do with the wild and lasting fame of Dressler's co-star Charlie Chaplin.

Yet Dressler's other co-star also had much to do with the popularity of "Tillie's Punctured Romance," both upon its release and afterward. For it's difficult to imagine "Tillie's" reaching the level of success it did without the presence and performance of

Mabel. Without question "Tillie's Punctured Romance" was a star vehicle, and Mabel was about as big a star as could be found in Hollywood at the time. The combination of she and Charlie supporting one of the most popular entertainers in the world in her motion picture debut proved to be too much for audiences of the time to resist.

The First Feature Length Comedy

In spite of the fact he became one of the most influential entertainers on earth, there is simply no denying that Chaplin learned from Mabel. "Charles Chaplin and Harold Lloyd were muggers in their early efforts," wrote *Los Angeles Magazine's* Michael Ventura. "They quickly adopted and adapted Mabel Normand's approach." Writing for *The* Guardian, Jay McCarthy quoted film historian Raymond Lee's assertion that "a study of her (Mabel's) films, made before Chaplin came to this country, shows entire routines, gestures, reactions, expressions, that were later a part of Chaplin's characteristics." Ventura and Lee were correct in their analysis.

While it's true Chaplin at times tried to imitate Sterling early in his motion picture career, the influence of Mabel became clear as he developed as a screen comedian. Perhaps Mabel's most significant impact on the man was the way in which she could give her characters dimensions. Chaplin's early work generally presented him as pesky and antisocial. Such characterizations are good for comedy, of course, but a true artist – and Chaplin was nothing if not a true artist – eventually looks to add dimensions to characterizations.

A creatively ambitious Chaplin needed to look no further than Mabel, with whom he continued to work on numerous films. Mabel, after all, could be the "Madcap Mabel" audiences loved, but she could also be empathetic Mabel in works like *Mabel's Busy Day* and *His Trysting Place*. As Chaplin's career progressed, his Tramp was ultimately a sympathetic figure in spite of his occasional flaws. Making an audience laugh is wonderful. Yet, as Chaplin learned working with Mabel, endearing yourself to an audience can be an even greater accomplishment.

Still, Chaplin would soon part ways with Keystone. Mack was not known to pay his actors well. Indeed, even Mabel at the time was only making $125 a week, a fortune at the time, sure, but not nearly as much as other top stars. In short, she was not being paid market price for her hard work and talents. Indeed, Mack's stinginess would over time cost him the likes of Sterling, Chaplin, and Arbuckle. With that in mind, Mabel herself later defended Mack by stating, "Mr. Sennett had to count the pennies because he was allowed a very small sum to make his pictures." Before Chaplin left, however, Mack cashed in on the Englishman's exploding popularity. He was arguably cheap, but Sennett in his own way, was also a master craftsman.

At the time, Keystone's motion pictures, indeed comedic movies in general, consisted of one or two reels of film, which made a work ten or twenty minutes long respectively. With his wildly popular girlfriend in his camp, along with Chaplin and the just hired Marie Dressler, however, Mack was ready to make the first feature length comedy, one a full five reels in length, with his team of comedic all stars.

"I was still making two-reelers almost exclusively but it was decided to let me graduate," Mabel told the *Los Angeles Examiner* years later. Sure enough, Mack's stars, and comedy itself, were about to graduate into a new format – feature films. Countless motion pictures had been made at the Keystone studio. As Chaplin indicated in his autobiography, three stages inside the studio were occupied by three separate crews filming three different movies simultaneously (the noise of a busy studio wasn't a matter for concern in the silent era). Plots were come up with on the fly and the pace was rapid, in keeping with the frantic nature of the films themselves.

Now, however, Mack had popular source material to work from in the form of *Tillie's Nightmare.* He also had a very expensive stage star making her cinematic debut. In short, he needed to make good on his investment. Top stars become top stars for a reason, however, and Mabel, along with Dressler and Chaplin, was able to carry out the large-scale proceedings effectively and professionally.

Mabel and Chaplin had been working together for some time and Mabel hit it off with the older Dressler, though there was a media rumor that the two were rivals and that a race between car fanatic Mabel's four-cylinder Stutz Bearcat and a Fiat owned by Dressler had been arranged. The race, however, was merely a promotional gimmick to stir up interest before the film's release. Indeed, Dressler proved to be a friend throughout some of Mabel's most difficult times.

Tillie's Punctured Romance was released in November of 1914 and went on to become a notable success. The first comedy feature in history proved that comedies didn't have to be confined to ten or twenty minutes in length in order to appeal to an audience. Once again, Mabel was a part of history, and a huge part at that. As shady Charlie Chaplin's equally shady girlfriend, she takes part in scamming Dressler's wealthy but barbaric heiress. And, being Mabel, she proves she has a conscience at the end. Yet, popular though it might have been at the time, *Tillie's Punctured Romance* can be a bit of a slog.

The opening and closing moments are impressive, with theater star – and main attraction – Dressler stepping out from behind a curtain. In the opening she transforms into the character of Tillie and in the end, she brings out Mable and Chaplin. Yet *Tillie's Punctured Romance* is, at points, tedious slapstick. There are only so many trips, falls, slaps, kicks, and punches that can be presented before tedium sets in. What works brilliantly in comedic shorts becomes tiresome here. While some of the locations, including the Castle Sans Souci, stand out and impress, the film has energy but not momentum. *Tillie's Punctured Romance* represents feature length comedies in their infancy. For that fact alone, however, it's worth the watch.

Which isn't to say *Tillie's Punctured Romance* doesn't have its positive attributes. There's no shortage of natural comedic ability here. Dressler shows she is a gifted comedienne, as, of course, does Chaplin. As for Mabel, she appears at times to seamlessly morph inside her own character, which is unusual for a comedic performance of the time. For instance, Mabel appears lost in her thoughts at some moments during the film. The keen viewer will also occasionally catch sight of Mabel rubbing her nose absentmindedly while in high end attire or while at a ball. Mabel uses the moments where she's not the center of attention to subtly, almost organically, convey the essence of her character to the viewer. Mabel, like castmates Dressler and Chaplin, was a comedienne who took comedy seriously.

Despite the flaws to be found in *Tillie's Punctured Romance*, fans and critics were extremely impressed with the finished product. The *Reading Times*, the *Abilene Daily Reflector* and the *Fresno Morning Republican* all presented readers with positive write ups. Roughly six months after its initial release, the *Daily Times* wrote two gushing pieces on *Tillies*, promoting how expensive it was to make as well as how groundbreaking it was to cinema. Describing the film as "a screamingly funny six reel Keystone picture," the *Times* heaped praise on the production, writing that "roars of laughter have greeted the screen capers of Chaplin, Marie Dressler and Mabel Normand everywhere 'Tillie' has been exhibited." It might not have been art, but *Tillies Punctured Romance* showed just how far the genre of comedy might go.

In time, Mabel pushed that genre even further along.

Franz Ferdinand

The heir to the throne of the Austro-Hungarian Empire was a stubborn man. Sophie Chotek may have been a mere "lady in waiting" among the imperial upper crust, but young Franz Ferdinand was in love and that was all there was to it. Suffice to say, Franz' uncle, the Austro-Hungarian Emperor, was none too pleased. A future emperor was supposed to marry someone of his own rank, after all. Bad enough that his nephew had the insane idea of modernizing the Empire, now he had the temerity to marry someone beneath his rank? Outrageous! Again, though, Franz Ferdinand was a stubborn man. He went ahead and married Sophie against his uncle's wishes on the condition that Sophie could never be Empress and that none of their children could ever be heirs to the throne.

The Emperor had bigger things to worry about than his nephew's choice of spouse, however. The world was becoming a very dangerous place. His ally Germany was on the rise, the powerful nations of France and Great Britain were none too happy about it, and Serbian nationals within his own empire were most distinctly displeased about their treatment at the hands of his government. The Emperor had to be careful. Nations and empires around the globe had allied themselves into various groups. What happened to one nation or empire impacted all the others.

There was good reason, then, for the Emperor's nephew and heir to visit Bosnia in the early summer of 1914. Bosnia was home to a population of ethnic Serbians who resented the way the empire treated them. It all made perfect sense. Of course a journey to Bosnia was dangerous, as a revolutionary group known as the Black Hand operated there. To the heir to the Imperial throne, however, it was worth the trip. On the 28th of June, Franz Ferdinand and his beloved wife Sophie arrived in the Bosnian capital of Sarajevo. The Black

Hand, however, knew of the visit in advance and subsequently put its own plans in motion.

On the way to the Sarajevo town hall, a bomb was tossed at the car Franz Ferdinand and Sophie were travelling in. The bomb didn't hit its moving target, exploding instead just behind it in the convoy, harming several members of the imperial entourage. Rather than rushing to safety, Franz Ferdinand and Sophie continued on with their plans, traveling on to the town hall, where Franz Ferdinand, being a boorish type by nature, proceeded to yell at the mayor. After the town hall ceremony, the stubborn Franz Ferdinand decided to go to the nearby hospital where the wounded members of his entourage had been taken.

His driver took a wrong turn. Then the engine stalled. Then the world changed. A Serbian radical standing – or stationed – nearby outside a deli hopped onto the floorboard of the car and subsequently shot Franz Ferdinand and Sophie in the neck and abdomen respectively. With his dying last words, Franz Ferdinand begged Sophie to survive for the sake of their three children. Both husband and wife were dead within minutes. A month later, the Austro-Hungarian Empire, with the backing of powerful Germany, declared war on Serbia. Russia subsequently backed Serbia. England and France went on to back Russia. Soon the entire world was in a war that would literally cost millions of lives and alter the course of history forever. The United States itself ended up getting into the fray, losing thousands of lives of its own.

It's worth asking how a shooting in front of a deli in eastern Europe led to the deaths of countless people from literally every inhabited continent on earth. As some have argued, what happened that terrible day in Sarajevo was merely the trigger – or the excuse, depending on how one looks at it – that started a deadly global conflict which by that point was pretty much unavoidable anyway. Either way, what became known as the First World War may have largely been fought in Europe, Asia, and Africa, but that didn't stop its impact from reaching all corners of the earth – including New

York and southern California, the twin bases of the American motion picture industry.

Not yet the global powerhouse it would become as a result of its eventual entry into the war, the United States was slow to join in the fray. Indeed, American troops didn't engage in combat until the later portions of the war. Once America was in the proverbial mix, however, the motion picture industry did its part, presenting films designed to entertain, rally the public and earn money for the American cause. Movies and celebrities also took on a patriotic role.

"When the United States entered World War I," wrote Professor Leslie Midkiff DeBauche of the University of Wisconson, "the film industry seized the opportunity to convey the government's messages to the American people. A number of federal departments and agencies routed educational programs and propaganda through the variety of channels the film industry made available." Before America entered the fray, however, much of the country was against the effort to bring the United States into the war. America hadn't been directly involved with any of the conflicts, after all.

The sinking of the British merchant ship Lusitania, courtesy of a German torpedo, proved to be the final straw. Numerous Americans perished among the one thousand plus victims of the attack. Although the German embassy had warned that ships traveling under British flags were open targets beforehand, the sinking of the vessel riled the American public to the point where it joined in the fight. There would be no turning back until the fighting finally came to an end in November of 1918.

The war, both before and after America's entry, had a profound effect on Mabel, leading the star to make bold statements regarding her positions on the conflict. Without doubt, Mabel was someone secure in her beliefs throughout her life. The First World War, however, impacted her in a profoundly personal way by striking close to home.

"Queen Of the Movies"

"The true function of the film is to show that which could not be shown on the stage." This quote, attributed to an "Expert" in a 1915 article by *Motion Picture Magazine* is nonetheless accurate in its assessment of movies at the time. For films did what stage plays couldn't – which is part of the reason why actors like Mabel, who could fly in a plane or a hot air balloon or race along a speed track or complete a daring dive, became so popular. It was just the right moment in time for someone with her unique abilities, though she showed she could evolve her brand of comedy over time.

Sure enough, the many movies Mabel proceeded to make with Arbuckle after Chaplin took his leave of Keystone often presented Mabel as more than put upon. Although the "Fatty and Mable" movies, as they're known, can sometimes delve into the sentimental, they generally have the same wacky style of outcomes her films with Chaplin had. Arbuckle, however, was a completely different kind of performer than Chaplin. At his best, Chaplin's performances are all about Chaplin. A solid actor like Mabel could more than hold her own, but as a whole Chaplin wasn't a world class collaborator. It simply wasn't where his talent as a performer could be found.

One of the best Fatty and Mabel films of 1915 was *Mabel and Fatty and the Law*. Fatty is married to Mabel in the film but has a wandering eye. He hooks up with another woman in a park where "no spooning" is allowed. Fatty goes to jail, where Mabel, after getting together with the other woman's husband, bails Fatty out and subsequently cracks him. While the short film clearly deals with some unethical decisions in about as an innocuous manner as possible, justice is served in the end, in screwball Keystone style, no less.

Fatty and Mabel's Married Life is another 1915 standout. A wacky film in the Keystone style, Fatty is away while Mable thinks "foreign robbers" are trying to break into the house. Turns out it's just an Italian organ grinder looking for his missing monkey, which he eventually finds in the house after much mayhem. The movie is surprisingly progressive for its time considering Mabel sees in the end that the Italian character is just a man who loves his monkey and is not a thief.

Fatty and Mabel at the San Diego Exposition, another 1915 pairing of Mabel and Arbuckle, is much like the title says. A Chaplin look alike makes a cameo and at least parts are clearly filmed at the exposition itself. As usual, things descend into slapstick madness. *Mabel and Fatty Viewing the World Fair at San Francisco,* on the other hand, is more of an on-site documentary than anything else, with the two stars soaking in the sights and sounds of the World Fair. Mabel is her energetic, fast-moving self, here, very curious about some of the things she sees. As an eerie side note – the Hotel St. Francis is featured here, which is where Arbuckle threw his infamous party years later.

Yet Mabel was known as more than the co-star of Arbuckle's at the time. Nor was she simply known as a cute, daring, and unique comic. She was, if anything, a person people simply wanted to know more about, a celebrity in the truest sense of the word. *The Photoplayers Weekly* reported that year that famed botanist Luther Burbank "made a special trip to the rose gardens" owned by Mabel, presumably at her address on the corner of "Marathon and Melrose Hill," which was described as "a big two-story house in a semi-colonial style." The article, which referred to Mabel as the "Queen of the Movies," made it clear Burbank was impressed with the star's skill as a gardener.

Mabel was admired for more than just her gardening, however. In a *Photoplay* piece that year, Mabel was presented in a photo being made up – presumably for a film or photoshoot. Under the photo was a quote Mabel gave to Grace Kingsley: "Put your mind on the fashions and anticipate changes; it's not hard to tell what the next style will be. Silks, velvets, satins and flowered or striped materials are best in pictures." Mabel was finally getting to wear the kinds of clothes she had dreamed of wearing when she modeled for artists and photographers in New York. Except now she was no model – she was someone regarded as an expert in women's fashion.

It was certainly a good time to be Mabel Normand. As Kristine Brunovska Karnick writes in *Hysterical! Women in American Comedy*: "In 1915 *Moving Picture World* ran a movie popularity contest, which Normand won as 'Female Comedian.'" With regular checks from Keystone amounting to well in excess of two-hundred thousand 21st century dollars a year for film work alone, Mabel made more than double what President Woodrow Wilson earned per year. Not all was perfect, however.

Although Mabel was certainly making an impressive amount of money, she wasn't making as much as her peers. Chaplin left Keystone in order to make over two times as much money as she did. And, wildly popular as Chaplin was, it was virtually impossible to imagine he was worth two and a half times as much money as the single most popular female movie star in the world. Indeed, by that point in their respective careers, Mabel may well have been as popular as Chaplin was. What's more, other stars, such as Ford Sterling had stepped away from Keystone. On top of all that, Arbuckle within the year was lured away to Paramount by what was then the biggest financial offer in motion picture history - a breathtaking one million dollars.

Yet, contrary to what is often said, Stephen Normand states that Mable and Mack WERE indeed engaged to be wed. And for Catholic Mabel, marriage was a serious endeavor, one to be taken with the utmost seriousness. In short, it would take more than a financial gripe to get her to turn on the man who asked her to spend her life with him. Sadly, Mac does not appear to have been an individual of overly strong character. When it came to Mack, Stephen says that "money overruled everything else." To make matters even more precarious, underpaid though she was, Mabel was earning more than even the most qualified accountant of the time could imagine, and so she put her trust in her fiancé when it came to money. All would remain well – provided Mack was loyal.

Mae Busch

"Imagine if you can," the actress Mae Bush once wrote in an article which circulated throughout the United States, "a girl who has not been accustomed to wealth and luxury. This girl comes to Hollywood and suddenly a picture company dumps more money in her lap every week than she ever dreamed could be brought together at one time." Her article, penned in 1929, was not an apologia but a plea for understanding. For the Australian born actress had, until recently, pretty much had it all. And then she lost it.

As Busch herself put it, "the girl goes Hollywood." What she meant was that "one loses all sense of perspective, all sense of judgment. The money is rolling in. More money than we had ever hoped for, more money than many of us knew existed; and we don't know what to do with it." Although Busch may not have known what to do with the fortune she had earned as a film actress, she certainly appeared to know how to make it disappear. When the article was published, Busch was down to less than five hundred dollars while caring for a sickly father. How far she had fallen.

Now she asked Superior Judge Marshall McComb of Los Angeles to have mercy on her, as she no longer even had access to the small bit of money she had left. The Court had placed an attachment against it. As she stated in her article, which described the elaborate sums of money she had spent on clothes, parties and other symbols of an elaborate lifestyle, her money had "gone out steadily. And the result has been that I have had to go to court as I did and let it be known how low my funds were."

Suffice to say, Busch indicated that her private ruin and public humiliation had taught her a valuable lesson – and that she could learn from her mistakes. McComb decided to give her a chance. The attachment was lifted, and, sure enough, Busch stayed true to her word and made a comeback for herself. By the thirties, she was known as Oliver Hardy's perpetually agitated wife in the popular "Laurel and Hardy" films. What's more, she continued making films into the 1940s, while she was in her fifties. When she died in 1946, she had been in the movie business for over twenty-five years.

Born in Melbourne, Australia to musician parents, Busch was taken to the United States when she was still a young child of six. Her parents then sent her to St. Elizabeth's Convent in New Jersey, where she stayed for around four years. Busch claimed she learned to sing in the convent, which led to her becoming a performer herself when she left. After performing on Broadway, Busch made her way onto the vaudeville circuit. Upon seeing Busch perform, Mack offered her the chance to join up with Keystone. Busch accepted. She went on to stay until 1916, making more than fifteen films for the studio.

Perhaps what led to Busch's standing out was her versatility as a performer. Chaplin himself called Busch "the greatest actress on the screen." This assertion may certainly be open for debate, but there's little doubt that Busch was a high energy, thoroughly engaged performer who was often so focused – or what today is referred to as "in the zone" – that she seemed unaware that she was performing before motion picture cameras. In short, Busch had the deep courage required to be a performer. Yet a performer requires more than just courage. A performer needs talent and passion. Judging from Busch's surviving film work, it's clear the woman had an abundance of both.

While it's true Busch worked in a variety of genres for a number of studios, she ultimately is most well known for her work as Oliver Hardy's fictional wife. There's good reason for this, as Busch certainly holds her own with the famous comic duo of Stan Laurel and Oliver Hardy. A look at the duo's first "talkie" film, "Unaccustomed As We Are," allows the viewer to see Busch launch into a diatribe against Hardy while the puzzled Laurel stands by watching. Hardy turns on a record to break the monotony of Busch's gripes, only for Busch to organically and unknowingly start griping to the music. It's a wonderful bit of comedy, one that clearly required exquisite skill and timing on behalf of Busch in order to be pulled off so successfully.

By 1947, with about one hundred and fifty films under her belt and now in her mid-fifties, Busch appeared in her final film, "Ladies Man," where she made a cameo. By the time the film was released in February of 1947, Busch had been dead close to a year. At the time of her passing, Busch had been married to Thomas Tate. Before that Busch was married to John Cassell and Francis McDonald respectively. She had no children, to her lasting regret. Indeed, the woman had even once composed a somber poem about not being able to conceive that was published in "The News, New York":

BARREN!
by
Mae Busch
Never to see your image in my arms
Nestling at my breast –
Tiny lips draining the milk of my
life –
Tiny hands clutching the tendrils
of my heart –
Why does God create barren soil,
when He forever fertilizes it
with His rain?
His sun, His softly warm winds?
Is life forever to go on wanting?
With naught for my arms but the
head of men,
Naught for my heart but their lash?

Looked at as a whole, however, it's clear Busch had herself an impressive career. She rose, she fell, then was able to once again get back on her feet. Even more impressively, she was able to do so after she was past the point of being a young starlet. Ultimately, it was her talent that provided her with her career. If she wasn't a Hollywood icon, there was – and is – no arguable way the woman can be considered a Hollywood failure. Her work as an actor, after all, is still available and ready to stand on its own.

Although not overly well known in the 21st century, Busch is nonetheless a part of Hollywood history as much for an incident that occurred between her and Mabel as for her countless screen performances. The incident changed Mabel's life forever, changing the course of her career, and even her overall outlook on life. And neither woman's story can be told without attention being paid to the other.

Beyond The Breaking Point

"The most frightening thing of all," Chaplin wrote of his start at Keystone, "was the fact that the great Ford Sterling was only getting fifty dollars a week more than I, and other members of the company three dollars a day who I thought were very good actors. All this gave me a great deal of anxiety." By 1919 Chaplin was forming his own studio with Mary Pickford and her husband, adventure star Douglas Fairbanks. Needless to say, he was already one of the highest paid – if not THE highest paid - entertainers in the world by that time, having long since left Keystone in the rear view mirror.

Chaplin's success, as well as the control he had over his own material, was phenomenal. Here was a man who got to do what he wanted as an artist, when he wanted. What's more, Paramount studios eventually offered Arbuckle more money than even Chaplin had been offered when he left Keystone. With stars like Sterling and Mace leaving and returning it was obvious that Keystone was not a place where popular comedians stayed employed. The pay, frankly, didn't often meet the popularity of the studio's stars.

Mabel, of course, was the exception. As Stephen Normand pointed out, she and Mack were indeed engaged, with Mabel even having an engagement ring (when Mack actually popped the question remains a mystery). What's more, her family had gone west to meet him. In 1915, however, things came to an abrupt halt. Although the details remain vague, the impact of the incident in question was profound, altering Mabel's career, personal life and even her overall outlook on life. "All the family were inside," Minta Durfee said of the evening in question. "And up comes this cab driver with Mabel with blood all over from top to bottom, where this awful Mae Busch had struck her."

According to Stephen Normand, Mabel had walked in on Mack and Mae. Although Stephen argues the two weren't having an affair, they were certainly caught being too close for comfort. Suffice it to say Mabel went off on Mae, who subsequently and brazenly struck her. The ugly moment not only ended the engagement of Mable and Mack, it arguably turned Mabel's world upside down, for now she saw things as they were. Not only was Mack paying her less than she was worth, not only was he ornery to be around ("She found Mack very difficult," Stephen claimed), not only had he put off marrying her, but he was also now caught being untrustworthy. On top all that, Mabel was assaulted and physically wounded by the very woman Mack was being untrustworthy with.

Such events are, and were, commonplace in Hollywood. Mabel, however, couldn't be considered a typical Hollywood Star in any era. For instance, she had stayed loyal to Mack in a town and industry where she was young and considered quite beautiful. "No Charlie," Chaplin claimed she had once said to him after he had kissed her, "you're not my type, and neither am I yours." Mack, it seems, had a type. It was Mack, after all, who had come up with the idea of his "Bathing Beauties," attractive girls appearing in bathing suits to entice potential Keystone viewers, just around a year earlier. Mabel, of course, had previously been filmed in a bathing suit numerous times – and Busch was filmed in a bathing suit as well in that year's *Settled at the Seaside* with Charlie Chase. Throwing in the fact that Mack had previously worked in burlesque theater, and it now became obvious to Mabel just what kind of man he truly was.

Perhaps worst of all for someone like Mabel was the fact that she was a devout Catholic who, according to Stephen Normand, likely had sex with Mack outside of marriage. She had trusted the man she thought would become her husband, had even put her soul at risk, she believed, and for what? For him to spend time with the likes of Mae Busch? The entire matter clearly must have struck the bleeding Mabel to her core all at once that evening. Sitting at the Arbuckle's, she must have realized she and Mack had different plans for their future the entire time.

She had wanted to be wife, business partner, and undoubtedly parent. He, on the other hand, probably wanted her to marry him once her star started to dim. Then she could stay home with the children or smile idiotically by his side at film premiers while he focused in on one Mae Busch after another. Undoubtedly, Mabel must have felt foolish for having allowed herself to have been blinded.

Mack, however, had allowed himself to have been blinded as well if he actually believed his brilliant, hyperactive fiancée would someday allow him to make her a captive housewife with a blind eye to his dalliances. Did he really not know Mabel at all? As the chaotic evening turned to day, Mack must have been awake with worry. Not only had he just lost a fiancée, but he had also enraged the one person he truly needed for his studio – Mabel. As long as he had a huge star like Mabel in the studio lineup, the likes of Chaplin, Sterling, and Arbuckle could come and go. Should Mabel now decide to leave, however, he would no longer have that security. In a sense, he was now at the mercy of the young woman he had disrespected. Mae Bush was talented and quite attractive, but she was no Mabel.

And Mack knew it.

There is no doubt that once the shock and the pain from her injury started to subside, Mabel began viewing matters objectively. It was obvious Mack would have to come to her to make amends. He couldn't afford the news that he had been disloyal to the most famous comedienne on earth to reach the public. Mabel was seen by fans as wholesome, which wasn't entirely untrue. He, on the other hand, was seen, if at all, as being a prominent film big shot. There was no way he could win a public relations battle against the likes of Mabel, and he knew it. And again, he needed Mabel financially. Perhaps Mack even felt genuine remorse that early on and hoped he might get Mabel back somehow. If so, he was grasping at imaginary straws.

Mabel was never romantically involved with Mack again.

Vincent Chiappa

"The Reverend Father Vincent Chiappa of Loyala College, Los Angeles, will preach a mission next week in the Italian language for those of the Italian tongue at St. Joseph's Church, East Bakersfield," the "Bakersfield Morning Echo" informed its readers in late April of 1926. At over seventy years of age, Chiappa was known as one of the oldest Italian missionaries in the United States. Born in Piedmont, Italy in 1852, Chiappa, according to "Our Sunday Visitor," had "entered the Society of Jesus on June 1, 1871, when he was about nineteen years of age." He came to the United States in 1872 and was ordained a priest at Woodstock College, in Maryland.

Going west, Chiappa found himself in San Francisco, teaching at the College of Saint Ignatius, as well as at Santa Clara. After getting sick and becoming an assistant director of the Jesuit novitiate in Los Gatos for a while, Chiappa was then sent to the Mission Band and "preached throughout the Northwest." Chiappa then went on to be a pastor in Lewiston, Idaho, before moving on to Spokane, Washington where he became "the spiritual father of the young scholastics" at Mount St. Michael. The cleric finally found himself as the Chaplin of Loyola in Los Angeles in 1924, where he remained until his death in 1929.

Chiappa was clearly an intellectual. In 1910, for instance, he preached a sermon on "The Catholic Church, Origin, Nature and Extent of Her Authority," wherein he discussed matters such as the Church's "Claim on Mankind," and "Church and State." Yet Chiappa was also a man of action, performing Catholic missions that could last for over a week, such as one held at Saint Patrick's Church in Oakland in 1911 that lasted ten days. Children were seeped in the faith while two masses were celebrated, and two sermons preached daily.

Naturally, being a missionary, Chiappa was interested in more than just preaching to his flock. While carrying out a mission in Montana, he made it a point to announce that those who weren't Catholic were especially welcome. It may seem strange that a Catholic missionary would operate in the United States of the 20th century, but America at the time was a vastly Protestant nation. What's more, some Catholics were seen as being disconnected from their faith in the vast American landscape. On top of that, there were always the poor and marginalized to serve - a priority of acute importance for Jesuits.

It should come as no surprise then that Chiappa celebrated mass for his fellow Italians in their native language. Nor should it come as a surprise that he held a mission for Native American children from California's Sherman Institute, a school designed especially for Native Americans, giving "40 or 50 the children their First Communion." Yet Chiappa worked with more than just the marginalized and downtrodden and local parishes. Being the Chaplin of Loyola in Los Angeles meant he was quite close by to the booming motion picture industry.

One of the more notable film writers of the silent era, Herbert Howe, wasn't a Catholic though he wrote of a movie star friend of his who had encouraged him to visit Chiappa. "There is one priest who is a miracle-worker," he recalled the friend telling him. "He saved my life, God love him. I wish you would let me introduce you to Father Chiappa, a very old Italian priest. You like Italians, don't you?" Howe assured the friend that he would indeed like to meet this priest he had heard spoken of in such high regard.

True to his word, Howe made his way to Loyola College the following day to meet with the 72-year-old priest. "I entered the little office and talked with Father Chiappa," Howe remembered, "a man of Christ-like gentleness over whom earth no longer had power." The non-Catholic press man was admittedly impressed. "When he died," Howe wrote of Chiappa's death half a decade later, "I felt I had lost an unfailing friend. Such is the instant power of fine personality." People may not have shared the old priest's beliefs, but it was clear he had the ability to win himself admirers.

And the film industry was already filled with people who were learning that fame could be a burden as well as a blessing. Plus, with untold amounts of money at stake, those performers had the burden of knowing that fortunes and the careers of their co-workers rested on their shoulders. No small thing. On top of all that, virtually all of the film industry consisted of transplants from areas outside of California. As Howe learned, however, Mabel, the movie star friend who had introduced him to Chiappa, was particularly drawn to the elder Chaplin.

"I am a Catholic," she said to Howe, "but don't hold that against the church." Mabel, Howe found out, took her Catholicism very seriously. Indeed, Chiappa told Howe that Mabel financed an entire wing of an Italian orphanage. Stephen Normand himself revealed that there are letters from orphanages, as well as convents, thanking Mabel for her considerable financial support, which helped fund not only orphanages, but also children's charities both in the United States and Europe. These were donations, however, Mabel never wanted made public in her lifetime. A Catholic, after all, was not one who was supposed to look for praise.

Yet to Mabel, Vincent Chiappa was more than just a conduit through which she could funnel money to charitable causes. As she told Howe, he had saved her life. One suspects he was there for support and guidance when life became dark for Mabel indeed. Howe referred to Chiappa as Mabel's "Father Confessor," yet a confessor does more than hear confession, and Chiappa appears to have been able to offer Mabel – who was always ready to admit she was no saint – the kind of support she was looking for when life as she knew it began falling apart.

Mabel Normand Studio

There's a popular belief that Mack's autobiography is an insincere grasp at positive self-promotion. This may largely be true, but in the pages of the book, the man does seem to be sincere in his guilt regarding his treatment of Mabel. If not, why not be more self-defensive in those pages where he fondly writes of "the actress who ate ice cream for breakfast"? Of course, no one can tell what's in a person's heart, especially as life winds down, but it seems Mack was a man who simply couldn't rise above his selfishness. His weakness, in short, was too difficult for him to surmount. Mabel appeared to have been keenly aware of this after the Mae Busch incident. What's more, Mack was well aware himself at that point that Mabel was on to him.

And he needed Mabel to make movies. The problem for Mack was that, by and far, Mabel WASN'T making movies. The fact remains that, cloudy as the exact details of the incident might have been, Mae clearly hurt Mabel quite badly when she struck her. It's been said she hit Mabel with a shoe – or even a vase. Whatever it was, Mabel was effectively out of the film business until she healed – both physically and emotionally. For his part, Mack seems to have tried to keep the true details of Mabel's injury under wraps. Still, the media soon caught on to just how severe the situation was, even if they didn't understand what exactly had happened. They may not have known what led to Mabel's distress, but they certainly were aware that Mabel had been hurt badly.

Under the banner headline "Mabel Normand Fighting Death," the *Los Angeles Times* wrote that "While medical science waged a desperate battle for her life, Mabel Normand, famous film star and comedy queen, was unconscious and rapidly sinking today. Her physician, Dr. O.M. Justice, early today, stated that the chance for her recovery was slight." The report went on to state that Mabel had been unconscious for several days and "that no rally is expected today…from her sick room at the Baltic Apartments."

The story concluded with the assertion that "Miss Normand's illness is attributed to an accident in the studio of the Keystone company, of which she is a leading lady, a little more than a week ago. It is stated that the beautiful star fell, sustaining injuries to her head. Since the fall Miss Normand has suffered concussion of the brain and not once since the accident has she uttered a coherent word." One obviously had to ask whether Mabel's condition was as serious as reported or if hyperbole was involved. She did, after all, recover fully with what appears to have been no lasting damage. Regardless, other publications ran stories on Mabel's condition throughout late 1915.

On November 7th, *The Baltimore Sun* reported that Mabel was over her "serious illness," but world be avoiding work while she took a lengthy vacation. On December 12th, *The Fresno Morning Republican* wrote in one story that Mabel was injured on set when Arbuckle fell on her, then claimed in another article in the exact same edition that she had been involved in a plane crash on November 17th with fellow Keystone star Charlie Chase. Years before radio was in popular usage, decades before television was in popular usage and close to a century before the internet was in popular usage, all variety of tales regarding Mabel's injury seemed to appear at various times throughout the later part of 1915.

Yet, amid the journalistic chaos, a piece of news appeared on September 11th in *The Tacoma Times* that gave an indication not only of Mabel's future, but also of the future of comedy: that a new $500,000 Keystone studio was being built for Mabel. Indeed, Mabel was now to head the Mabel Normand Feature Fim Company. She may have been injured, she may have had her heart broken, but how many stars had their own studios named after them, as Mabel now did? Her future would be her own, and she would make it as she wished.

Nursing a broken heart can be a strange experience. One reflects. One grasps for clarity and a degree of perspective. Finally, one must accept the fact that it's time to move on or to stay a stationary victim of the past indefinitely. While recuperating physically and emotionally, Mabel realized that she had to move on – but on her own terms. She would work with Mack, yes, but she would now make the kinds of films SHE wanted to make. The days of silly Mabel were over, both on and off screen. She was still a good time prankster, but Mabel now, at her core, was considered a serious force in the industry.

A rare positive aspect of heartbreak is that it can lead a person to reflective depths otherwise unknown. That may have been the case with Mabel, for she now wanted her work to have a degree of artistry to it. She would still – and always – be a comedienne, but now she was also an artist keen on bringing her own personal vision to the screen. Mack, who was now with Triangle Studios via merger, may not have been happy with this new Mabel, but he needed his star back before the cameras again. Plus, there was likely a degree of guilt involved.

"On December 26, 1915," wrote Marilyn Slater and Marie Squiciati, "Mabel Normand left Sennett in Edendale to work at the Triangle Studios in Fort Lee, New Jersey with Roscoe Arbuckle, Minta Durfee (Mrs. Arbuckle), and several Keystone players. Here they made the dark comedy *He Did and He Didn't* and a few others." Slater and Squiciati also wrote that "Roscoe and Mabel staged a mock funeral and buried an actual Chinese slapstick and their ties to Sennett's ways." Mack, simply put, was no longer calling the shots as he had in previous years. In fact, Mabel, who was now close to her family on the east coast, wasn't particularly eager to rush back to the west coast.

"Normand returned to California in the summer of 1916," continued Slater and Squiciati, "to her own studio in Silverlake and her own production company." Not only did Mabel now have a studio to call her own, but she also had a studio that catered to her and her tastes. “She had full control of her work,” wrote Slater and Squiciati. “The ten-acre studio, built by her design and financed by Sennett was, it was believed, an apology for what happened between them.”

Mabel, the tiny young girl in the sweatshop, had made the jump from star to studio head. She was now set up to create her magnum opus.

Minnie Devereaux

It's easy to blur the past. Eras seem to collide, to seep in and out of each other, to be one in the same one instant, and then completely separate entities the next. Mabel's era is perhaps particularly hard for those of the 21st century to get a firm grasp of. The famous Old West of lore was still coming to an end in some areas during Mabel's time while the Jazz Age was on the verge of breaking out in others. People like Mabel would flew in planes and raced around in cars, but the horse drawn carriage was still in regular use, even in major cities. Modern, high-tech warfare was raging in the fields of Europe, but the lands being fought over were still being run by kings, as if it were still the Middle Ages. Without doubt, Mabel existed in a period of profound transition.

How hard it is, for instance, to reconcile the fact that Mabel's "A Dash Through the Clouds," which saw her flying on an airplane while shooting a gun, came out just weeks after the sinking of the Titanic? Or that Harriet Tubman was still alive when Mabel arrived in California in January of 1912? Such facts have a way of putting matters in perspective while at the same time blurring that perspective. The truth is that Mabel, high diving, speed race loving, gun toting, airplane adoring Mabel, was very much a part of the turning of the page, as it were. Indeed, she helped, and was actually among those at the forefront of, the evolution of traditional America to what would be modern America. Still, a country's past can't be denied.

"Minnie was 'Earth Woman,' daughter of Chief Plenty Horses, head of his tribe," proclaimed Mack's own hype publication, the egotistically named "Mack Sennett Weekly." Chief Plenty Horse was well known for going about killing a member of the American Military in revenge for the brutal Massacre at Wounded Knee, where hundreds of Lakota, many of whom were women and children, died

in a battle with American soldiers after one Lakota, who by that point had been double crossed and half starved, refused to surrender his weapon (In fairness it should be noted that news of the slaughter came as no surprise to high ranking American military officials, who themselves were angry at the treatment the Lakota were receiving beforehand, but were unfortunately powerless to do anything about it despite their best efforts).

As for the "Minnie," the article writes of, she was Native American actress Minnie Devereaux, part of Mack's team of character actors. What has to be kept in mind is that the Hollywood system, much like the system today, loved to lie to make the lives of their performers appear more colorful. Mabel, for instance, was said to have been born in Atlanta, as if working class Staten Island simply wouldn't do. It's doubtful Minnie was any exception, though one never knows. Ultimately, the Minnie of "Mack Sennett Weekly" was the Minnie the public was presented with. Not only was she the daughter of the infamous Chief Plenty Horses, she herself claimed to have been witness to the events at Little Bighorn, where General George Armstrong Custer was wiped out along with his men by Lakota warriors a good forty years earlier.

"'Can't remember because I was only eight years old?' Minnie snorts. 'You forget I was an Indian then, and an Indian does not forget. I remember the happenings of those days better than the things of yesterday, for the white man has taught me how to forget. You write things on paper, you lose the paper and then is gone. We did not write down our thoughts but stored them away in memory.'"

This is a strange quote in that it indicates white American readers, even before the 1920s, had begun to embrace the view that Native Americans had been gravely wronged. Yet the quote still rings of stage acting, of engaging in stereotypical dialogue to capture the reader's attention. Minnie here seems to be more of a writer's idea of a noble savage than a living, breathing, actual person arguing her case to a skeptical audience. With that in mind, there's no defeating the argument that these WERE Minnie's actual words, or that she truly was at the Battle of Little Big Horn, or that she was the daughter of Chief Plenty Horses. There simply appears to be no definitive proof one way or another. Still, one can suspect the truth lies beyond that which on the surface appears to be an obvious fabrication.

And to be sure, minorities and outsiders were indeed treated stereotypically in the silent era. Mabel's surviving films are relatively free of such ugliness, yet it can still be found on occasion. A greedy Jewish stereotype here (perhaps even one played by a Jew), characters performing in blackface onscreen there, stereotypical figures aren't bouncing out of Mabel's film resume, but they can, at times, sadly be found. Strangely, the nature of such things doesn't even appear to have been questioned by the film industry at the time, at least not among those who operated and/or emerged from the Keystone empire. For instance, Mabel, whose own mother's family had come from long suffering Ireland, was said to derogatively refer to producer Hal Roache as "that thick necked Mick." Such attribution, clearly deemed unacceptable in the 21st century, were largely ignored at the time as simply being a harmless aspect of the nature of the business.

With that being said, evidence strongly suggests that Devereaux had a close and positive relationship with Mabel, appearing in numerous films with her, forever playing the mature adult to Mabel's impulsive young ladies. Candid photos taken after working days, also indicate a natural friendship between the two women. Indeed, one of these photos shows a picture of Mabel and a film crew sitting around a large bonfire one night. The crowd is loaded with smiling white faces, yet it's Devereaux who sits close to the smiling Mabel.

“Mickey”

“You see I have a hobby that dovetails beautifully with my work here. It’s studio house keeping, or, rather, studio home keeping,” Mabel told film journalist Pearl Gaddis of her new studio in 1916. “Efficiency comes first of course, but I didn’t see why a studio should be a huge, unlovely barn of wood. So I planned for comfort and beauty, as well as efficiency. That explains the rugs downstairs, the adorable balcony, and the attractive dressing rooms.” Gaddis described the studio as “having ever so many feminine touches that make it artistic as well as businesslike, comfortable as well as efficient.”

Mabel now not only had her own studio, she also had the freedom to make the kind of film she herself now wanted to make. And what Mabel wanted to make was a movie that focused on character, and that, while still a comedy, dealt with timeless themes and also contained drama and adventure along with the humor. After heartbreak and a splash in the face of cold reality, Mabel was determined to enrich here work with larger subjects that mattered to her – subjects such as class, the desire to rise above one’s lot in life, and, of course, loyalty. It would all be rather Dickensesque, which was exactly what she wanted.

In May of 1916, the *Chicago Tribune* announced that James Young would be directing Mabel in a “four-reel comedy drama in the special Mabel Normand studio.” By January of the following year, the *Tribune* informed readers that Mabel, who had been away from the scene, was heading her own studio. She was to make four movies a year, all features. *Mickey*, readers were informed, would be the first film. The article also added that *Mickey* would be a more mature comedy for Normand. A few months later, in April, the *Butte Miner* reported the mystery of where Mabel was had been answered. She had been busy making a feature film called *Mickey* with her own studio. That same month the *Santa Fe New Mexican* informed readers that it had been announced that Mabel had taken a year away from films in order to work on *Mickey*.

The buzz around *Mickey*, which was indeed the film Mabel had been making at her studio, was intense. Then again, the shoot was lengthy. What's more, the film was extremely expensive for its time, costing a full quarter of a million dollars to make. Filming primarily occurred at the Mabel Normand Studio, though parts were also filmed at Lake Arrowhead and Exposition Park, both in California. Some other portions of the movie were filmed at a Phoenix racetrack.

Indeed, it was while in Phoenix that Mabel and Minta Durfee took time to take part ia a Peace Rally per the request of Arizona Governor George Hunt, in the hope of keeping the United States out of the world war which was currently tearing up the globe. Mabel had previously been the feature attraction at a huge "Peace Day" at the 1916 Panama California International Exposition where, according to Slater and Squiciati, "thousands of California children paraded on the fairgrounds to watch Normand dig a 'grave' and bury the symbols of war: a sword, a gun, and a pistol. Then she planted a symbol of peace, an olive tree, atop the grave of the instruments of war."

For the Phoenix event, Mabel provided "Peace Garden" pins for the children there. Mabel also wanted fruits and vegetables, along with the olive tree and weapons, planted so that the focus would be on growth as well as the avoidance of war. "Mabel Normand Global Peace Day," which occurred on November 16th of 1916, proved to be a huge success. Mabel carried out the ceremony of burying weapons alongside two veterans of the Civil War, again firmly presenting herself as an opponent of war. Her opinions changed over time, but for the moment, pacifism was something Mabel clearly felt quite strongly about.

Overall, it was an extremely busy period for Mabel. She had showcased her forgiving Catholicism earlier that summer when a man tried blackmailing her, telling Mabel he had information on her that she absolutely didn't want to be made public. Mabel agreed to pay the man off in her Baltic Apartment suite on Orange Street – but when the blackmailer arrived, he found the police waiting for him. Not only was Mabel unwilling to give the man money, she went to the authorities on the matter, who subsequently arranged the sting operation. Unbeknownst to the blackmailer, the apartment was tapped, and policemen were hiding in the closet. "The whole affair was terribly exciting," claimed Mabel while admitting: "I was frightened once or twice. It all seems so mysterious and strange to me."

The blackmailer ended up being one Raymond A. Swett, a Los Angeles doctor who was down on his luck. "I have a wife, child and father dependent on me," he wrote to Mabel while in custody. "They will be the ones to suffer if you see fit to go on with the prosecution. I have come to you clean with my story of wrongdoing, and now ask that you show clemency for their sakes if not my own. Will you kindly consider and give your answer to the bearer?" Mabel, who was originally willing to charge the good doctor, had a change of heart.

"While I feel that I am doing an injustice to the public at large by not prosecuting Dr. Swett to the full extent of the law," she said. "I am constrained to hear his plea for clemency on account of his wife, child and father, whom I find to be wholly dependent on him for a livelihood…I feel perfectly willing to drop the case as it stands and have Dr. Swett released to his wife and child."

Without doubt, it was an interesting time to be Mabel Normand. Indeed, it must have seemed like a lifetime ago when she caught Mack and Mae Busch together, seemingly behind her back, in 1915. However, Mabel was determined to make her mark as an artist in Hollywood. No longer was she simply a star. No longer was she simply a writer and a director. Now she was a producer. Not only that, she was a studio head, and *Mickey*, in spite of all else transpiring in her hectic life at the moment, came to life via her design.

Without doubt, there would be practicality mixed with Mabel's artistry on the project. The world was at war, a war the United States might soon find itself embroiled in. Untold thousands of lives were being lost on a regular basis. The appetite for kicks to the rear and bricks to the head was unquestionably on the wane. Keystone presented a harmless kind of violence, true, but people were now exposed to enough real-life violence when they opened the newspaper each morning. The silly antics were put on hold for *Mickey.* At the same time Mabel was sure to make her pet project be a comedy first and foremost.

In order to make what was essentially a very big movie as easy as possible to bring to life, Mabel brought in her own team both in front of and behind the camera, including Deveraux, Durfee, and longtime Keystone regular George Nichols. Meanwhile director F. Richard Jones, who Mable had overruled Mack on hiring for the job, was tasked with keeping everything under control and moving forward. Again, *Mickey* was quite an expensive project. What's more, it took a considerable amount of time to film, the process bleeding from 1916 into 1917.

The end result, frankly, is very impressive. The production values are spot on for the time. The story – a real story – is compelling. Mabel is completely unique and appealing in the title role. The genres smoothly transition from one to another. Even the ending is moving. Viewing the film over one hundred years after its creation, it's obvious why it went on to be such a huge hit...and why Mabel saw it as a crowning achievement. Essentially a reworking of the classic Cinderella story, the film presents classic elements and scenarios, then meshes them with Mabel's unique film persona.

Mickey is a bumpkin who lives in a mining shack and who spends her time playing with the local critters and skinny dipping in the nearby pond. Being a teenager, she obviously drives her father – played by Nichols - up the wall while her pipe smoking stepmother – played by Deveraux - tries keeping her on the straight and narrow.

Mickey is sent east to meet wealthy relatives. Once they find out her father's mine is worthless, however, they put Mickey to work as a maid. This doesn't suit the precocious Mickey at all, who doesn't seem capable of avoiding such antics as sliding down a banister, accidentally knocking over a grandfather clock and stuffing cherries from atop a cake into her mouth.

Things come to a boil as Mickey attracts both an upright wealthy suitor, as well as a creepy rich predator, learns the family mine has hit pay dirt, then gets wind of a plot her east coast relatives have to steal her family's newfound fortune. In order to save the day, Mickey finds herself in elaborate scenarios, wherein she puts the skills she learned back home to good use. She rides a horse in a high stakes race, gets into a car chase, fends off a would-be rapist, and somehow survives hanging from a mansion window high off the ground, all while bringing matters to a just and satisfying conclusion.

"I dwell on 'Mickey,'" Mabel would go on to say, "because it is my best work and because it is a historic picture." Perhaps Mabel's biggest dare, *Mickey* paid off not only by showcasing her talent and ambition, it also broke new ground in cinema, being the first major film to so effectively cross genres. All other movies which combine comedy, drama and romance are arguably *Mickey's* descendants. Mabel's masterpiece introduced the world to the romantic-comedy feature, with some high stakes action thrown in, to boot.

All, however, was not perfect. Stephen Normand states that Mabel's tuberculosis once again activated while making the film. Mabel may have simply viewed it at the time as a common cough combined with slight fevers, but eventually the truth revealed itself. When one considers the fact that the overworked Mabel not only had acted and produced the film, but also had performed her own daring stunts as well, it's clear the overall toll on her body was considerable.

Equally awful was the fact that Mack, being Mack, decided to once again take advantage of Mabel. According to Stephen

Normand, he told her *Mickey* wasn't any good and offered her 25 thousand dollars for it, saying he would "shelve it." Suffice to say, Mabel agreed, allowing Mack to shelve *Mickey* until the right moment came for him to release it, thus providing himself with a huge financial windfall without having to pay his former fiancée another dime. In short, Mack had not only scammed Mabel in love, but had now scammed her out of an enormous amount of money, as well.

Samuel Goldwyn

"My early boyhood was spent in Europe," Samuel Goldwyn wrote in his autobiography, "and I was just fourteen when, absolutely alone and with no friend or relative to greet me, I arrived in New York City." Born to a Jewish family in Poland, Goldwyn was one of six children whose father sold used furniture. Before the age of ten, he was sent to England where his name was changed from Gelbfisz to Goldfish. The young man then made the long journey to the United States in 1898. America at the time was a land of well over sixty million people, many of whom were now coming in from Europe in search of a better life.

The competition for a young man to get ahead was, to put it mildly, challenging. Goldwyn, however, seems to have had a gift. After moving near the Adirondacks, the recent arrival to the United States took up selling gloves. He ended up being one of the top salesmen in America. Goldwyn, in short, knew how to make a product appeal to people. It was a skill that would serve him well throughout his life. Goldwyn, who had arrived in his adopted homeland alone and unsupported, was able to quickly become a success story through ambition, yes, but also through focusing his talents on endeavors he could thrive in.

It's doubtful, after all, that Goldwyn's abilities would have served him well in the field of professional baseball. As a salesman, however, the man's personal skill set could thrive. Flush with his success, Goldwyn moved to Manhattan and married Blanche Lasky, whose brother, Jesse, worked in the theater as a producer. Yet Goldwyn simply wasn't the type to remain contented. Whether it was through imagination or sheer ambition, he convinced his brother-in-law and Cecil B DeMille to get into the movie business. While it was certainly a risky endeavor, it was nowhere near as risky as travelling alone from Europe to the United States in order to set out on his own.

The team's first foray into film was "The Squaw Man," a western that surprisingly focused on race relations between whites and Native Americans. The 1914 film was, it's been argued, the first feature length motion picture to have been made in Hollywood. "It scored immediate success," Goldwyn said of the film. "Our second play established us even more firmly." The partnership between the three men proved long lasting, for Paramount Pictures, still famous and operating in the 21st century, directly stemmed from that relatively small collaboration.

Goldwyn's partnership with Lasky couldn't survive his divorce from Blanche, and so he teamed up with Archibald Selwyn and his brother, Edgar Selwyn to form the Goldwyn Company in 1916. As a result he once again changed his name – this time from Goldfish to Goldwyn – and decided to stock the company with popular stars. The company also presented the world with its trademark, Leo the Lion, which is still used by Metro Goldwyn Mayer to this day. Ironically, Goldwyn himself had nothing to do with Metro Goldwyn Mayer, as the shady dealings of a distributor he trusted led to Goldwyn's being dumped from the company before it made the transition.

Never one to be denied, however, the determined Goldwyn focused on making high end films that were distributed to various studios such as RKO and United Artists. With his own contracted players, he could rent out stars to other studios, sometimes for considerable sums of money. On top of being the producer of such films as "Porgy and Bess," "Guys and Dolls," "The Best Years of Our Lives," and "The Secret Life of Walter Mitty", Goldwyn was also known for his "Goldwynisms," which were sayings of his that were oftentimes odd or simply senseless.

"Anyone who goes to a psychiatrist should have his head examined," was one. "A hospital is no place to be sick," was another. "I never liked you and I always will," was yet another. Yet Goldwyn's uniqueness wasn't always pleasant to those who had to deal with him. The man was known for recasting his films, much to the dismay of

those involved. Furthermore, Goldwyn was also known for his fiery temper. In short, he wasn't known as an easy man to work with. One person Goldwyn himself admired enormously, however, was Mabel.

In his autobiography, Goldwyn presented a story of Mabel coming to his rescue when he was going through a difficult financial time. "Mabel came up to my desk and handed me a long envelope," he wrote. "'What is this?' I asked her. 'My Liberty bonds,' she answered. 'There are only fifty thousand dollars' worth of them, but if they may tide you over you can have them.'" Goldwyn was rightfully stunned. No one expects someone to simply hand them close to what would in the 21st century amount to over half a million dollars, much less a young woman in her twenties. There the money was, though, in a single envelope, his for the taking, with no requirement to pay it back.

"Those interested in the personality of Mabel Normand," wrote Goldwyn, "can receive no more illuminating introduction to her than the incident just sketched." Goldwyn also wrote of a time when Mabel, visiting a struggling family with a young child struck with tuberculosis, slipped a thousand dollars into the young girl's hand. "Gifts from her," Goldwyn writes of Mabel, "come unprovoked as manna."

Goldwyn outlived many of his contemporaries, passing away in 1971 at the age of 91, leaving behind a monumental personal legacy as well as a family that became firmly ensconced in the industry. In his autobiography, written fifty years before his death, Goldwyn viewed the film industry as something that was indeed impressive, but that was also in need of improvement. "When I think of the glow which pictures have brought to so many lusterless lives all through the world, I am tempted, indeed, to overlook all the defects of the industry and to dwell only upon its perfections." He may have contributed to the defects as well as to the perfections, but there is no doubt his impact was phenomenal.

And if it hadn't been for Mabel, Goldwyn may well not have been able to reach the heights he eventually did.

A Thousand Dollars A Week

In July of 1917, Mabel sent a telegram to Mack at the Los Angeles Athletic Club. "Signed today," she wrote. "Got duyn(sic) 1 year and option Graham very satisfied said much better than expected start work Sept 1 company said I didn't look well must rest and go away until then winter studio Florida so I won't be able to peep at you ever again wanted you to know I signed although you never wire. M July 24 210am." There were two major bits of news to be found in this messy, not particularly well worded, message. First, Mabel had signed with Goldwyn Company. She was no longer tied to Mack or the now crumbling Triangle Company he was a part of. Although she would no longer have her own studio, as Mabel Normand Studio was under the failing Triangle Banner, she was now finally getting the kind of star treatment she had long deserved.

The second major bit of news to be found in the telegram was the fact that Mabel was beginning to look unwell – unwell enough to trouble her future employers. She'd have to go to Florida to recuperate before working for Samuel Goldwyn's company. Her tuberculosis, which had reappeared during filming of *Mickey*, was starting to show. "That day," Minta Durfee would recall of a day on the set of *Mickey* where Mabel was scheduled to hang precariously from a roof, "in the morning, she and I were talking, she said 'Oh, I better take my goop,' - she always called it 'goop,' Because I feel like I'm gonna have a little hemorrhage.' 'Well,' I said, 'Don't do your work, don't do that scene today, do something else dear.' And she said, 'Oh no, that's the way the schedule goes. No, I'll do it."

Sadly, Mabel's illness worsened over time. She wasn't even 25 years old when she signed with Goldwyn, but the clock was already ticking. What's more, Stephen Normand claims that about this time, Mabel, who had obviously been going through a strenuous and difficult time, thanks to Mack, Mae Busch, and overwork, had begun seriously drinking – something that, like tuberculosis, would plague her for the rest of her life. What's more, Stephen also claimed that the Normand's suffered from depression, something that people would learn more and more about Mabel as time went on.

All of this has led to a longstanding and century-plus long rumor about Mabel being a drug addict who indulged in heroin and/or cocaine. Such accusations can be lodged at anyone, of course, and are impossible to refute. The truth, however, is this: **No serious evidence has been uncovered that Mabel was addicted to, or even used, illicit drugs.** Mabel was sickly and suffered from depression. She became alcoholic after suffering from considerable physical and psychological trauma. Mabel was also, when healthy, hyper-energetic by nature. These are irrefutable facts. Rumors of illicit drug use are, on the other hand, simply unsubstantiated.

In spite of the considerable problems Mabel had and was continuing to face, forward progress was being made. She was being paid 1,000 dollars a week under her new contract, which amounts to between twenty-to-twenty-five thousand dollars a week in the 21st century. What's more, Goldwyn and his team were treating Mabel like royalty. Not only was she now being presented as a famous comedienne, but the world also saw an entirely new side to Mabel, thanks to both the Goldwyn public relations team… and herself.

It's been generally assumed that the Goldwyn Company employed a strategy that presented a new, serious Mabel who was well read and who wanted to make films with more maturity than her previous fare. While it's true Mabel wanted to be presented in a more serious light, it's untrue to claim that the new, more serious Mabel was the product of a Hollywood marketing team. Indeed, as early as January of that year, while she was still with Mack, the *Chicago Tribune* was reporting that Mabel planned to make more mature films than the early slapstick titles she had first exploded onto the scene with. Sure enough, *Mickey*, though a comedy, had far more seriousness to it than Mabel's previous films.

The idea loudly espoused by some that artistry, literary appreciation, and a degree of seriousness were beyond the grasp of the former sweat shop worker from Staten Island is utter snobbery. To believe a woman who helped expand the notion of what a screen comedienne could do, who mentored some of the biggest names in show business, who directed, wrote, and produced pictures as well as ran her own studio, all before the age of thirty simply didn't possess the gravitas needed to create cinematic art or understand a book by a well-regarded author says more about the person who thinks such things than it does about Mabel herself.

With that being said, there's no doubt the Goldwyn Company wanted the public to grasp onto Mabel's artistic inclinations. Yet the Company also put its money where its mouth was. While there were articles about Mabel's reading habits and intellectual curiosity, there was also the fact that Mabel's films with the Company looked polished, with impressive sets and an attention to detail Mack wasn't apt to indulge in. Still, as Slater and Squiciati stated, "Mabel was always bigger than any film she appeared in." In other words, people paid to see the Mabel they knew, not necessarily the Mabel the Goldwyn Company, or even she herself, wanted them to see.

Both Mabel and the Goldwyn Company learned over time that, in truth, the public wasn't as interested in "the new Mabel Normand" as they were in a Mabel Normand who made them laugh. It took some time, but Mabel eventually was able to again combine her artistic desires with films the public would embrace. It is ridiculous to say her work with the Goldwyn Company didn't bring in attention, money, and accolades, but the truth is the surviving and available Goldwyn films starring Mabel didn't pack quite the punch her previous films had tended to.

Fortunately for Mabel, her career got a second wind due to the most unlikely of events.

Edith Wilson

"I myself, never made a single decision regarding the disposition of public affairs. The only decision that was mine was what was important and what was not, and the very important decision of when to present matters to by husband." These words from former First Lady of the United States Edith Wilson, were written as an answer to the question of how much power she held while she and her husband Woodrow occupied the White House. The White House's own website made it clear how the United States' government viewed Wilson's tenure as First Lady. "After the President suffered a severe stroke, she pre-screened all matters of state, functionally running the Executive branch of government for the remainder of Wilson's second term."

Born to a wealthy Virginia family in 1872, Edith is said to have not left her hometown of Wytheville until she was twelve years of age. Three years later, she was studying music at Martha Washington College. In 1896 Edith married Norman Galt, whom she had met in Washington, DC while visiting her sister. During the twelfth year of their marriage, Galt died unexpectedly. Fortunately for Edith, the jewelry business belonging to her and Galt was able to provide for her. While a widow, Edith met Wilson, then already the President of the United States, who himself was anguishing over the loss of his wife, Ellen, who had recently died of Bright's disease.

Described as "a man who depended on feminine companionship," Wilson found himself falling for the forty-plus year old widow. He and Edith were married by the end of the year. It was an unlikely story, for sure, as rarely did a United States President get married while in office. In fact, only Grover Cleveland and John Tyler had previously gotten married while leading the nation. Still, it was reported that the couple got along extremely well, which was good news for those worried about a President who had been in mourning due to the loss of his first wife.

Still, life certainly wasn't easy for the middle aged couple. Less than a year and a half after Edith and Woodrow were married, the United States was pushed into entering the First World War. Leading the nation during the bloodiest conflict in the entire history of humanity was no small task, and it obviously led to what must have been an inordinate amount of stress. Yet matters became even more stressful for the couple after hostilities had officially ended. Not only had the U.S. military lost over one hundred thousand lives during the conflict, the entire world was essentially determined (futilely, it was sadly proved) to prevent such a slaughter from occurring again. As her husband's biggest supporter, Edith remained by Woodrow's side both literally and figuratively.

"Edith Wilson submerged her own life in her husband's," the White House wrote, "trying to keep him fit under tremendous *strain. She accompanied him to Europe when the Allies conferred on terms of peace." In the midst of the post-war madness, Wilson dreamed up the "League of Nations," which was essentially an early version of the United Nations. Not only did Wilson fail to achieve his dream, he ended up having a massive stroke in 1919. Half paralyzed and clearly quite ill, Wilson nonetheless remained in office – no doubt to the consternation of those who felt that Edith was now President by default. Edith, on the other hand, believed she was merely doing what was required.*

"She did not initiate programs or make major decisions," the White House wrote, "and she did not try to control the executive branch." Indeed, the First Lady referred to herself as her husband's "steward." Wilson retired in 1921 and the couple subsequently remained in Washington, though not, obviously, at the White House. The former President died in 1924 at the age of sixty-seven. Edith, on the other hand, lived until the age of eighty-nine, passing late in 1961, "a highly respected figure in the society of the capital." *Edith had written an autobiography called "My Memoir," in the late*

1930s and had taken part in the inauguration ceremony of President John F Kennedy eleven months before her death.

*Wrote the "AP" at the time of Edith's death, "she retained in her old age the charm and erect carriage of a grand lady." By the mid 1990s, Edith was being viewed as perhaps having started a trend where First Ladies eventually "*began to hire separate staffs of their own, take more public roles in policy and personnel decisions, and lead important reform movements." *In her own way, then, Edith Wilson was something of a trendsetter.*

There was no doubt that Edith had in her a boldness which had allowed her to act as she did on her husband's behalf. During the war itself, Edith engaged in war effort activities which previous First Ladies might have found to be men's affairs. Edith made sure that the public saw her as part of a national effort to defeat tyranny, someone not afraid to embrace the culture at large during such a frightful and historically altering time. Sure enough, she happened to meet Mabel, who at the time was one of the few people as, if not more, well known than she was.

It would be easy to assume, of course, that the two women had little in common. While this was true in large part, there were some similarities between the well-bred Virginian and the uneducated young entertainer from Staten Island. First off, they would not allow the fact that they were women to prevent them from leaving a mark on a society still run largely by men. They also weren't afraid that some might not approve of their personal boldness. Different though they unquestionably were, the two women had notable commonalities that few other women – or men – of the time did.

"Dark, Windy Days and Chocolate Cake"

"'I love dark windy days and chocolate cake.' Miss Normand announced with perfect gravity, 'and storms, when houses blow down.'" So Norbert Lusk wrote for the February 1918 edition of Picture-Play Magazine. Lusk's job had been to interview Mabel, but the quirky star appeared to have him puzzled. "Chocolate cake," she told him, "is the one thing I never get. People always keep it from me. That's why I have decided it is my favorite food." Mabel then went on to speak in a way that may or may not have been serious. "But I never eat it – or anything else – when I am acting," Lusk quoted her as saying. "'Food makes me too contented." She yawned lazily over her coffee. "And I don't want to be lazy anymore. A year of rest is enough for anyone. Now I want to come back – *hard.'"*

Sure enough, Mabel had come back hard after getting to work with Goldwyn. In 1918 alone she starred in seven movies released by the company. After an almost two year absence from the screen, Mabel was everywhere, in the media as well as in theaters. The Lusk interview is telling in that it showcases the free flowing thought process and speech of Mabel. Indeed, those who knew her spoke openly about her fast moving thoughts and motions. Her odd seeming interviews weren't performance art. The woman could literally switch from serious to comical in a single sentence, all the while assuming the listener was keeping up with her.

There was indeed no one quite like the hyperactive Catholic girl from Staten Island.

"Because of that sense of the comic, Mabel Normand cannot be serious wholeheartedly," Lusk wrote to the readers of *Picture-Play.* "She is the true spirit of mischief. Early in the chat, her interviewer gave up all hope of putting a question to her – or, rather, of recording an answer." Those who wanted to learn more about Mabel certainly had the opportunity to while she was under contract to Goldwyn. It appears she was ubiquitous in 1918, popping up in outlets big and small.

One outlet for instance, wrote of Mabel's sending an autographed photo of herself to a Mexican fan who had been arrested for stealing an image of her from a theater lobby. Another outlet, the *Pittsburgh Daily Post* provided readers with a largely fabricated look at Mabel and her past. The *Winnipeg Tribune* wrote of Mabel accidentally dropping her knitting into the orchestra while watching the movie *Thais* from the front row of the Lexington Theater, while the *Muscatine Journal* wrote of how Mabel had encouraged the works of O Henry to be filmed because they placed the comedy squarely in the situation rather than in action…a professional, nuanced distinction if ever there was one.

Not all of the press Mabel was receiving, however, was positive. The *Tampa Times*, in a piece that was a bit of an outlier, essentially accused Mabel of being a diva in a paragraph long article. The story reported that Mabel had apparently fired her maid for repeatedly not being around to get her water at Goldwyn Studios. She also apparently fired her butler after hearing him express pro-German sentiments. While perhaps untrue, there was no doubting that Mabel's pacifism had evaporated as the United States entered the war.

According to the *Winnipeg Tribune* Mabel, while addressing military officers and civilians at Jacksonville Florida's Hotel Mason, told the audience that "whenever anyone tells you that Germany has always been friendly to the United States, make him eat his words by reminding him that the Hessians fought against Washington to prevent the birth of the republic." But she wasn't done. "Don't make your fight solely against the Kaiser," she continued. "Get after everything and everyone German. We'll never win if we wait for a revolution by the German people. They love their 'god' too much for that."

Chilling. And not particularly in keeping with her faith.

Had the fact that her brother had joined the Marines had something to do with the harshness of Mabel's comments? It certainly must have made the war quite personal to her. Perhaps learning of the hardships endured by the families of fallen soldiers had something to with it. Mabel gave considerable sums of money to orphanages, after all. Or perhaps it was the booze she was now consuming that led Mabel to speak so harshly. As her nephew Stephen Normand himself plainly stated: "She had a problem drinking." Gin was Mabel's drink of choice, and Stephen spoke of her sitting at the Sherry-Netherland hotel in New York, where she often lounged with friends and her flask of gin.

Still, Mabel remained popular. Though not as popular as she had been in the early days of her career at Keystone, she was relevant enough to watch a screening of one of her Goldwyn films with First Lady Edith Wilson. The film was called *Joan of Plattsburg* and was a modern retelling of the Joan of Arc story. Joan of Arc was enormously popular at the time, just a few years away from canonization. By transforming her story into a comedy with serious themes, Goldwyn was able to get a ton of press for the wartime film.

Unsurprisingly, Mabel took the role of a modern-day Joan quite seriously, the *Greenville News* reporting that Mabel studied Joan of Arc paintings and statues at New York's Metropolitan Museum of Art to prepare for the role, as she wanted to study the expressions. Indeed, Mabel may likely have been thrilled when she was asked to watch a screening of the film with the First Lady at Krandals' Knickerbocker Theater in DC. on June 4th. The show was sponsored by the *Children's Year Campaign Committee*, which the First Lady helped lead. Mabel was called to the First Lady's box to speak with her for about 10 minutes before the show and appeared onstage after the film had ended to speak to the audience. She was on stage when someone asked if, since she had brought the California sunshine, had she brought the moonshine, too?

A stray wisecrack? Or a sign that her reputation was changing?

Like other stars such as Chaplin and Pickford, Mabel did what she could for the troops by supporting the sale of Liberty Bonds. That fall, while at Madison Square Garden, she addressed a gathered crowd to encourage them to buy bonds that evening. "Give us a kiss for a bond?" asked someone in the crowd. "How large a bond?" Mabel asked in return. The man said a thousand dollars, leading Mabel to laughingly agree to the bargain. A thousand dollar bond was sold, a kiss was delivered (no doubt on the cheek, as Mabel's tuberculosis had returned), and twenty-thousand dollars total went on to be earned for the war effort that evening. Regardless of what else was going on in her life, Mabel still knew how to turn on the charm.

And that charm soon provided Mabel with her greatest success.

Alexei Nikolaevich Romanov

He was supposed to inherit the entire Russian Empire. Instead, he was dead before the age of fourteen, murdered alongside his family in completely brutal fashion. The empire he was to inherit had been overthrown from within, when he and his family were deemed too dangerous and vile to continue existing. It was an intensely disturbing end for a life that wasn't allowed to reach adulthood. While it's true the young man's father had not been an effective ruler, the nightmare ending to his life, as well as the lives of his wife, children and others, is rightfully regarded as an act of wanton and extreme cruelty.

Yet life wasn't always severe for the family of Tsar Nicholas II and his wife, Tsarina Alexandra. Surviving photos and motion pictures show what appears to be a tight knit clan swimming, vacationing, and relaxing. There was more to the Imperial Family of Russia, then, than the starchy uniforms, political meetings and military displays so frequently seen in documentary footage. Indeed, it's been argued that the Tsar and Tsarina were enormously physically attracted to each other – not something one pictures when thinking of a royal union. There is little doubt of Nicholas' love for Alexandra, for he stood by his wife for good or ill, in spite of what enemies, friends, and even his own family felt.

Sure enough, Nicholas married Alexandra against his family's wishes, or, at the very least, in spite of their concerns. Alexandra's own grandmother, England's Queen Victoria, feared the attractive young girl simply didn't have what it took to be the Empress of Russia. Still, Nicholas was in love and that was all there was to it. The fears of Victoria and others, however, soon appeared to be well founded. Alexandra was not warm to the Russian people, as her mother in law, Maria Fedorovna, Nicholas' mother, had been. Considering the fact that Nicholas' own grandfather had been assassinated, it was clear the monarchy wasn't exactly on solid ground. His own wife's aloofness to his subjects couldn't possibly have been considered helpful.

Things went from awkward in the beginning to completely worrying as time went on. Although they had four daughters, Nicholas and Alexandra needed to have a son as heir to the throne. As unfair as it was, Alexandra took a lot of the blame for circumstances well beyond her control. She simply couldn't decide what kind of child she wanted, after all.

Finally, in 1904, the couple had a son, Alexei, much to their and the nation's relief (it's admittedly hard to imagine people in the 21st century thinking a leader had a be a male). Matters wouldn't be joyful for too long, however. Alexei, the couple learned, was afflicted with hemophilia, a hereditary disease his great-grandmother Queen Victoria of Britain had. Internal bleeding, the hallmark of hemophilia, could be deadly. In other words, the male heir to the throne of the Russian Empire might not live long enough to survive his father.

To have a son with such a severe illness no doubt had to be heartbreaking to his parents. Alexandra, however, made things go from bad to worse by becoming enthralled with a trendy mystic named Gergory Rasputin. She became convinced that the crude Siberian could heal Alexei. She also reportedly trusted the man so much that she wanted her husband to take Rasputin's advice about political matters. The situation subsequently went to from bad to outright alarming. Ultimately, Rasputin ended up being assassinated by a number of Nicholas' own officers, who had decided the country could take no more of the man's influence. It all proved to be too late.

The First World War was devastating for the Russian military, so much so that Nicholas decided to go to the front lines to take control of matters himself. Yet, while he was away, the Russian Revolution erupted. While trying to rush back to the capital of Saint Petersburg, his train was stopped by revolutionaries, and he was forced to abdicate his throne. The mighty Russian Empire was no more. While there's no doubt the insolated outlooks of Nicholas and his wife contributed to the matter, there can be no denying that history itself was turning a page. The days of royalty dynasties were by and large finished, save for ceremonial purposes.

Of course, things don't instantly change by a signature on an abdication document. A bloody civil war erupted between the revolutionaries and those loyal to the Tsar and his family. In the meantime, Nicholas, Alexandra, their children, and members of their household staff were held as prisoners, ultimately ending up at a large home known as Ipatiev House. With news of troops loyal to Nicholas, known as White Russians, moving in, members of the Bolshevik party, which was far more organized and deadly than its competitive factions within the Revolutionary moment, decided it was time to kill the entire family.

Moving the prisoners to a basement room, a ragtag team of killers slaughtered the entire family, along with the few remaining members of their staff. It was a disorganized, bloody, and sadistic affair. Some of the Tsar's daughters had jewels sewn into their dresses, which meant the bullets being fired at them wouldn't pass. They ended up being bayoneted in that dark, smoke filled chaotic basement, not even being given the solace of dying quickly. Afterwards the victim's bodies were tossed into holes dug in the woods.

Although they came to a horrifying end, the Russian Imperial family were more than just characters in a tragedy at least somewhat activated by their own political dysfunction. This was a tight knit group, not perfect for sure, but a loving unit, nonetheless. In fact, they were said to enjoy movies. And whose films did they have copies of? Mabel's. Like millions of others, Alexei was a fan. The family's collection of Mabel films has reportedly survived to this day and now rests at the Heritage Museum.

Hollywood Pioneer

It's been said that a theater owner who was short a film to show had been given a copy of *Mickey* simply because there was no other movie available to give him. If this were truly the case, then it proved to be one of the more remarkable tales in cinema history – for *Mickey*, the film Mabel was assured would be a dud should it be released – was instantly and explosively popular once it was finally introduced to the public in late 1918. Just how popular was *Mickey*? Popular enough to become one of the very first films to earn over a million dollars. What's more, the movie played and played and played for year after year. Referred to as "the film of the century," *Mickey* held the box office record as the world's most successful film until the very late 1930s.

"At first everybody thought it was a flop," Mabel later said, "and it was actually shelved for nearly eighteen months. It cost only about one hundred and fifty thousand dollars, including the earlier failures, but it took in more money through the box offices than any picture ever made in proportion to its cost." Mabel, who had been deceived by Mack, now no longer a part of the Keystone Empire, was the star of perhaps the most successful movie in history up until its time. Bigger than anything Chaplin had done. Bigger than anything Arbuckle had done. Or Mary Pickford. Or Douglas Fairbanks. Or any number of the other top stars. It was her film, a film she herself had created, no less, that topped all others.

Mickey was the rare movie that proved to be as much a social phenomenon as it was a film. The *Springfield News-Sun* would go so far as to print a whole page virtually dedicated to Mabel and *Mickey*. In one article, Mabel was said to feel like people now only saw her as the character of *Mickey*. Another article focused on co-star Minnie Devereaux, while yet another related a possibly true story of Mabel talking to an expert equestrian on set (where Mabel did stunts with a horse). Still another told of two cats in *Mickey*, each one symbolizing different classes of people. There was even an article about how Mickey's attitude in the film led to attainment and to successfully dealing with war (it was a rather intelligent piece, frankly). Aside from the plethora of ink dedicated to *Mickey* related stories, there was also on the page *Mickey*-related ads for Racine tires, Colombia Records, and the MD Levy Company.

Mickey was big news, and big business. Unfortunately, Mabel received the fame and the accolades she deserved, but not the money. Mack had seen to that. Although she was well paid for her efforts, Mabel, the captain of the ship that was *Mickey,* received a small percentage of what someone else in her position would have. According to Stephen Normand, Mack was aware of the film's quality before its eventual release but told Mabel that it wasn't any good in order to pay her just twenty-five thousand dollars for it. Then, rather than keeping *Mickey* shelved, as he had indicated to Mabel he would, Mack subsequently cashed in on the film's wild success when it went on to earn an untold fortune.

Mabel didn't even see money from the song *Mickey*, which was inspired by, and eventually played at, the movie. Not that such a small matter as a song mattered much to Mabel (it allowed for theater tickets to be sold in music stores). Mack's double crossing of her, however, must have once again served as a reminder of how ultimately untrustworthy the man was.

Still, even with all the justified bitterness that must have come with her film's success, there was a large part of Mabel which was thoroughly pleased. *"Mickey" Wins Commendation Of Movie Reformers* read a March 1919 headline in the *Lansing State Journal*. "In her role here," the article read, "Miss Normand does some real acting that makes one sit up and take notice." While the lengthy article had an annoying habit of presenting the film as a product of Mack Sennett's talents, it certainly showered credit upon Mabel's performance, which represented something new, even to her most ardent fans.

"From first to last," the unnamed writer stated, "Mabel Normand does exceptionally clever work in this picture, and here is a name that can always be depended upon to make itself felt at the box office." Sure enough, Mabel's combination of star power and creativity made *Mickey* the film it was, not the supposed brilliance of Mack. In *Mickey* her performance switched from comedy to drama and back to comedy again seamlessly. Mabel also performed stunts and exuded a physicality unusual even for her. Whether it was hanging on a dangerously high windowsill, jumping atop a horse, or generally showcasing boundless energy, Mabel here proved herself to be an action star and literal stuntwoman as much as she did a multi-faceted actress.

This was something new. Having directed parts of the movie herself Mabel acted as studio head, director, star, and stuntwoman in the production of *Mickey,* a film which arguably became the most financially successful movie ever, and that just so happened to be released at a time when women still weren't allowed to vote. With the creation, release and enormous success of *Mickey*, Mabel had solidified her position as a Hollywood pioneer. "*Mickey* played to more repeat dates than any picture ever made," Mabel said, "and to this day the industry prays for another picture like it. I don't know how many healthy fortunes all over America got a fine start from *Mickey*."

One of the appealing things about the film is that it did, in a very real sense, mirror Mabel's life in such a way. For like her film, Mabel was the product of a Cinderella story. What other way to explain her virtual rags to riches transformation from child laborer to film celebrity, from a sickly girl from a working class shoreline enclave to a glamorous star who was able to collect cars and expensive jewelry with the ease of someone shopping for groceries? Like Mickey in the film, Mabel was someone who was able to employ her unique set of talents to get ahead in life.

And that was something audiences of the time could truly appreciate. America was a growing nation in the early 20th century, filled with immigrants and natives alike who believed there was an "American Dream," one that not always led to fame and fortune, but one that could still largely guarantee opportunities most other parts of the world simply couldn't. Mabel was proof of that guarantee, which is another likely reason why she was so pleased with the film that ultimately proved to be her greatest screen success. There was, after all, a lot of Mabel to be found in *Mickey*.

F. Richard Jones

"F. Richard Jones was the director," Mabel said of "Mickey", "and the picture proved to be the first real big comedy hit of the industry. By virtue of having been the star of that picture," she continued modestly, "I became a very valuable young lady and I too began to get $1000 per week." True enough. Indeed, over time it could be safely said that Jones ended up being Mabel's favorite director, for their partnership lasted for close to a decade. Although they certainly didn't work together all the time, their collaborations clearly gave Mabel a sense of artistic satisfaction, something she felt wasn't being derived from some, if not all, of her other work.

"He was the only director," Harry Carr wrote of Jones in the "Los Angeles Times" years later, "other than Sennett himself, who ever could get anything out of Mabel Normand. Under his direction, she became the greatest comedienne that has ever been seen on the screen." Indeed, Chaplin himself was to argue that Mabel needed the right person guiding her in order for her genius to flow. True? Impossible to tell, really, though Mabel certainly performed well under her own direction. Still, both Carr and Chaplin make an interesting argument, especially Carr in regard to Jones.

Yet Mabel wasn't the only one to understand the level of Jones' talent. According to the "Internet Movie Database": "Stan Laurel credited Jones with teaching him about film comedy, as opposed to comedy for the stage." A keen distinction. Later in his career, Jones was credited for creating a successful "talkie" when he directed the sound film "Bulldog Drummond." Indeed, it was not only his first and only "talkie," it was also the last movie the man ever directed. Like Mabel, Jones suffered from tuberculosis, which eventually caused his early death before the age of forty in 1930.

His brief life, however, had been nothing if not memorable.

Jones was born in St Louis and went on to become a member of the local film community. As Betty Sherman Corp wrote, "Jones worked in the film laboratory and other departments but his real interest lay behind the camera, creating the visual product." He ultimately moved on to California where he teamed up with Mack. After penning a few scripts, Jones finally found himself in the role of director. Still, Mabel had to push for Jones to direct "Mickey." By directing such an enormous hit, however, Jones found himself to be a director of note.

An interesting point of Jones' professional relationship with Mabel is the fact that, by the time "Mickey" was filmed, Mabel had the ability to indulge her artistic ambitions. Jones, however, saw himself as a craftsman, nothing more. Films were to be constructed, in his opinion, not elevated to art through heightened creativity. Mabel clearly disagreed, but it can't be denied that their partnership worked. By aspiring to artistry, Mabel kept Jones from creating a flat, unimaginative movie. By remaining a grounded professional, Jones appears to have been able to keep Mabel's creativity from sailing off into flights of fancy.

At least he appears to have been able to most of the time.

Carr wrote of an incident on the set of "Mickey" where "Harem Scarem Mabel," as he called Mabel, truly left a lasting impression. "One day while they were working on a big set," he stated, "that a friend drove up alongside in a car and Mabel walked over to speak to her. She got in the car and didn't return for two weeks." While the timespan here seems at the very least a bit exaggerated, Mabel was certainly known to do unexpected things on a whim. Yet Jones was clearly able to get the best work possible out of Mabel, something which clearly required a give and take approach. All the success in the world simply couldn't keep Mabel from still being the hyperactive Catholic girl from Staten Island. And so Jones gave Mabel the leeway she needed, such as allowing her to have the song "When Francis Dances With Me" playing constantly on the set for one of their films.

Anything to get Mabel in the frame of mind needed to succeed before the camera.

After working with Mack for whom he directed over forty films, Jones landed with Mack's competitor, Hal Roach, and held the positions of "production supervisor" and "supervising director." Afterwards he worked with the likes of D.W. Griffith, Laurel and Hardy, and Douglas Fairbanks. His talents brought him to numerous studios such as Paramount and Goldwyn. Had he not died young, it would have been interesting to see how Jones would have continued on in the "talkie" era.

Although he was married three times in total, the other major woman in Jones' life – aside from his professional relationship with Mabel - was Irene Lentz, who reportedly started off at Keystone as an actress before moving on to become a studio costume designer of some note. Indeed, Lentz continued designing costumes for some of the most famous films in history in the decades leading up to and away from the Second World War. Sadly, she took her own life on November 15th, 1962, letting it be known beforehand that she wished to be buried alongside her late husband, Jones.

Never a publicity hound, Jones wasn't particularly well known outside of the industry – even during his prime. Still, he was most certainly an important director and all-around industry professional. He made many films, after all. On top of that, he directed "Mickey," a groundbreaking film if ever there was one. What's more, as time went on Jones proved to be an extremely loyal friend to Mabel, remaining steadfast throughout some of the most challenging portions of her life. Mabel had certainly been there for him when it came to providing Jones with the chance to direct Mickey. Jones returned the favor when Mabel needed a hand in kind.

Back To Mack (Professionally)

"My pictures with the Goldwyn Company were not particularly good, in my opinion," Mabel someday reflected. Although very few of her movies made with Goldwyn have survived, those that have give every indication that Mabel was correct in her assertion. Although provided at times with impressive sets and otherwise strong production values, Mabel's Goldwyn work appears more forced than organic. She may have moved beyond the wild free for all her films with Sterling, Chaplin and Arbuckle often descended into, but fans still expected Mabel's work to be funny and entertaining. One gets a sense of awkwardness while watching Mabel's surviving Goldwyn films, as if a square peg is trying to be jammed into a round hole.

Not that Goldwyn didn't try to take Mabel's career in impressive new directions. The company's marketing of Mabel was nearly ubiquitous. Examples abound. The *Edmonton Bulletin*, for instance, wrote about director George Loane Tucker discovering that Mabel was "a first rate dramatic actress." The *Baltimore Sun* wrote of Mabel staring in a wartime food conservation film for the United States Food Administration where she comically showed that rice flour could be used to make pancakes instead of wheat flour.

What's more, the *Calgary Herald* indicated that Mabel designed her own bathing suit for a film. The *New Britain Herald* reported that "Mabel Normand insists on carrying everything she buys," while also posting a poem about Mabel which first appeared in the *Albany Evening Journal.* The *Herald* also ran an article on the same day about the nuance of Mabel's clothing in one of her films, where her character appeared simple but was in fact wearing trendy New York attire. This particular article indicated that Mabel had say when it came to her screen costumes.

One particularly interesting article about Mabel appeared in the *Los Angeles Herald.* If more than a simple media creation, the story it tells speaks volumes not only about Mabel, but also about the fame that surrounded her. According to the article, Mabel was in San Francisco to film boat scenes for her upcoming Goldwyn film *What Happened to Rosa.* A swarm of fans crowded around the set, much as fans of films have continued to do in the hope of seeing stars over the decades.

"One thing Mabel detests," the *Herald* wrote, "is public gatherings where she is stared at, so she prepared to fool them. Her costume was a Spanish girl's dancing flimsy, so she just put on a big bathrobe, borrowed a slouch hat from Director Victor Schertzinger, slung a towel over her shoulder and with dark glasses over her nose and a pair of prop man's boxing gloves under arm, she arrived at the wharf in a taxi, got out and stalked through the crowd while they waited eagerly to see 'Mabel.'"

What makes this piece fascinating, if true, is that it showcases what the daring Mabel's limits were and were not. She was happy to perform in a bathing suit – which was unusual for a female celebrity of the time. She was even happy to perform in a body sock, as when she appeared to be skinny dipping in *Mickey.* And indeed, Mabel was fine performing in a sexualized – albeit mildly sexualized – costume in *What Happened To Rosa.* This was not, to be sure, a woman who was uncomfortable with her body. Yet Mabel was not one to flaunt herself around, either for the public or in private.

She wasn't, for instance, like Mack's troop of *Bathing Beauties,* who were essentially employed solely to look attractive. Mabel was a comedienne after all. Whether she was in a bathing suit or a gown, Mabel was performing. She had modeled before. As a film actress, she was a performer first and foremost. Simply put, the article hinted at a less freewheeling Mabel than the one that has sometimes been presented. Not all sources of information on Mabel, however, are – or have been - so kind.

For instance, rumors of a promiscuous Mabel are, like her rumored cocaine and heroin use, unsupported by any existing evidence. And yet they continue to exist. Contrary to some opinions, it had been remarked that Mabel never had a man overnight in her home. This, subsequently, led some to indicate, again without evidence, that Mabel may have been a closet lesbian. In truth, Mabel was only known with any certainty to have been romantically involved with two people – one being Mack and the other being the man she would marry later in her life.

As for Goldwyn, the studio was more interested in furthering Mabel's career than in rumor. Therefore, it tried placing Mabel in all variety of roles. While she appeared erotic at times in *What Happened To Rosa*, she likewise appeared as a goofy looking down home character in *Sis Hopkins*, a Joan of Arc aspirant in *Joan of Plattsburg,* and a circus performer in *Jinx.* Ultimately, however, Mabel's output at Goldwyn proved to be disappointing. Writing for the *Los Angeles Times,* Antony Anderson gave a poor review for *Joan of Plattsburg,* arguing that Mabel "is keeping her mouth open all through the play. She makes Joan look like a semi idiot, which is perhaps correct enough." A harsh review, to be sure, but surviving films from Mabel's time at Goldwyn, of which *Joan of Plattsburg* is not one, are far from Mabel's best work, as she herself was to acknowledge.

The Floor Below, a Goldwyn flick, was recently discovered. Mabel here is a lowly employee at a newspaper who goes undercover among some rich folks to expose a crime. The reader cards are in Dutch, so perhaps it's hard for those who don't read in the language to follow the action. Still, while Mabel's face dominates here, as always, the film is strangely confusing and, in the end, serious and enigmatic.

What Happened to Rosa is another Goldwyn film of Mabel's that has happened to survive. The production value is obviously stronger here than most of Mabel's Keystone works, but not the off the wall, high energy humor. Mabel's admittedly funny, though, as a woman who thinks she's a Spanish beauty. There's not as much running around here, however, as Mabel was now closing in on thirty and the tuberculosis tragically appears to affect her performance – although she does swim in the film.

Goldwyn had a problem. What had always made Mabel shine was her uniqueness. Yet it was easy to see other stars such as Mary Pickford, Norma Talmadge, or even Mae Busch starring in Mabel's Goldwyn films. Before she signed with Goldwyn, on the other hand, it was nearly impossible to see anyone other than Mabel starring in Mabel Normand movies. Goldwyn realized this after the booming success of *Mickey*. He even tried a more Keystonesque approach to Mabel's films after *Mickey's* enormous success. Nothing, however, seemed to work as it was supposed to.

It perhaps wasn't much of a surprise then when *Variety* reported on February 11th, 1921, that "Mabel Normand is back on the Mack Sennett lot and under contract for that producer for a number of productions." The article went on to read that "The contract between the comedienne and the producer is said to involve approximately $1,000,000," which would be about sixteen million plus dollars in the 21st century. The money may have been too good for Mabel to refuse, but she was also aware that Mack was the studio head she worked best under. Besides, Mabel made sure Mack paid her well this time around.

She also had F. Richard Jones directing her next picture for Mack, *Molly O'*.

Virginia Rappe

Whatever it was that led to Virginia Rappe's death at the age of 30, two things can be assured: First, that it was certainly a tragedy. Secondly, that Roscoe Arbuckle certainly wasn't directly involved with it. Few would argue with the first fact. The second fact, however, wasn't embraced until after Arbuckle's career and reputation had been shattered. Hollywood's first major scandal still reverberates to this day, and with good reason. Starting with the death of Rappe, the media decided to go hunting for scandals – and celebrities were big game. It was a hunt that's continued well into the 21st century.

The lead up to Rappe's death can be traced to Labor Day weekend, 1921, when Arbuckle, who had just signed an enormous contract with Paramount, decided to flee his Los Angeles mansion in his Pierce-Arrow. His destination was San Francisco, where he hoped to kick back with some friends and enjoy himself during the long weekend. He and a few others grabbed three rooms at the lush Saint Francis' Hotel and ordered some booze – which was illegal at the time - and had some people up. Music played. The drinks flowed. More people arrived.

One of those people was Rappe, who had just turned 30. A designer and actress, she had arrived with a friend of hers named Maude Delmont and made herself at home at the party. After trying to get into a bathroom supposedly occupied by an amorous couple, Rappe made her way at some point to Arbuckle's empty room. According to reports, Arbuckle entered sometime later and the two were alone for several minutes. At any rate, Arbuckle eventually came out, stating that Rappe needed help. Finding the girl ripping her clothes and anguishing in pain, the guests called a doctor.

Rather than be sent to a hospital, Rappe was sent to another room, where she inexplicably stayed for several days. Arbuckle returned to Southern California only to learn that Rappe had died after he left San Francisco. He was subsequently arrested for rape and murder. The charges were nearly as explosive as the media orgy which followed them. Arbuckle ended up going not through one, not through two, but through three trials before he was acquitted. The jury of that final trial apologized to Arbuckle for all he had been through.

The truth was that there shouldn't have ever been a first trial. Doctors examining Rappe's body declared there was no sign of sexual assault. What's more, it was determined that the poor woman had died from a ruptured bladder. "The doctor who treated Rappe at the hotel," the Smithsonian stated, "testified that she had told him Arbuckle did not try to sexually assault her, but the prosecutor got the point dismissed as hearsay." Nothing seemed to be enough to stop a politically motivated prosecutor from charging Arbuckle, the argument being that the heavy star had caused Rappe's insides to explode by forcing himself atop her. It was a flimsy premise to put it lightly.

On top of that, Maude Dumant, the woman who had arrived at the party with Rappe and who subsequently became the prosecution's prime source of information, was found to have sent messages to lawyers stating: "WE HAVE ROSCOE ARBUCKLE IN A HOLE HERE CHANCE TO MAKE SOME MONEY OUT OF HIM." No matter. Arbuckle was ruined. Even his acquittal couldn't save the man's career. The newspapers sold a lot of copies making the man a villain, after all, and there was absolutely no way they were going to admit wrongdoing on a large scale. The jury claimed Arbuckle was innocent, but the media had made sure he'd be guilty in the court of public opinion.

The reality, though, was that Arbuckle wasn't charged with being a deadly deviant, not really.

He was charged with not being the man audiences thought he was. The man people saw as a smiling bumpkin or a frazzled husband onscreen was actually a cigar smoking partier who liked to drink illegal booze while enjoying the company of attractive women. He was not, simply put, the Fatty Arbuckle everyone knew and loved. That Arbuckle was no violent sexual predator mattered not – especially with newspapers placing the available facts on the back burner in favor of "exposing" the man. Rather than attempt to view the entire person, the public – which had never experienced such a scenario before – went from viewing Arbuckle as a teddy bear to viewing him as an outright monster. Finding the truth somewhere in the middle appears not to have occurred to most people at the time.

Largely overlooked in all the chaos, of course, was the story of Rappe herself, a woman who tragically died young. "It's worth considering," Clemence Michallon wrote pointedly in "The Independent", "why so many versions of this story present it primarily as the tale of a man who lost his career, when it began, first and foremost, with a woman losing her life." Although she's been presented as everything from a woman of loose morals to a proponent of just causes, the inarguable truth is that Rappee was a determined and resourceful young woman who applied herself at whatever she did, be it acting before the camera, designing clothing, or offering advice to other young women in print. In short, she deserves to be seen as a three dimensional person who died under tragic and painful circumstances, not reduced to second billing in a real life courtroom drama.

Of course, the media couldn't have been happier with the very lucrative results offered by the Arbuckle trials. They had now taken down one giant of popular culture. How many more papers might they sell if they found another celebrity to target? It was a question on everyone's mind in the movie industry. Stars might still be presented as royalty, but now there would forever be targets on their backs. True or false, their reported sins would now become front page news. Paramount and the public turned on Arbuckle, after all. Other studios and the public could just as easily turn on someone else.

The hunt was on.

Molly O'

Articles on Mabel, like one printed in *The Victoria Daily Times* in June of 1919, may have kept Mabel in the public eye, but they eventually didn't do her film career any good. Although it was nice to read that Minnie Devereaux had made a pair of moccasins for Mabel ("Many days and nights she worked on them.") – such public relations pieces weren't helping Mabel's reputation as a performer. Critics were lukewarm before the release of *Mickey*. After its impact was felt throughout the industry, they simply wanted less of the Mabel that Goldwyn had been offering.

The fact that Mabel, too, wanted less of that Mabel, must have made the transition back to the untrustworthy Mack seem all the more reasonable. Now that she and Mack were back in business again, Mack may well have believed their failed romance might rebloom, if so, he was sadly mistaken. Mabel was done seeing Mack through romantic, trusting eyes and that was all there was to it. Both knew, however, that they could help each other's careers immensely. And so, with Mabel's favorite director, F. Richard Jones, at the helm, production began on *Molly O'*, a massive project that, in contemporary parlance, was designed to be a blockbuster.

While Mabel's time spent with Goldwyn wasn't successful, Mack was smart enough to know a sharp strategy when he saw one. Nothing if not keenly aware, Mack realized that Goldwyn's extensive use of marketing and public relations could indeed be successful if combined with a project that worked well for Mabel. "Molly O' was a large and important production for the Mack Sennett Studio," wrote Mabel expert, Marilyn Slater. "It was advertised as his first feature drama. The amount of promotion was extensive from the very beginning." Hoping to match the success of *Mickey,* Mack aimed not only to make *Molly O'* big news, but to attach the production with other big news, as well.

"One of intriguing uses of the newspaper to entice interest in Molly O'," wrote Slater, "was the tie-in with an accident of Pensacola blimp, which had wrecked in March of 1921 just as the filming of Molly O' had begun and the ZR-2 in August. The promotional material included the blimp story." The literally high-flying finale of *Molly O'* was to take place on a blimp, and so, as Slater put it, "the public reading the story of the filming of the blimp sequence at the end of Molly O' would have been very aware of the accident in Pensacola."

The ethics of promoting a film on the backs of the forty-four people who had perished in the Pensacola blimp disaster (body parts were eventually found along with the debris) were shaky as best. Mack was nothing if not an opportunist, to be sure, but it is worth adding that the finale of *Molly O'* indeed had features common to the real life disaster which had happened only recently. This was simply a horrible coincidence. The truth was that the blimp-centered finale of *Molly O'* was likely going to be a big part of the media's attention, whether or not a very real tragedy which had much in common with the movie's climax had occurred or not.

Yet the production had more than an enormous budget and the challenge of enormous set pieces to worry about. There was also the matter of Mabel's friend, Arbuckle, who was currently going through his courtroom drama before the rapt attention of the entire world. Mabel and Arbuckle were not only close, but they had also been one of the most famous duos in show business. Arbuckle's recent movies had already been pulled from theaters. Would the public truly wish to see Mabel onscreen again after it had tossed aside her friend and screen partner?

The answer ultimately appears to have been a resounding yes. Although the movie didn't reach the financial, cultural, or popular heights of *Mickey*, it was a huge hit, nonetheless. And, in honesty, there's a lot to like about *Molly O'*. Very entertaining in the first half, the film gets strangely dark, intense, and even sensual in the second half...but the finale involving the blimp and a water plane is like a 1920's version of a *Mission Impossible* flick. *Molly O'* is, in short, pretty, impressive, and very cool. Mabel is Molly – a working class girl who hooks up, Cinderella style, with a wealthy nice guy. Before arriving at the happy ending, however, Molly has to rise to the occasion repeatedly.

Strangely, there's not a whole lot of humor here, if any, from Mabel. Mack was actually telling the truth when he announced the film as his first dramatic feature. Yet Mabel employs her own dramatic skills to strong effect through her very notable facial expressions. Mabel was changing as a performer to be sure, but the change also came with some new nuance to her performances, as well as some much bigger budgets than she had previously worked under. Either way, the public appeared to be enjoying the transition. *Molly O'* proved that *Mickey* was no one-off. Mabel had a vision for where she wanted her career to now go and the vision was proving to be a popular, satisfying, and lucrative one. The material Mabel now worked with was personal, as well. Hers may not have been a genuine Cinderella story, as those presented in *Mickey* and *Molly O'* were – but her biography, from humble origins to the heights of wealth and society, was very close to one.

"A visit to almost any equipped store," wrote *The Tacoma Daily Ledger* around the time of the film's release in December of 1921, "will reveal in its stock a 'Molly O'' something. There are 'Molly O';' candies, lingerie, shoes, tea biscuits, sport hats and playing cards. Hairdressing parlors are offering 'Molly O'' curls and manicure sets. A new and imported brand of silk is being marketed under the name of 'Molly O'.' The astronomers in the Mt. Wilson observatory are even looking for a new star to name 'Molly O'' it is rumored."

With the tragic fiasco that was the Arbuckle scandal not having too significant an impact on Mabel's success, Mack could breathe a sigh of relief. Mabel had now been in the film industry for over a decade. Close to thirty years old, she had successfully gone from precocious young star to an established attraction. So confident were Mabel and Mack at this point, that production of a new film, one titled *Suzanna*, starring Mabel and directed by Jones, would soon begin.

By the time *Suzanna* would reach theaters, however, Mabel's life had changed forever.

William Desmond Taylor

The man remains one of the film industries' greatest enigmas. An urbane, knowledgeable, likeable and talented individual, William Desmond Taylor was nonetheless not the man anyone had likely assumed he was. As a film director, Taylor was a far cry from the New York based family man he had previously been. As a family man, he was a far cry from the ranch hand he had previously been. As a ranch hand, he was a far cry from the privileged child in Anglo dominated Ireland he had previously been. And all of those aspects of Taylor were a far cry from the dashing British officer he became during the First World War. Taylor, in short, was, and remains, a mystery. Still, mysterious or not, the man was a flesh and blood human being, one who was both fascinating and successful.

Taylor's real name was William Deanne Tanner, and he was born in Carlow, Ireland, on April 26th, 1872. He came to the United States in the later part of the 19th century, and reportedly got a job on a ranch where his skill on a horse did him well. It appears he was competent throughout his life, so it's understandable that the young Irishman would be respected on a rugged western ranch, a place where skills and a strong work ethic were imperative if one were to be accepted.

Perhaps awash in the belief that America was the land of opportunity, Taylor became an actor before finally ending up on the east coast where he opened an antique shop in New York City and married Ethel May Harrison in 1901. The following year saw Taylor becoming a father of one, Ethel having given birth to a daughter they named Ethel Daisy. Home life apparently didn't suit Taylor well, however, for in 1908 he completely abandoned his wife and daughter, leaving them thoroughly in the dark as to what had happened to him.

Changing his name from William Deanne Tanner to William Desmond Taylor – not doubt to throw off the scent of the wife and child he had cruelly deserted – Taylor found himself acting, doing odd jobs, and even prospecting for gold. Finally, late in 1912, the man made his way to Los Angeles and a new kind of life.

"I entered the pictures as a sort of compromise," Taylor told "Motion Picture" in 1915. "I had made several attempts to get away from the stage, and my last venture had been along the lines of mining, when the annoying persistent call of the stage came again, and, as I did not fancy the small and stuffy dressing rooms and the continual study, I came to the coast and deliberately tried to get into the motion picture game."

After getting a start as an actor, Desmond made the move behind the camera. "On the evidence," writes Anthony Slide, "of the few William Desmond Taylor films which have survived (preserved at the Library of Congress, the International Museum of Photography at George Eastman House, and the UCLA film and television archive) it is obvious that he was not a great director." While he was clearly capable of putting a film together, Taylor appears to have not left anything particularly memorable in the annals of film history, save for his own personal biography.

One doesn't have to be a master at one's craft in order to be successful, however. One simply needs to be professionally capable, and Taylor certainly appears to have been that - capable enough at least, to direct around sixty films between 1914 and 1922. Taylor could not have worked with the likes of Mary Pickford if he were less than up to par as a director. Yet Taylor was able to stand out from his peers not because of the quality of his work, but for what today might well be considered activism.

"Taylor was considered a leading figure in the film industry," writes Slide, "during most, if not all, of his directorial career. His work on the studio floor and in promotion and defense of the film industry made him an important figure in the late 'teens.'" The man proved to be even more outgoing than some may even have first

thought when he joined the British Army during the First World War – although he was in his forties at the time.

"In the summer of 1918 with other recruits; I was Provost Sergeant," the "New York Times" quoted Stuart Cooling, one of Taylor's fellow soldiers, as saying. "He (Taylor) was very quick to learn and became a Lance Corporal in two weeks, a Corporal in three weeks, a Sergeant in five weeks, and a company Sergeant Major in two months. Then we went to England and he got a Lieutenant›s commission in the Army Service Corps of the British Army. His men worshipped him--would do anything for him."

Although he never saw action in the war, Taylor was able to return to directing films in California afterwards knowing he had earned the respect of his fellow soldiers. The man was not without his issues, however. Although he never married again after abandoning his family, Taylor was engaged for a time to actress, Neva Gerber, who spoke of him suffering from profound depression. Added to the combination of having left his family and randomly changing the course of his life more than a few times, it's little wonder that Taylor is seen as an enigmatic figure today.

Yet Taylor was nothing if not charming. Young star Mary Miles Minter appears to have been in love with the man. And, although she may not have been in love, Mabel was thoroughly fond of, and quite close to, Taylor in the early 1920s. She appears to have viewed the director as a kind of intellectual mentor, which was a role Taylor gladly played. Their friendship, however, ended up drawing the kind of publicity neither could have ever imagined. Or wanted.

“Under A Terrible Nervous Strain”

“I had known Bill Taylor casually for years,” Mabel told the *Los Angeles Examiner* of her friendship with Taylor. Although they both worked in Southern California’s film industry, Mabel reported that the two never had much to do with each other until one evening in the early 20s. “We were at a dinner party one night and sat beside each other,” she said. “The party wasn’t particularly interesting and we began to talk about various things, the screen, books, life in general. I found him extremely well informed and I liked his viewpoint of things. He was a brilliant man, a man of remarkable intelligence.”

There was a lot about Taylor that would appeal to someone like Mabel. For starters, he was nice, which was something that couldn’t always be said about the gruff Mack. What’s more, Taylor, like Mabel, was a literary person living in a less than literary community. Indeed, Mabel’s father, Claude, told the *New York Times* that Mabel saw Mr. Taylor as a reading guide. Needless to say, the two became fast friends. Although they didn’t see each other all the time – both worked in the film industry, after all, which could lead to quite a bit of traveling – their relationship was quite close.

There are those who have stated the two dated, and it’s easy to see why. Taylor had a locket on his keychain with Mabel’s image in it. What’s more, it was inscribed with the words “To My Dearest.” Furthermore, the two had a written correspondence known as the “Blessed Baby” letters due to the fact Taylor actually referred to Mabel as “Blessed Baby.” Mabel made it clear, however, that her friendship with Taylor was no love affair. “You see,” Mabel said, “just in a jest, Mr. Taylor called me ‘Blessed Baby’—it started at dinner parties we attended together. And just to tease him, I called him--this great, big, stern-minded man--’Baby’ in return. They were used in our letters; strictly in fun…Our letters exchanged were mostly 'joshing' ones, frivolous and jesting about the trivialities we had come upon since our last meeting. "

Perhaps Taylor was indeed in love with Mabel. As far as Mabel was concerned, however, theirs was more of a mentor-student relationship. "To me," she would say of Taylor, "he was always a kindly adviser in my efforts at mental improvement and to all who knew him he was an inspiration to the nobler and loftier things of life." The events of February 1st, 1922 would put a spotlight on the relationship between the older director and famous star – who was still in her 20s at the time.

As day worked its way into night, Mabel found herself in downtown Los Angeles getting silverware engraved for herself and for some friends. After dropping items off in her safe deposit box. Mabel decided to call her maid, Betty Coss. "I told my maid I thought I would stay downtown for dinner and see a picture," said Mabel, "but she said Mr. Taylor had phoned several times and said he had a book for me that I had been trying to get. It had been a cloudy day and no one was working on location or on 'outside sets.'"

Betty encouraged Mabel to pick up the book from Taylor, then head home to her own bungalow on West 7th Street and relax. Mabel had to be on the set of *Suzanna* at eight the next morning, after all. Mabel agreed that it seemed like a good idea, so she had her chauffer drive her to Taylor's bungalow on Alvarado Street. "He was having dinner," she said of Taylor, "and I sat at the table with him for a few minutes and then told him I was going home as I had to rise early. He said he would go to the car with me, and as we were walking he said he had a lot of work to do, but might call me about 9 o'clock to see how I liked the book. But he never called."

She would never speak with the man again.

"In the morning," said Mabel, "while I was making up to go on location for 'Suzanna,' my telephone rang. It was a friend who lived in the same court with Taylor. She told me that his butler was running up and down the court shrieking that Bill was dead." After first being told that Taylor had suffered a heart attack, Mabel soon learned that the truth was actually much darker. Taylor had been murdered overnight. A single shot fired from inside his home had sent the director falling to his death before his desk. Mabel was struck to her core. Taylor was dead and she and her chauffer were the last people to ever see her friend alive.

"It was a terrible shock," she said. "I liked and admired him so much. And I had talked with him only twelve hours before. I phoned the studio that I could not work that day and took off that remnant of my make-up that had not already been ruined by tears. As a matter of fact it was three weeks before I returned to work." Just how badly did Taylor's death affect Mabel? Badly enough that she literally collapsed in front of Taylor's casket at Saint Paul's Episcopal Cathedral days later at her friend's funeral.

Being the last person (along with her chauffer) to actually see Taylor alive meant that Mabel was the focus of much police attention. The *New York Times* reported that "a motion picture actress" had been put through what police called a "long and grueling examination," that actress, of course, being Mabel. On top of that, the "Blessed Baby" letters were missing. What's more, a pink nightie was found on Taylor's property. Lastly, Taylor's valet, Henry Peavey, told the media Mabel had informed him she and the director were to be married. No wonder the *Los Angeles Record* reported her as being "under a terrible nervous strain."

The police, however, simply had no real reason to suspect Mabel was the killer. First and foremost, witnesses had Mabel at home or on the road with her chauffer when the murder occurred. What's more, there was no legitimate evidence of an engagement, or of a fight, or of any kind of hostility, between her and Taylor before the director was killed. Soon enough, the *New York Times* presented readers with the following:

"Claude G. Normand, Mabel Normand's father, who leaves at 127 St. Nicholas Avenue, New Brighton, S.I., said last night that he had received a message from his daughter in which she said the District Attorney and the police had absolved her of any responsibility for the murder of William Desmond Taylor." The *Times* also wrote that "about five years ago she (Mabel) bought a house valued at $25,000 and gave it to her parents."

Perhaps most importantly, there were others who might have had real reason to see Taylor dead. Ultimately, though, there wasn't enough evidence to charge anyone with the crime. Strangely enough, no one was ultimately indicted for the murder. To this day, the killing of William Desmond Taylor remains unsolved. As for Mabel, she may have been innocent of cold blooded homicide, but she was about to be treated as if she were a public menace, nonetheless.

Some in the media had found a new target.

William Randolph Hearst

It appears that in many ways publisher William Randolph Hearst has been unfairly vilified over the years. One of the most powerful men in the world during his time, Hearst was also one of the wealthiest. The man ran for president (and lost) and it's said he started the Spanish-American War, and was thrilled with the business the Arbuckle trial brought to his numerous publications. Forgotten is the fact that Hearst at the time had no governmental power with which to wage a war and the fact that Arbuckle himself went on to make movies with Hearst's longtime mistress Marion Davis. While he certainly wasn't a saint, William Randolph Hearst wasn't the man Orson Welles presented in his 1941 film Citizen Kane.

Indeed, when viewing Hearst through a 21st century perspective the word "unwieldy" comes to mind. Figuratively speaking, he was too big to keep himself from indulging in his political impulses, just as his empire was too big to keep some of his reporters on the journalistic straight and narrow. Was anyone able to remind Hearst, for instance, that a war with Spain might have severe consequences, that it was ultimately a matter of life and death? And was he even aware of the fact some of his reporter's first articles after the Arbuckle scandal broke focused on mocking the man's weight? The answer might well be no in both instances. Still, emperors are responsible for their empires just as journalists are responsible for the articles they print.

And Hearst was very comfortable being an emperor.

"William Randolph Hearst," wrote biographer David Nasaw in "The Chief: The Life of William Randolph Hearst,"... "was a huge man with a tiny voice, a shy man who was most comfortable in crowds; a war hawk in Cuba and Mexico but a pacifist in Europe; an autocratic boss who could not fire people." Hearst was, in many ways, a walking, talking contradiction. In this he was no different

than most if not all people. What separated Hearst from others was, frankly, his wealth. For the man was born wealthy.

His father was a highly successful miner and United States Senator, and Hearst grew the family fortune to unimagined heights.

After attending Harvard, Hearst was literally given "The San Francisco Examiner" from his father and kicked off a career as a publisher. "The Examiner" was only the beginning for Hearst, who moved on to take control of many publications. His New York circulation war with fellow publisher Joseph Pulitzer saw Hearst swipe top names from his competitor, while cutting costs and engaging in an often hyperbolic reporting style designed to bring in readers.

It was the war with Spain, however, that brought Hearst the most attention and notoriety. Passionate in his beliefs, Hearst felt that Spain should be cast out of Cuba, where a revolution was occurring. As the New York Times wrote, "Mr. Hearst saw the insurrection then occurring in Cuba the makings of spectacular newspaper copy." Hearst got his war, but he also received a large degree of fame as well. "When the United States declared war on Spain on April 24th 1898, Mr. Hearst became a national figure."

As a result of his power, wealth and popularity, Hearst was able to be a two-term member of the House of Representatives. He then tried to earn the Democratic nomination for President in 1904. Only 41 years old, Hearst was backed by none other than legendary attorney Clarence Darrow. Yet a famous reputation, coupled with wealth and notable support, couldn't win Hearst the party's nomination. That honor went to Alton B. Parker, who had won over twice as many votes as Hearst had. Undeterred, Hearst ran for Mayor of New York twice, and Governor of New York once. He was defeated in all three elections.

Less than a decade later , Hearst entered the motion picture business. "The Perils of Pauline" starred Pearl White and was a notable effort from Hearst's studio. Ultimately though it was the very attractive Marion Davies who would be widely seen as Hearst's contact with the motion picture industry. Not only did Hearst work to make the talented Davies his star, she became the married father of five's mistress for the rest of his life. Needless to say, Hearst was well over forty years Davies' senior.

One of the facts – aside from journalistic hyperbole – that Hearst is best remembered for is a property he never lived to see completed – the imposing "La Cuesta Encantada," in San Simeon, California. Featuring hundreds of opulent rooms and designed in regal European fashion, the structure known as "Hearst's Castle" was (and remains) like some of the articles that appeared in Hearst's newspapers: nearly jaw dropping in its excesses. Yet, as the Hearst Castle site indicates, the man had to move off the property in 1947 due to ill health. Hearst died in Beverley Hills at the age of 88 in 1951.

Although Hearst's papers could be said to have ruined reputations, Hearst's own reputation was attacked by Welles' Citizen Kane, which, although far from an exact biography of the man, presented Charles Foster Kane, a tycoon clearly based on Hearst, in a far less than positive light. Welles may have been a cinematic genius, but it's clear he viewed Hearst as a target ripe for the picking (Welles' was originally said to have planned his film on the life of someone like famed back robber John Dillinger but ended up instead focusing on Hearst and many of his perceived shortcomings).

While it's unfair to vilify Hearst outright, some who wrote for his papers performed what could only be described as reputation assassinations in print. This was true of Hearst reporters Edward Doherty and Wallace Smith, who attacked Mabel with maliciousness, inuendo, and outright falsehoods that had such an impact that they've remained with her reputation to this day. With that in mind, it's fair to add that other Hearst outlets, like "The San Francisco Examiner," treated Mabel favorably throughout the years. Perhaps then the Hearst Empire's treatment of Mabel and others may stand out as an example of a media universe capable of doing as much harm as good. Something that remains as true today as it did in the early 1920s.

Media Assault

"Mabel Normand," the *San Francisco Bulletin* wrote nearly a week after the murder of Taylor, "who was among the last persons to see William Desmond Taylor, director, alive, made a number of declarations 'on her word of honor' to newspaper interviewers." There was no doubt that, funeral aside, Mabel dealt with the death of Taylor gamely at first. To reporters she made it clear that her relationship with Taylor was a platonic affair. "Get it straight," she said,"our friendship was based on comradeship and understanding." So, she wasn't in love with Taylor? "On my word of honor, no."

It was then that Mabel was asked a strange question. "It has been hinted he gave drug parties," the *Bulletin* quoted a reporter as saying about Taylor. "Did you ever hear of them?" Mabel was quick to respond. "Never in God's world," she stated, "never, on my word of honor." Mabel then went on to address another matter that was annoying her. "And, oh please," she added, "say that I never heard of that pink silk nightrobe they say is missing from Mr. Taylor's apartments."

It was a brutal time for Mabel, to be sure. She had been the last person to see Taylor alive, after all. Plus, there were the rumors of drug parties, as well as the rumors of her and Taylor having been engaged. Perhaps worst of all, Taylor's cook, Henry Peavey, claimed she had asked him if other women had come to visit Taylor at home. "He ought to be ashamed of himself," Mabel said of Peavey to the media. "I saved him his job once when Mr. Taylor wanted to fire him."

It's understandable why the police moved on from Mabel, as there was – simply put – no "there" there. What's more, Mabel was consistent in her stories. As recently as the day after the murder, for instance, Mabel told the *Los Angeles Record* that: "If I had been engaged to marry Mr. Taylor, I would be only too proud to acknowledge it." And that assertion, as well as other assertions Mabel made in regard to Taylor, never altered.

While she may have been cleared by the police, Mabel had other people to worry about. For members of the media were starting to circle. Of course, it would be wildly irresponsible to argue that the media as a whole took the occasion of the Taylor murder as an opportunity to destroy her. Indeed, many, if not most, news outlets simply transcribed the news as it arrived, that is to say, in a professional manner. Smears sell, however, and numerous reporters decided, without provocation, to mop the figurative floor with Mabel's reputation due to bold careerism, intense personal dislike, or perhaps both.

Mack, who had also been questioned by law enforcement, had Mabel stay at a home on Foothill Avenue in Altadena in order to avoid the crush of the press. She was, to be sure, in a state of near breakdown. But who, really, could blame her? A close friend had been murdered, and her name was associated with that murder. What's more, Taylor's hidden past life, which included the abandonment of his wife and child, began to emerge, no doubt making Mabel wonder if her dark night of the soul would ever come to an end.

Desperate to clear his star's – as well as his former lover's - name, Mack had his studio release a statement which basically reiterated the facts of the case: That Mabel showed up to borrow a book, then went home before the murder occurred. "That is the way her name became connected with the case," the release stated. "Miss Normand has the sympathy of the entire country through the accidental connection of her name with this regrettable tragedy, for she has been completely exonerated of any connection with it."

She may have been exonerated by the police, but some in the media were just getting started. First, the *L.A. Herald* altered a picture of Taylor on set with costumed actress May McAvoy so that Mabel's face was on McAvoy's body. What's more, she and Taylor were then moved so that they appeared closer together than Taylor and McAvoy had actually been. The reason for this apparently was that there were no pictures of Mabel and Taylor together, so one was simply created.

Yet the *Herald's* fiddling with photos was nothing compared to the writing of Edward Doherty, which appeared in *New York News* just four days after the Taylor murder. "Mabel Normand likes to go to parties with the fellows of the film," he wrote snarkily, "and many a party she has enlivened by her wish for 'horseback rides'." But he wasn't done there. "'Mabel wants horsebackie rides," she'll say and climb up on the back of a willing friend, to be ridden around the cafe, shouting, singing, laughing, waving her arms. Great times when Mabel's around." Doherty's sneering and mocking condescension of Mabel continued for years.

Yet he had competition when came to Mabel bashing. Wallace Smith went straight for the figurative jugular in the pages of the *Chicago American*. One week after the Taylor murder, Smith wrote of "one of the actresses mentioned time after time in the life and death of Taylor, the man of mystery." Smith then went on to mention "an amazing record of her escapades from practical jokes that would have shocked the notorious Dirty Club of London through a dozen scandalous love affairs to downright crimes." In case readers still couldn't grasp who Smith was referring to, the reporter then made it crystal clear:

"All done by a woman," he said, "a victim of drugs, who is loved by millions for her innocent pranks on the screen."

"It was not to be lightly considered," he added, "how far the protection of the movie millions might go to shelter these pets of filmdom. Already ugly rumors run through Los Angeles of attempts made to bribe those most vigorous in pushing the investigation."

It could be argued, of course, that only a handful of reporters went after Mabel's reputation. That, however, would be to downplay how effective the printed smears were. Mabel was never looked on the same by the American public after the Taylor murder, a crime which she had absolutely nothing to do with. Even to this day, the version of Mabel conjured up by the pens of Doherty and Smith is strong enough that many believe it was the real Mabel. Indeed, even respectable outlets continue to write of Mabel's "cocaine addiction" and/or "promiscuity." Well into the 21st century, Mabel continues to stand as irrefutable proof that smears sell.

The question, of course, is why these rumors were spread to begin with. It's safe to assume that certain journalists were looking for anything that might make Mabel the next Arbuckle – whose own legal problems were still raging at the time – and that her having been cleared by the police left them scrambling. Still, even with the thrill of taking down another celebrity, there seems to have been something else in play among certain determined members of the media.

The answer might be found in what should be a footnote in the Taylor affair. While being questioned about the night of the murder by police, Mabel revealed that Taylor had joked with her upon finding peanuts in her car along with a copy of the popular general information paper the *Police Gazette.* The fact that Mabel, who was supposed to indulge in fine literature, also consumed peanuts and lowbrow publications, made Taylor laugh good naturedly. To some in the media, however the news spurred an intense resentment. Mabel, it seems, was nothing more than a pretender to these people, which made her worthy of scorn and mockery.

"It must have been with pain and anguish," one journalist wrote snidely, "that the screen fans read how Mabel Normand, pictured as a devotee of Voltaire and Nietzsche, testified that on her way to William Taylor's house on the fatal night she stopped at a newsstand to buy a bag of peanuts and a copy of the *Police Gazette.*" Indeed, another journalist went in for all out mockery. "Between old Mister Nietzsche and the *Police Gazette,*" this journalist wrote, "it's no wonder that Mabel is nervous and confined to her bed." It appears, then, that classic snobbery was a primary source of hostility towards Mabel. Mark Lynn Anderson keenly points out that:

"While many of the jokes made about Normand's cultural pretensions sought to expose the star's long- purported interests in highbrow culture as nothing more than a publicity sham, these jokes also betrayed a deep-seated uneasiness about the possibility that one might, indeed, read Freud and the *Police Gazette* as similarly interesting expressions of modern times."

William H. Hays

If anyone had told Will Hays at the beginning of the 20th century that he would someday become primarily known for being arguably the most powerful man in the film industry, he might well have laughed. For Hays, to his very marrow, was a product of American politics. Yet, like it or not, Hays is today remembered primarily as being what journalist Eric Gardner calls "the man whose battle against cinematic indecency either squelched filmmakers' creativity or fostered Hollywood's Golden Age." He may have led the fight to get Warren G. Harding elected President of the United States, but Hays' greatest contribution to American society – for good or ill – was the impact he made on Hollywood.

A product of Indiana, Hays was born in the town of Sullivan in 1879. He became the head of the Republican Party and was just forty-one years of age when he led the charge of Harding's successful presidential campaign in 1921. Hays was rewarded by being made Postmaster General of the United States. Although popular until his death in office in 1923, Harding and his administration were subsequently exposed as being one of the most amoral and corrupt in history. In fact, as recently as 2008, the New York Times referred to Hays as "the venal chairman of the Republican National Committee and later Harding's postmaster general."

Yet with Hollywood awash in the early 20s with tales from the Arbuckle trial, the Taylor murder, and the untimely deaths of such stars as the beautiful Olive Thomas, the film industry's' reputation was taking a severe hit. Giving up his administration post, Hays went west to become, as "The Associated Press" put it, "the author of Hollywood self-censorship with the Hays Code." Hays was brought in, perhaps laughably in hindsight, to clean things up. "Life had been good to Will Hays," wrote author Laton McCartney of Hay's decision to become a moral arbiter of creative works before the Harding administration met with real consequences, "though he still looked like a weasel."

Hays found quite a home for himself amongst those of the film universe as President of the Motion Picture Association. "While some industry heavyweights objected to Hays as the moral arbiter," the "Los Angeles Times" claims, "he was recognized for guarding filmmakers' right to self-regulate at a time when seven states already had provisions for government censorship." Needless to say, Hays made his presence felt by supporting the studio's ban of Arbuckle from making movies after his acquittal. Arbuckle had been found not guilty in a court of law, but a scapegoat was needed to get things off on the right track. Arbuckle, then, had to go.

In hindsight, the sheer irony of a high-ranking member of what might well be the most thoroughly and gleefully corrupt administration in presidential history traveling west to inject the movie industry with some old fashioned morality would be laughable if it weren't so blatantly hypocritical. The man who led an open adulterer in Harding to the White House, the father of an illegitimate child he refused to publicly recognize or acknowledge, was going purify showbusiness? Indeed, that would be the party line – and all parties were going to stick with it.

Yet, as "PBS" put it, "Hayes was merely a spokesperson. Since he had very little power to change the content of films, the criticism escalated, exploding into a national crisis when sound technology gave the movies a voice." Hence, the Production Code came to be. Per "PBS": "the Production Code spelled out specific restrictions on language and behavior, particularly sex and crime – two sure-fire box office draws. It prohibited nudity, suggestive dances, and the ridicule of religion. It forbade the depiction of illegal drug use, venereal disease, childbirth, and miscegenation." Needless to say, the Code ruled supreme for decades.

By the early 1950s, however, the code's grip on American cinema was finally released when it became clear that filmmaker's works fell under the protection of the First Amendment. By that time, however, Hays had long since retired. His work done, Hays had left Hollywood in 1945. He died at his Indiana home 1954 at the age of 74. He had come a long way from being head of the Republican Party, but there was no doubting the man was one of America's premier fixers. He kept scandal from destroying the presidential ambitions of Harding, then went on to perhaps save the financial ambitions of Hollywood.

Did he, though?

What's strange about Hays' Hollywood mission is that its primary focus – at least at first – appeared to be film stars like Arbuckle, who, although proven innocent of a violent crime, nonetheless was found hosting a booze-soaked prohibition party when Virginia Rappe fell ill. While Arbuckel's films were basically innocuous, America found the whole affair unseemly. Still, while Catholic organizations may have pressured Hays to clean up the film business, it generally came across as tame in comparison to the post Code film industry of the second half of the 20th century.

In truth, Hays was a wonderful attorney. In other words, he was always there for the people he represented. His job wasn't correcting the adulterous Harding or correcting his wayward eye, for instance. His job was to make Harding look upright. The same could be said of the film industry. His duty was to get, then keep, that industry out of trouble. This is clearly evidenced by the fact that the man never targeted Mabel, no matter how searing matters might be. For whatever reason, Hayes never saw Mabel as a threat to the film industry. His stance proved to be one less stress in Mabel's life.

An interesting question is what Hays thought about his expertise at handling reputation destroying scenarios. Was he somehow a proponent for what he believed was a greater good? Or was he simply a man who felt the morality of a situation (or the lack thereof) shouldn't interfere with the work at hand? Perhaps those were questions only the man himself could answer.

Europe

There was still work to be done. Her friend may have been murdered. Her reputation might have been in the process of being tarnished, but Mabel was a film star, and *Suzanna* eventually had to be completed. Therefore, after less than a month in seclusion, Mabel returned to Mack and Jones to complete work on her latest film. This was undoubtedly challenging for a woman who was clearly and understandably wiped out by several brutal weeks. Like many religiously oriented people, however, Mabel turned to her faith when life became rather dark. As Mack himself said, "All during her devout but casual life Mabel Normand professed and practiced the Roman Catholic faith." Stephen Normand added that Mabel "was actually quite a religious person" whose Catholicism helped get her through difficult times.

By spring, then, Mabel's work on *Suzanna* was done and Mabel was ready for a much-needed vacation. Reporters were still hounding her, after all, plus her film work, combined with her tuberculosis and the overall stress of the Taylor murder, made a holiday almost necessary. "Mabel Normand, film actress," The *New York Times* wrote, "will go to Europe in June, it was announced at her home here today. Her plans call for visits to London, Paris, Berlin, Rome, Naples and Madrid."

Mabel travelled with Juliette Courtell, a friend from the Oakland area who spoke French. Once they had made their way across the Atlantic, the two women joined up with another friend, Perry M. Charles, who was kind enough to make preparations. "When do you sail?" Mabel asked Charles via telegraph. "Might be able to go along. Want you to work for me. Anything you say goes about salary. Might be better your going ahead to fix things up, then return to America with me, London, Paris, Berlin, etc. Love. Mabel."

On June 13th 1922 Mabel boarded the opulent liner *Aquitania* in New York enroute to Great Britain. She would have traveled sooner, but because she didn't work during Holy Week, production ended up being delayed on *Suzanna*. Mabel had good reason to be excited. On top of touring, she planned to visit her bother Claude, who had served in the war with the United States Marines. Before getting on board, however, Mabel was asked by the assembled media about the Taylor murder. *"Please don't discuss that," she said. "I've been running away from it for months. That is one of the reasons I am going away to get a rest."*

Once the journey actually began, Mabel was able to enjoy herself. According to Mabel expert Marilyn Slater, Mabel was a serious tourist. "She was a list maker," wrote Slater, "a reader, a listener and a learner." While in Great Britain, the American star made it a point to meet authors she admired. "Among the persons whose friendship began in late summer of 1922," she was to later write, "were George Bernard Shaw and H. G. Wells." Mabel was also thrilled to make the acquaintance of *Peter Pan* creator J. M. Barrie. "He made me think of Peter Pan grown old," Mabel claimed. "He wears a shawl."

The journey to Europe proved to be nothing if not memorable. An international star, Mabel found herself at one point dangerously pressed by a mob of fans while in London, though she gamely made it a point to be warm to the crowd. Suffice to say, Mabel was quite warmly received during her month in England. Unfortunately, she was actually learning how to curtsy, as the Prince of Wales birthday was approaching, when the Irish Republican Army assassinated a member of Parliament, causing the festivities to be called off.

Yet after her month in Britain, it was off to the continent itself. Rather than hopping on a boat, Mabel took advantage of the still new airplane service, which had begun running a few years earlier, in 1919. As always, however, Mabel found herself running late, so late that a vehicle had to be quickly round up in order to get her to her flight on time. Having accomplished the goal successfully,

Mabel and Juliette Courtell found themselves arriving in France in under three hours.

Paris proved to be a city where Mabel could indulge in her love of fashion. *Photoplay* ran a two page spread on her Parisian attire, ranging from a Silver Evening Cape ("of silver cloth brocaded in great mauve flowers") to a Heavy Crepe Street Costume ("a clever mixture of sophistication and extreme girlishness"), to a Brown Velvet Hat ("almost audacious in its youth and coloring"), to her "favorite hat - a tightly wound turban also of (heavy) silver cloth," to numerous other items of high fashion.

Not only did Mabel, the former model, enjoy being a style maven, but she also was required to look her best on the Continent. For it was there that she met Max Linder himself, played the tables (apparently quite successfully) at Monte Carlo's Casino de Pourville-Sur-Mer, attended the horse races at the resort of Deauville, and was the guest of King Albert and Queen Izabella of Belgium, whom she had previously hosted in southern California.

Perhaps most interestingly, a member of the Egyptian royal family decided to court Mabel while she was abroad. Indeed, Prince Ibrahim went so far as to inform the media he'd give up his royal title for the American movie star. Although Mabel politely refused his marriage proposal, she attended the races with the Prince while they were in Deauville. Once again, it was good to be Mabel Normand. At least for a brief moment, the devastating events of the previous winter were literally half a world away. Still, while she certainly enjoyed herself in Europe, Mabel also tended to more serious matters.

She may have gone from being a pacifist to a woman determined to punish Germany throughout the course of the First World War, but Mabel made it a point to visit Germany on her trip to Europe. What's more, she went to Berlin's Adson Hotel where the American Relief Association was located to speak with Bill Hashell. In truth, Mabel was moved by the condition of the largely decimated post-war Continent. She was especially troubled by those children who had lost their parents. Although she kept such things quiet, Mabel went out of her way to support numerous orphanages in Europe, besides the one she supported for Father Chiappa.

Aside from charitable causes, Mack had also wanted Mabel to search for shooting locations so that some of his films might be shot abroad. In all, however, Mabel's eight months abroad gave her the time away from the United States she needed. Eventually, however, it was time to head home. *Suzanna* was now playing in theaters and there would surely be more work to be done. Hopefully, the dark intensity of the previous year had been abated.

"Mabel Normand is at last back in Hollywood," the *Wichita Eagle* wrote on March 11th, "Miss Normand denies the wedding rumor regarding herself, admits to having all kinds of new Paris clothes, and is said to look plump and radiantly happy." The rumors of a marriage had clearly been making the rounds, for Mabel addressed the matter directly to the *Daily News.* "Do you think I could have kept it a secret this long if I were engaged?" she asked. "Besides, I've just bought a world of clothes – enough to frighten any husband away." After reporting that Mabel had receipts for nine entire trunks of luggage upon her return to the United States, the *News* stated that Mabel "was in the best of health."

Her return, at least early on, looked like it might be free of the scandal that had consumed her life before her journey across the ocean.

Edna Purviance

"Edna Purviance," the "Los Angeles Times'" headline read, "Once Chaplin Film Star, Dies...Retired Actress Had Played In Many Of Comedian's Two-Reelers Of Silent Era." The subsequent article, which was accompanied by a picture of the deceased as a young woman, appeared on page thirty-nine of the "Times" January 16th, 1958, morning edition. The piece was less than two columns long, briefly describing the life of an actress whose time in the spotlight had clearly come and gone. Referring to Purviance as "Charlie Chaplin's long ago leading lady," the "Times" informed readers that Purviance had passed at the Motion Picture Country Hospital in Woodlawn, California at the age of sixty-one, and that memorial services would be private.

It was a quiet, unassuming end for a woman who had reached heights most couldn't possibly imagine. Unlike most peoples', Purviance's death warranted a short news article in a major American paper rather than a simple obituary. The aging former actress' passing, however, was not top news. This was understandable, of course, as Purviance had been away from the public eye for many years. Indeed, the only reason Purviance had been in the public eye to begin with was because of Chaplin. And, when the self-absorbed superstar no longer had use for her, Purviance slowly began fading into obscurity. At least that's the story that's been told (reality is often a more complex matter than the rumors it's mistaken for). A life, however, is not – or should not – be defined by one person's interest in another, no matter how long or short a period of time that interest may last.

In other words, there was considerably more to Purviance's life than her years spent as a muse, lover, and costar of Chaplin's.

Like Chaplin, Arbuckle, Mabel, and others, Purviance came from a humble background. She was born in Paradise Valley,

Nevada, in 1895. Paradise was a thriving town due to the fact that it supplied the local silver mines, but Purviance left Paradise with her family while only a toddler, moving to Lovelock, Nevada, where the family got involved with the hotel industry. After graduating from high school, Purviance and her then widowed mother moved to San Francisco. Her mother returned to Nevada a short time later, but Purviance remained and worked as a stenographer.

The young woman's life changed forever when she met Chaplin, who was looking for a leading lady, in 1913. If reports are to be believed, Chaplin met Purviance at the Saint Francis Hotel, but walked away unimpressed. When he saw Purviance at a party afterward, however, he was charmed – and more importantly, impressed – when she pretended to be hypnotized by him. Here was a woman who could go along with a joke – something that was essential for a Chaplin leading lady. Purviance must have been dazzled when she was lifted from obscurity into stardom by the motion picture star.

Although she doesn't have the on-screen magnetism of a Mabel or a Mary Pickford, Purviance is very good in her films with Chaplin. What stands out besides her charm, confidence, and a natural comfort of being in front of the camera is the unique dream-like quality Purveance gets in her eyes at certain moments. There are times where she appears to be looking beyond the moment, beyond the physical set she's on, beyond the here and now, to a distant future perhaps, or to a distant past. It's all very effective. Little wonder, then, that Purviance went on to make thirty-four films with Chaplin of which "The Tramp," "The Kid" and "The Idle Class" were only a few.

While Chaplin could open the door to fame and a robust income, he could not be relied upon to be a faithful boyfriend. They met when she was nineteen and he twenty-five. Some time well into their personal and professional partnership, Purviance put an end to the relationship. A short time later, Chaplin wrongly thought he had impregnated sixteen-year-old Mildred Harris. Months later, the couple was married. Surprisingly, if not shockingly, enough, Chaplin continued to pay Purviance for years after their film and romantic partnership had ended. No one would ever accuse Chaplin of being a great beau, but there was clearly something about Purviance that, at the very least, pulled at his conscience.

Needless to say, after staring in her own feature, "A Woman of Paris," Purviance eventually went on to have a full life for herself. She wed airplane pilot John "Jack" Squire in 1938, and the couple stayed together until Squire's passing in 1945. Purviance never married again. She and Jack were said to have had a successful marriage, which separated it from Purviance's shaky relationship with Chaplin. With that being said, Chaplin reportedly resumed giving Purviance monthly checks once she had become a widow (the payments had ceased once Purviance had married Squire).

Although generally remembered today as an early co-star of Chaplin's, Purviance was able to make a life for herself on her own. It's also worth noting that, while successful, Purviance appeared to possess a refreshing degree of honesty. "Now," wrote Hazel Simpson Naylor in 1918, "nine out of ten celebrities, when asked what they consider caused their success, will announce: 'Work--good, hard, never-give-up work.' But not so Edna Purviance." When asked about the source of her success, Purviance, for better or worse, was positively gleeful. "Just luck," she answered, "wonderful, wonderful luck. I am the happiest girl in all the world. Here I am just turned twenty-one. I have everything I want--things I should never have dreamt of obtaining—and it's all due to luck."

Some may have found that kind of bold, joyful frankness off-putting, but Mabel – who indeed found her success through the grind of brutally hard work – obviously didn't mind. She and Purviance, after all, were famously close. At least that was the case for a time. Dark clouds returned, however, and this time, they did not disappear under the sunlight of a voyage to Europe.

The Extra Girl

"After *Suzanna* was finished I went to Europe for a long rest," Mable said. "I returned completely cured of the things that had broken me physically and were threatening to wreck my mind." Indeed, the diminutive star seemed to have been much happier upon her return to the states, visiting her family and staying in New York City. "I returned from Europe on the Majestic about the middle of September," she said, "and stayed around New York a few weeks, visiting friends and seeing the new shows and pictures. Then I went on to Hollywood, Sennett having telephoned me that he had a fine comedy for me."

Suzanna had been released while Mabel was in Europe. Indeed, Mabel may have been surprised by audiences' reaction to the film. "Suzanna made a lot of money," she said, "part of which I got, and the Taylor case notoriety didn't seem to hurt it at the box-office." Indeed, Mabel earned her money while making the film. "There were two little bears in the original play," she said, "and I used to wear a wide leather belt which we covered with honey. The bears soon learned to toddle along beside me, licking at my waist and pawing at the heavy belt. One day one of them got his claws inside the belt and almost tore me to pieces."

Mabel, obviously, was concerned. Director Jones, however, didn't seem overly alarmed. "I screamed to Dick, 'Dick, your bears are killing me!' and leaped frantically around, trying to break that agonizing, clawing clinch. Instead of gallantly rushing out to rescue me, Dick yelled through the megaphone: 'Be brave, my girl! Don't weaken. It's the best shot of the picture'. So I had to lay off for a week till the scratches healed." Again, Mabel earned her pay making the film.

Unfortunately, *Suzanna* in its completed state is lost to history (at least until someone discovers a finished copy of the film). There's not a lot there for the contemporary viewer, but there's something different about the portion of the film that remains. Mabel was around 30 at this time, obviously not as young as she once was. Yet she's still energetic and dances like there's no tomorrow. There's a deliberateness here to the comedy, though, which doesn't serve her talents well. With that in mind, she remains a cute screen presence, as always. The film is also perhaps a bit slow moving. The fact Mabel was working on *Suzanna* when Taylor got shot might add something to the strangeness of it. This clearly isn't a standard flick in the traditional Mack Sennett style.

Mabel, however, returned to form in the new comedy Mack had in mind for her now that she was back in America. The new film became a defining work because it was one of the few films at the time to actually be about the movies. It also turned the classic Cinderella story Mabel had been applying to her features on its head. Here a girl left a humble background to find great success in Hollywood – only to realize great success couldn't be achieved. Rather Sue Graham, Mabel's character, learned that things such as family and simplicity lead to a far greater happiness. It was a new, mature theme for Mabel to work with in a film, one which she might have developed after having fallen on some hard times in Hollywood herself thanks to the Taylor killing and Mack's betrayal.

"It was a good picture, all right," said Mabel, "and called *The Extra Girl*; but I soon found that he (Mack) hadn't sent for me until he had spent an awful lot of money trying to find another comedienne to take my place. So I made him give me three thousand dollars a week and a percentage of the profits." The relationship between the former lovers was now entirely professional – and even awkwardly professional at that. Mabel was still willing to work for Mack, but she demanded to be treated as an expensive and popular star if he wished to employ her talents.

While filming *The Extra Girl*, Mabel once again nearly got terribly hurt by a dangerous animal. A lion was needed for the film and Mabel insisted on one she was told was too young and dangerous.

On set the lion, named Duke, behaved well enough at first, so it was decided that Mabel would walk it around the studio lot for a scene where Sue Graham, her character, absentmindedly and without looking, mistakes the lion for a dog. The scene was going fairly well until Jones stepped back while filming a reverse dolly shot and fell, alarming the lion and terrorizing Mabel. As a horrifying side note, Duke was subsequently rapped on the back of his head by his "trainer" while Jones and another man on set had pitchforks with which to save Mabel should the situation call for it. In an era where children could still be expected to hold full time jobs, the humane treatment of animals was, sadly, not a high priority.

With that in mind, the production was winding down to completion in the later part of the year. "*The Extra Girl* was finished and ready for release just before Christmas, 1923," said Mabel. "I had been feeling quite ill during the latter part of the picture and resolved to go to a hospital for an operation immediately after the holidays. Those festive days passed pleasantly and excitingly enough, and I received many beautiful presents."

The treatment of animals on film sets aside, things seemed to finally be going well once again for Mabel. No doubt she felt that she could survive the rumors, suspicion and sense of loss that had hounded her less than two years earlier. It had all been a harrowing experience, to be sure, but Mabel must have sensed that Christmas season that she had perhaps survived it. And indeed, she might have – but another violent incident was on its way, one with which she once again wasn't directly involved, but brought about a storm of furious repercussions, nonetheless.

Courtland Dines

In 1906, a prominent Denver attorney went to the home of his neighbor, a sixty year old mill owner and millionaire and assaulted the elderly man with a whip he also used on his dogs. Reportedly encouraged by his own violence, the lawyer then proceeded to repeatedly punch the elderly man in the face. The millionaire's daughter and wife pulled the lawyer off his victim, only to see a gun fall out of the lawyers' coat. They told the lawyer there was a sick person upstairs. The lawyer responded by saying he wasn't afraid to kill four people. When the lawyer himself passed away over twenty years later, he was remembered as a powerhouse of the Colorado legal system.

Money can provide freedom from a great many things – including consequences.

At least that's the case at times.

At other times, however, consequences, sometimes severe and even unfair, impact rich and poor alike. Such was the case of the wealthy lawyer's son, Courtland Dines. Unlike his father, Tyson, Courtland seemed to be a rather charming man at all times. "The most delightful fellow you ever met," The "San Francisco Examiner" wrote of one associate's opinion. And, to be sure, photo evidence presents a smiling, good time Charley. Dines, it seems, was a world class bon vivant. He certainly wasn't his father (indeed, Courtland had reportedly talked to his father's victim before the assault about the family feud that was transpiring and walked away without violence or chaos), but the man doesn't appear to have had great aspirations, either.

By the time he had made his way to southern California, the younger Dines had married and divorced twice. "I want eleven months of perfectly straight married life," he said, "but I've got to have about one month out of the year for play." Courtland's ex-wives, attractive and from wealthy backgrounds themselves, responded that Dines wanted eleven months of play to one month of serious marriage. Dines, no doubt, was a dyed in the wool playboy, and he found quite a home for himself in Hollywood – at least for a bit.

Even for a son of privilege, Dines must have been amazed at his fortune when he began dating none other than movie star Edna Purviance. While he admitted that he regretted his marriages and never planned on marrying again, Dines easily settled into the southern California party scene. He may have been running out of money, but he certainly wasn't running out of good times. Besides, his friends were enormously wealthy. As the "San Francisco Examiner" put it, "money was the least of their troubles with that crowd." He may well have felt like the good times would go on indefinitely. It paid to be the beau of Edna Purviance, former love of the great Chaplin.

"Every afternoon I leave my office right after lunch," he said, "and we go to Mabel's house or to Edna's, or to the home of another actor." From there the party started. "We drink and play around," he continued, "and you never tasted such Scotch Highballs. It certainly is a lot of fun." From there, Dines explained how the party then moved to the water. "Then we have a new club called the 'Beach Club' at Santa Monica. We play around on the beach in our bathing clothes till we are tired, then we go into the clubhouse and drink highballs and smoke in our wet bathing clothes."

Suffice to say, it's likely none of this news pleased Cortland's father, much less his mother, Katherine, who was said to be an invalid as a result of Courtland's brother being killed in the war. To be sure, Dines was apparently known as someone who was out of control before he even left for the West Coast. He had gotten into several car accidents and would start drunken brawls for people commenting on, or even wanting to date, one of his attractive ex-wives. And while he wasn't known as an adulterer, the handsome Dines appeared to have had no problem attracting single women.

With that being said, Dines seemed to have a similar track record with employment as he did with marriage. It was reported that the playboy had been thrown out of both Holbrook Military Academy and Andover. He was reportedly now involved with the oil industry, though he had previously purchased himself a seat on the New York Stock Exchange and had been in the aviation service. Back home in Denver, "he was arrested for speeding many times."

Although he said he wasn't serious with Edna, Mabel said they were engaged. It would, in fairness, be easy to see how Dines and Edna would connect. They were both, as Edna put it, products of "luck." Edna had the luck of being Chaplin's chosen leading lady and Dines had the luck of being born into a high powered and obviously wealthy family. Edna was able to live off the money Chaplin sent her and Dines had his family to support him if things were to somehow go bad.

As for Mabel, she was busy having a grand old time for herself with her friends. In photos she can be seen horsing around with Edna and Dines. In one particular photo, Edna is on the deck of a boat smiling while Mabel and Dines stand over her laughing. Dines is lifting Mabel's dress a bit, showing a bit of an ankle that appears too thin to be healthy. Only those at the occasion could tell what the action in the photo was all about, though it certainly appeared to be part of a rather boozy affair. Indeed, the image looks as if it's presenting almost stereotypical 1920s excess, which it may well have been.

All parties, however, come to an end, and for Courtland Dines the party ended a lot sooner than he probably could have imagined. "We would not approve of a marriage to a screen star," his father stated. Yet disapproving parents were about to be the least of Dines' and Edna's concerns. As for Mabel, the immediate future may well have been even darker for her than it would be for her friends.

Another Shooting

The Extra Girl showed that Mabel's talent was continuing to develop. The movie had a real story – if not a bit of a disjointed one - with a good moral, and a surprisingly intense and violent ending. It also - being a Mabel Normand film - had humorous moments. Still, Stephen Normand pointed out that, though it was his favorite of Mabel's films, his aunt doesn't always look healthy in the movie. Be that as it may, at this point in her career, it must have been fascinating to wonder about what new directions she might take. Unfortunately, *The Extra Girl* was Mabel's last feature, which meant the world would be left with five full length features from Mabel: *Tillies Punctured Romance, Mickey, Molly O', Suzanna,* and *The Extra Girl*. Had Mabel decided to stay home during New Year's 1924, more feature length films may have been added to her resume. Sadly, however, that was not to be the case.

"A day or so before Christmas Edna Purviance and Courtland S. Dines came to my house," Mabel recalled. "When they dropped in that afternoon I was ashamed to remember that I hadn't bought a gift for him. I had a lovely big Christmas tree, and people had been coming in all day with their things for me and taking my gifts for them off the tree. So I whispered to Mamie Owens, my maid, to send Joe Kelly, my driver, across the street to a drug store to buy Dines a couple of military brushes."

Joe Kelly picked up the present, which was then strategically snuck into the branches of Mabel's enormous Christmas tree. Upon discovery, Dines started to open the gift, then apparently decided to unwrap it later. "I wish he had opened it," Mabel would go on to say, "for on so trivial a thing as his failure to do so hinged the second big scandal of my life!" Long story short – Dines accidentally left his gift at Mabel's. A short time later, on

New Year's Eve, Mabel attended a sumptuous dinner party at Mack's. After sleeping until noon the next day, Mabel got a call from Edna who told her that "she and Dines had been at a wild party in the Ambassador Hotel the night before, and were feeling pretty low, and for heaven's sake to dash over and cheer them up."

According to Mabel, she had Joe Kelly drive her to Dines' apartment at North Vermont Avenue around 5:00 PM, telling him that she would call him at her house when it was time to pick her up. By Mabel's telling, things began innocuously (if not legally) enough. "I found Dines and Edna needed cheering," she said, "and that the flat needed a lot of cleaning. So while he mixed a drink I took off my coat and grabbed a broom and a mop and a vacuum cleaner and fixed up the place. There were a lot of dishes in the sink, so I heated some water and washed them; and I emptied the ash trays and otherwise did a great maid act."

The fact that there was alcohol being served at the residence went on to haunt Mabel and her hosts. Booze was illegal at the time in the United States, after all, and had been for several years. Still, no one appeared to be worried. Indeed, the only thing that bothered Mabel at the time seemed to be the fact that she had left Dines' Christmas gift at home. Therefore, she called her maid, Mamie, and asked her to have Kelly bring the present over. "She suggested I come on home and get a good sleep," Mabel said, "because I had to go to the hospital quite early (to have her appendix taken out). But I told her not to worry, that I'd be home early enough as there wasn't to be a party that night."

The night proved to be longer than anyone expected, a fact evidenced in the next day's newspapers.

"TWO MOVIE STARS SEE C.S. DINES SHOT," the *New York Times* blared. "Edna Purviance and Mabel Normand in His Apartment When Oil Operator Is Wounded."

"MABEL NORMAN, EDNA PURVIANCE QUIZZED IN L.A. SHOOTING," screamed the *San Francisco Examiner*.

"FILM STARS ON GRILL," shouted the *Cincinnati Post.* "Mabel Normand Accuses Chauffer of Shooting Denver Oil King; Edna Purviance is Quizzed."

Needless to say, Mabel was back in the headlines from coast to coast and around the globe – though not in the way she could possibly have hoped. As for the events of the night in questions, Edna was changing out of her dress while Mabel and Dines were talking on the couch when Kelly arrived with the gift. Mabel's recollection of that night years later proceeds as follows"

"'Miss Normand,' he (Kelly) said, 'Mamie's worried about you. Don't you think you'd better come on home?'

"I told Mamie I'd be home a little later,' I replied. 'Go on down and wait in the car for me.'

"Just then Dines spoke up. He was a rather hot tempered individual.

"'Say, Kelly,' he said, 'where do you get that stuff, asking my guests to leave my house?› Get out of here and down in that machine where you belong."

"Kelly had evidently been celebrating the New Year or something after leaving me earlier, because before I could say anything, he turned on Dines with an oath, berating him for keeping me there when I was going to the hospital the next day, and swearing he wouldn't leave till I did. I started to scold him, when there was a confused lurching of bodies toward each other, an oath or two, and then three pistol shots that sounded like firecrackers."

Dines fell to the floor. Kelly ran out the door. Edna rushed into the room. "'My God, Mabel!'" Dines said as he lie bleeding. "Can you imagine -- that hophead shot me!" The police arrived moments later. Fortunately for Dines, the injury wasn't fatal. Dines was rushed to Receiving Hospital where it was discovered he had a 25-caliber automatic slug in his chest that didn't puncture his lungs, reported the *Times.* He was declared not badly hurt, and therefore subsequently sent to Good Samaritan Hospital. Meanwhile, Mabel and Edna went to the Central Police Station "where they wept copiously until their release after questioning." Kelly himself went to University Police Station and turned himself in.

Mabel did end up getting her appendicitis operation – at the same hospital where Dines was recuperating. The *New York Times* reported she was "doing very nicely" afterward. At that point, the same certainly couldn't be said for Mabel's career. Not only was it discovered that Jack Kelly had shot Dines with a gun owned by Mabel, it also came to be known that Jack Kelly wasn't really Jack Kelly. His real name was Horace Greer and, to Mabel's horror, he was an escapee from an Oakland chain gang.

Mabel may have thought at the time that things couldn't get any worse for her. If that were the case, however, she would have been mistaken.

Asa Keyes

In a city famous for colorful figures rising and falling within its limits, few have risen quite as high or fallen quite as far as Los Angeles based prosecutor Asa Keyes. In less than a decade, the man went from an esteemed figure of law, order, and justice, to a part of the same California correctional system he had sentenced so many men to. Keyes' was a story of corruption, hubris, and perhaps the effects of a dangerous amount of self-righteousness. When one is the very symbol of the public welfare, after all, how can one possibly be detrimental to that welfare? Rather easily, it seems, if one is to find the answer to that question in Keyes' biography.

Born in 1877 in Wilmington, California, Keyes went on to study law at the University of Southern California. Just after graduating, be joined up with the District Attorney's office in Los Angeles and began making a name for himself as a subordinate attorney. According to the "Los Angeles Times," an "unshakable integrity and a fearless demeanor in fighting crime as a deputy under John D Fredericks and later as a prosecutor under Dist.-Atty. Woolwine brought him before the public." Such a reputation served as good cover for later, more nefarious actions.

For the time being, however, Keyes appeared to have been an honorable public servant for the most part. Indeed, the man was very much involved in the investigation into the murder of William Desmond Taylor. There is even a well-known photograph of Keyes sitting at a table with Mabel and her attorney, Milton Cohen, discussing the case. Years later, former California governor Friend W. Richardson declared to the "San Francisco Call-Bulletin" that he knew who the killer was – and had evidence to prove it.

"A motion picture actress killed this director, and I have positive proof to this effect," he claimed. Naturally, the "Chicago Tribune" ran the article with the picture of Mabel and Cohen sitting at the

table with Keyes. Keyes brushed the assertion off as nonsense. "If Richardson has the proof why doesn't he produce his evidence now?" Keyes snapped. "No stone was left unturned then or since to uncover the secret of the murder." Not surprisingly, Richardson did not lead police to the killer of Taylor.

With that in mind, Keyes' early work clearly impressed his superiors enough for him to become District Attorney after Woolwine resigned from the position in 1923. By 1924, Keyes' found himself to be popular and well regarded enough to be officially voted into the position. Suffice to say, the man was not one to simply enjoy the prominence his position awarded him, at least not at first. Keyes' was nothing if not ambitious. Aside from ordering close to twenty-five members of the District Attorney's office to resign, on the Fourth of July, no less, Keyes, and his new team proceeded to cut trial times by a whopping sixty percent.

The salad days ended for Keyes in 1928.

"DISTRICT ATTORNEY KEYES IS ACCUSED!" read the explosive headline of the November 1st edition of the "Los Angeles Times." "Grand Jury Charges Willful Corruption."

Keyes was indeed in profound trouble, for he was being charged with nothing short of bribery, a major crime, especially considering that he was a district attorney. According to the prosecution, Keyes, along with others, took a bribe in a case involving Julian Petroleum, a company which was subsequently acquitted. The act led to Keyes' conviction and sentencing to San Quentin prison for five years. He reached out to the Court of Appeal, only to have his petition denied. Keyes ended up staying locked up at San Quentin for 19 months before being pardoned by Governor James Ralph.

"In the five years he was District Attorney of Los Angeles," "Time Magazine" wrote at the time of Keyes' conviction, "Asa Keyes (pronounced Kize)...sent 4,030 men and women to California prisons for every variety of crime. Last week he joined this criminal company himself, entered San Quentin Prison as a convicted bribe-taker, a betrayer of public trust."

After getting out of prison, Keyes did some work in Hollywood and tried to get back into the legal system as an attorney. He also sold cars and operated a bail bonds company. When he died of a stroke in 1934 at the age of 57, he was remembered as a high flying star who had crashed to earth in phenomenal fashion. "His health broken by his conviction," wrote the "Nevada State Journal" after Keyes had perished of a stroke, "and the 19 months he spent in San Quentin, Keyes outlived his parole by less than three years." At the time of his death, Keyes' attempt to be allowed back into the California Bar was still working its way through the system.

He may not have been able to redeem himself publicly, but Keyes had certainly made an impact in and around Los Angeles, where he had served. Aside from the Taylor murder and the Julian Petroleum case which brought about his downfall, Keyes had successfully prosecuted a child murderer named Edward William Hickman and had earlier on successfully prosecuted two men for taking part of a dynamite bombing of the "Los Angeles Times" that resulted in the deaths of several people.

Although Mabel had been familiar with Keyes due to the Taylor investigation, the two once again became legally acquainted as a result of the Dines shooting. It's hard to imagine Mabel ever thinking she'd end up in the midst of a highly publicized crime. It's even harder to imagine her thinking she'd end up in the midst of two. Whatever her flaws may have been, there was no doubt Mabel had an unfortunate knack of being involved with crimes she hadn't perpetrated. Yet many, if not most, at the time didn't appear to see things that way. It was one of her life's great misfortunes. Asa Keyes or no Asa Keyes, Mabel's reputation and career were rattled by violence in which she herself had no direct part.

Rumors Thrive

"Do you know whether Miss Normand uses dope?"

That question, quoted in the *Daily News*, was asked of Horace Greer by Police Captain Herman Cline. Greer, as noted earlier, was the real name of Joe Kelly, the chauffer under Mabel's employment who had shot Dines. Greer admitted that he had acted alone in the crime, but the police saw an opportunity to see if those Mabel drug rumors were true. Suffice to say, "Greer replied in the negative." Cline, however, wasn't done. "Do you know," he asked, "whether Dines was supplying Miss Normand with narcotics?" Once again, Greer replied in the negative.

"They tried him on a charge of assault," Mabel later said of Greer, "with intent to commit murder, and Dines good-naturedly helped exonerate him. Kelly was acquitted and, I think, taken back to finish his sentence on the chain gang. Dines left town and the thing died down." It didn't matter. Although Mabel could not be tried for the shooting of Dines, her career and reputation were open game.

"Dines fled to his family's home in Colorado," Slater and Squerciati write. "Chaplin rushed in to protect Edna Purviance." Mabel, however, had no such support system. "Mabel was left alone," Slater and Squerciati continue, "to hear Kelly (Greer) boast – out of order in the courtroom – that he shot to defend Normand's honor and would rather go to the penitentiary than testify and besmirch the reputation of that lovely, wonderful star, Mabel Normand. For this bit of acting he was acquitted of the attempted murder of Dines and Mabel Normand's reputation was permanently damaged."

Sure enough, as a result of the Dines' shooting, Mabel's movies were now being banned throughout the country. "Memphis Bans Normand Films Kansas Exclusion Also Sought," read a January 4th headline in the *New York Times*. "Hartford Theatre Owners Bar Normand Pictures," read another *Times* headline three days later. "Mabel Normand Films May Go Under Ban Here" wrote the *Pittsburgh Post-Gazette* on January 5th. "Mabel Normand films barred in several states," the *Miami Herald* claimed that same day. While she undoubtedly still had fans, Mabel was now persona non grata for a considerable number of the public, or at least a considerable number of society's power players. And the reasons surely went beyond the legal system.

As with Arbuckle, Mabel was guilty of not being the person people thought she was or wanted her to be. Mabel onscreen was a good natured, if often reckless, delight. Most who knew her would likely argue she was also good natured offscreen most of the time, as well. The public, however, was now seeing her as a woman involved with not one, but two shooting cases, one of which involved her own chauffer and her own gun (Greer had apparently swiped it out of a drawer containing some clothing) and the other which involved a murdered director. Coupled with the drug rumors and the fact that the Dines' story involved the consumption of illegal alcohol, the shootings made for a life altering impact of events. Plus, there were those who were all too eager to permantely squash the popular star.

"Mabel hated pretention and snobbery," Slater and Squerciati write, "and, with her great wit and intelligence, amused her friends by poking wicked fun at pretentions, those qualities that Hollywood society seemed to be built upon. She had made enemies, and they now had their day. This upstart, salty tongued, working-class Irish outsider with no studio, husband, or agent to protect her was fair game." Although she was certainly an alcoholic and at times was quite reckless, it's hard to match the Mabel of record with the Hollywood degenerate she was portrayed as.

There's reliable documentation, for instance, of such specific details as to whom Mabel reached out for bootleg alcohol, as well as which order of nuns she discreetly gave money to in order to support their orphanages. Yet zero reliable documentation has been discovered indicating Mabel ever purchased, received or used illegal narcotics. Zero. Yet the lack of evidence didn't matter. The hyperactive, eccentric star was a far cry from the average person on the street, so suspicion, rumor and innuendo were taken as fact.

And, although there is no denying Mabel was far from a perfect individual, the fact she never showcased her finest qualities in moments when such information could have helped her image indicates she was far from the caricature she was now portrayed as. Mabel, however, simply wasn't one to discuss her vast donations to orphanages, or the helping hand she showed to those who had recently failed in the industry. She didn't broadcast the story where she made a poor Irish immigrant feel at home in a Hollywood restaurant or the story where she offered Samuel Goldwyn financial support when he was desperate. To do so, after all, would be to make her good deeds about herself.

She had come a long way from her humble roots, but Mabel ultimately always remained the Catholic girl from Staten Island.

Fortunately, Mabel still had defenders. "Shall this young woman," asked Fulton Oursler in the pages of *Movie Weekly* on February 2nd, "be convicted before the bar of public opinion without a fair hearing? Shall her livelihood be endangered, her reputation besmirched, her pictures be barred on the strength of the most unreliable testimony ever uttered in the history of the world -- the careless and irresponsible reports of the popular American newspapers?" The answer appeared to be an unequivocal yes.

"Already boards of censorship in various states," Oursler continued, "trembling with virtuous indignation, have pontificated over the young woman. Her pictures have been censored off the screen by these dignitaries, although they know nothing more of the circumstances than what they have read of them in the sensational press." Unfortunately, for moral opportunists, it was all about the pose, a fact evidenced by the mayor of New Britain, Connecticut who, upon learning that one of Mabel's movies was shown in his city, claimed the showing of a Mabel film to be "sickening."

With all that was going on, however, Mabel understood she still had a movie to sell. "Because of the Dines scandal," she said, "the release of *The Extra Girl* was held up, and about the end of February I made personal appearances in a number of cities with the first showing of the film."

Mary Pickford

She had literally known Mabel from the beginning. Virtually as soon as a young Mabel stepped inside the Biograph Building at Eleven East Fourteenth Street, Biograph star Mary Pickford appeared to be enthralled by the slight young girl who had literally stepped in off the street. And while there's no doubt friendships ebb and flow over the years, it appears Pickford remained enthralled with Mabel throughout their lives. "It is given to few women in this world," Mabel would say, "to have such friends as I have in Mary Pickford and Norma Talmadge." She wasn't joking. Whatever could be said about Pickford – and many things could be said – there was no denying that the woman knew what it meant to be a loyal friend, whether it was fashionable to be one or not.

"After the dinner was over," Pickford had written of Mabel concerning a New Year's train trip across country one New Year's Eve, "we staged a motion picture comedy, and it was then we realized, almost for the first time, what a wonderful comedienne Mabel Normand was. She had been playing ultra-seriously in dramas. Because she was dark and the representative type of villainess, she was made to play the flashing-eyed creature of temperament whose very looks were stilettos in your heart and whose movements undulated like a snake crawling through the brush. The thousands who have laughed with her on the screen in her last few years of comedy perhaps have forgotten her as a heavy woman."

Again, Pickford had been enthralled with Mabel since the beginning. The fondness, of course, was mutual. Mabel was said to have kiddingly called Pickford a "prissy bitch," but Stephen Normand feels the report was inaccurate in that the language has essentially been spiced up over the years. With that being said, it's impressive to see what appears to be a lack of resentment from either woman regarding the other. Pickford, after all, was the biggest star at Biograph when Mabel was instructed to play her foil. Meanwhile, Mabel, who had been second fiddle to Pickford at Biograph, managed to arguably become Pickford's celebrity equal in a relatively short amount of time. Yet neither performer seems to have viewed the other as competition.

Indeed, D.W. Griffith once uttered words about Pickford that might well have applied to both women. "She has tremendous driving power in her," he said, "and a most remarkable talent for self-appraisal. She never 'kids' herself. The thing that most attracted me the day I first saw her was the intelligence that shone in her face. I found she was thirsty for work and information. She could not be driven from the studio while work was going on. She was – and is – a sponge for experience."

Still, as much as the two women had in common, there were vast differences between them. They both were born in the 1890's and came from humble backgrounds, true. And yes, they were both talented performers the camera loved, as well. And to be sure, they both also battled alcoholism, and dealt with their share of heartaches. Yet while there was no denying that both Mabel and Pickford were talented and driven, their respective careers, while both clearly successful, went down entirely different routes.

Although she had been born in Canada, Pickford was called "America's Sweetheart" for a reason. She was the very picture of wholesomeness, an actress literally able to play a child while in her 20s. As Pickford herself said: "I didn't act – I WAS the characters I played on the screen." In short, people went to see Mary Pickford movies to see Mary Pickford. The same, of course, could be said of Mabel – though after falling out with Mack, she focused on Cinderella type characters long before Pickford decided to go a more adult oriented route in the late 1920s.

When Pickford, along with Chaplin, Douglas Fairbanks, and others formed United Artists, however, they established themselves as true powerhouses in the industry. Mabel, sadly, never had the luxury to do such as thing, as she remained loyal to Mack, who clearly and repeatedly proved to be disloyal himself. The Mabel Normand Studio may have produced the biggest blockbuster of its time with Mickey, but the financial house of cards Mack had helped build it upon soon crumbled. Still, Mabel was smart with her money, even with her charitable endeavors and love of expensive cars and jewelry. The biggest difference between the two stars, however, was how the public reacted to them in trying times.

When Pickford left her husband and co-star Owen Moore to marry Fairbanks in 1920, her career was truly in danger. Unlike Mabel, however, Pickford was "America's Sweetheart," which meant her marriage to Fairbanks was not only accepted but embraced. The colorful, high-energy prankster that was Mabel, on the other hand, had to withstand social and media assaults due to crimes she hadn't partaken in. Image, after all, can go a long way. Pickford was the girl next door. Mabel was "Madcap Mabel." And that may have made all the difference.

The truth was that Hollywood queen Pickford could have easily stepped away from Mabel after the Taylor and Dines shootings. Rumors of drug use, promiscuity, and generally decadent behavior made her a dangerous friend to have if one cared about one's public perception. Pickford undoubtedly cared about her public perception – but that didn't keep her from publicly defending Mabel when the world was arguably moving on from her friend. The bottom line was that Pickford could have sat the moment out but didn't. Of course, Pickford is well remembered for being one of the biggest stars in history, which she most certainly was. Like many celebrities, however, there were more shades to Pickford's personality than she could have ever presented on the screen.

As Mabel's career and health began to decline throughout the 1920s, there were times when she was nothing if not a person in need of powerful friends. She was fortunate to have several of them, of which Pickford was among the most outspoken.

The Performance Of A Lifetime

Perhaps surprisingly, *The Extra Girl* proved to be a box office success. "Mabel, in the April of 1924," writes Mabel expert William Thomas Sherman, "went on a nation-wide movie theater circuit promoting *The Extra Girl* -- and to clear her name. The tour did manage to gain her sympathy, and the formal bans of her films were overtime ultimately lifted, with *The Extra Girl* actually ending up doing excellent business." Rather than trying to ride the latest scandal that had enveloped her out, Mabel once again found that it paid off to do the daring thing. With that being said, *The Extra Girl* would be the last major success of Mabel's career.

Without doubt, other than the success of *The Extra Girl,* 1924 was most distinctly a bad year for Mabel.

Aside from the Dines' shooting, there was also the subsequent trial of Greer, his shooter. Mabel perhaps felt that she was done with the whole sordid affair after she and Pruviance appeared at the initial hearing in January, but Los Angeles prosecutor Asa Keyes demanded she return to court while she was on her rehabilitation tour. "Los Angeles District Attorney Asa Keyes wants to make sure Mabel appears as a witness," the *New York Times* had written that April. "Mabel went back east before the preliminary hearing had been finished. The DA says it's 'essential' that Mabel's "evidence is essential to the case."

Mabel, who was in Detroit when she heard the news, was taken aback. "No subpoena ever was served on me in connection with the trial," she said, "and, of course it would be impossible for me to get to Los Angeles in time for the trial, which is set for tomorrow." She continued: "I am sure Mr. Sennett and my lawyers have arranged everything, or I should never have been allowed to go on this fifteen week's tour. My tour was delayed two weeks in order that everything could be properly arranged and I was told I would not be needed as a witness."

When Mabel finally took the stand back in Los Angeles in June, she made sure to leave quite an impression. "Dines Absent as Shooting Is Told," read *The Oakland Tribune's* page one headline. "Mabel Normand Is Riot at Trial." The page one headline of the *Los Angeles Times* that same day stated: "Miss Normand Upsets Court by 'Wise Cracks.'" It was indeed quite the performance, replete with Mabel regularly speaking in slang terms, perpetually waving her hands theatrically, and often presenting herself as a smart aleck. When she was sworn in, for instance, Mabel extended her arm fully upward, as if she were a child trying to see how far she could reach.

Her behavior was just as irreverent while under oath. "I cleaned up all the cigarette butts," she said while describing the events of the evening in question, "you know what those are, your honor – and we sat down and talked after I arrived there." When asked at one point where Greer was in the apartment, Mabel responded like a vaudeville version of a street kid. "I just told ya," she snapped. "Mr. Dines just let 'im in!" The defense made an effort to suggest perhaps it was Mabel behind the shooting, or at least that Mabel's drinking may have led to the risky atmosphere in the apartment that night. Mabel, however, wouldn't bite.

When shown her gun – which was the same gun Greer had used to shoot Dines – Mabel was asked if it was hers. "How should I know?" she cracked. "It looks too clean for mine." When shown an alcohol bottle and asked if it was the one employed at Dines' apartment the night of the shooting, Mabel was again ready with a tart response. "It looked like that and it didn't look like that," she said. "I've seen a lot of bottles in my young life."

Even the presiding judge wasn't immune from Mabel's antics. Asked how big a man the handsome Dines was, "the witness turned her back on the attorney, whirled in her chair and smiled sweetly at Judge Crail." After smiling himself, the judge tried averting her gaze. "Your honor," Mabel said before smiling at him once more. "I think Dines was just like you, your honor. May I say that?"

Yet even while performing, Mabel was able to show signs of temper. After being asked outright by the defense if she had asked Greer to shoot Dines ("I did not. Well, I should hope not!") Mabel was pressed about her claim that the shots sounded like fireworks. "Suppose I threw a firecracker at you!" she snapped. "Do you think you could remember everything, then?" The attorney responded by once again asking outright if Mabel had ordered Greer to shoot Dines. "For heaven's sake - no" she reiterated. "Why should I tell anybody to plug anybody anyhow?"

Mabel's performance in court that hot June day was the polar opposite of Pruviance's, who opted to behave in a sullen matter, offering little and readily showing her exasperation with the whole process. For whatever reason, Mabel decided to throw caution to the wind while on the witness stand. Perhaps it was because she knew full well that there was no way a jury would believe she was the driving force behind the Dines' shooting. Or perhaps, after the physical and emotional impact two years of battling scandals had brought her, Mabel was simply done with endlessly being judged and questioned by others. She was a comedienne, after all, and so perhaps she had simply decided to use comedy in the courthouse in order to fight back.

Whatever her reasoning may have been, it was obvious that Mabel was no longer going to treat such matters seriously. Had Dines died from his injuries, she may have acted differently. Since he had healed up nicely before returning to Denver, however, Mabel might have decided to treat the court proceedings as if they were something out of one of her old Keystone films. Her behavior that day on the witness stand may have been a slap in the face to courtroom decorum, but there was no denying as she stepped back out into the southern California sunshine that day, that Mabel had just put on the performance of a lifetime.

Al Woods

It was said he was a young man who literally ran away from home to join the circus. Born in Hungary in 1870 as Albert Herman, Al Woods moved with his family to New York's Lower East Side as a baby. It was also said that at as a youth, Woods was friends with future New York Governor and United States Presidential Candidate Al Smith. By the age of fourteen, however, the daring Woods decided it was time to get on with his life by joining the circus. Moving on to find himself in the theater business, the adult Woods reportedly made millions as a king of the American stage scene.

By the first decade of the 20th century, Woods had already made his name presenting popular melodramas such as "The Queen of the White Slaves" and "Confessions of a Wife." Indeed, Woods became successful enough to purchase his own theaters and was written of towards the end of the decade as a "New York theatrical man." Not that he saw himself as a high end producer. "All this high brow stuff may be very well," he was quoted as saying in 1908, "but 'The Millionaire' and 'The Policeman's Wife' played to $413 in Kansas City at a matinee and to $771 the same night. A show with a title like that can't lose."

According to the "Chicago Tribune," by the '20s Woods "had 25 road companies touring the nation at once." Woods also had a theater in New York. Although he produced plays as far away as London, it was Broadway where Woods truly made his mark, producing well over one hundred plays in Broadway's theaters (He claimed he produced over four hundred plays overall).

"Al Woods was interesting," The "Kingston Whig Standard" wrote, "because he did what many people have tried to do, and did it with great success: he gave the public what it wanted." Summed up, Woods gave the public entertainment without the pretense of art. His plays could be risqué by the standards of the time, but perhaps

that only led to their appeal. This may have especially been true in the 20s, an era where traditional American standards of morality were being brought into question and where rebellious behavior was in vogue.

Still, the suggestive nature of some of the man's productions certainly led him into a bit of trouble at times. For instance, in late 1921, New York authorities took Woods to court for his play, "The Demi-Virgin." Chief City Magistrate William McAdoo and other notables were put off by the play's supposedly immorality. "In view of all these expert and moral opinions," wrote the "Daily News" that November, "Magistrate McAdoo last week held Mr. Wood's in $1,000 bail." What exactly was it about the play that brought about such a reaction? Primarily, it seems, a scene involving strip poker. Fortunately for Woods, a Grand Jury refused to indict.

In sum, Woods appears to have been a world class character. "He greets everyone, regardless of sex, with: 'Hello, sweetheart,'" theater writer Sidney Skolsky stated. "All his business correspondence ends with: "With Love and Kisses.'" What's more, Sklosky wrote that "Douglas Fairbanks, Mary Pickford and Charlie Chaplin worked for him before they entered the movies. He let them go because they wanted more money. Chaplin was getting twenty-five dollars a week and asked for thirty." He may have been cheap, but Woods clearly knew how to be successful in show business. "A good script," Sklosky wrote of Woods, "he considers, is one that makes him forget his cigar has gone out." Sklosky also stated that Wilson "believes in luck and does most everything by hunches."

The Depression led Woods to declare Bankruptcy. Indeed, the man claimed that, as a result of the 1929 stock market crash, he had gone on to lose around four million dollars. He died in New York City in 1951 at over eighty years of age. "He made a large fortune," wrote the "Kingston Whig Standard" upon Wood's death, "he gave pleasure to millions, and he gave employment to thousands. He was a man of great charity, though not perhaps a man of great taste. And he gave the public what it wanted."

While he is primarily remembered for producing work that skirted the edge of social mores of the time, the evidence suggests Woods produced a wide variety of works – provided those works could earn a profit. Unlike Ernest Hemingway, whose novel "A Farewell to Arms" Woods produced for Broadway, Woods doesn't look to have been interested in having any of his works stand the test of time. He was a showman, yes, but he was primarily a businessman, and for most of his life a very successful one at that.

He may not have been an artist, but Woods was successful and interesting enough to be attractive to artists. He, in fact, was friends with George Bernard Shaw. He also worked with the aforementioned Chaplin, Pickford, and Fairbanks. Throw in an adaptation of a Hemingway novel and it was easy to see what Wood's allure would be for those interested in enriching their finances and/or careers. In a world now obsessed with cinema, Woods knew how to keep the theater appealing. And lucrative for those involved.

Perhaps it's not surprising, then, that Woods eventually teamed up with Mabel, another unconventional individual willing to take chances. Their pairing was brief, but it said a bit about both Woods and the famous film star. The Wood's production Mabel appeared in was called "The Little Mouse." Although it's title might have indicated it was a production for children, the play itself was most certainly for adults. To both Mabel and Woods, the endeavor would was the risk. The question, however, was whether or not the public would approve of their unusual endeavor. Clearly both Mabel and Woods suspected that it would.

"The Little Mouse"

After her performance in court, Mabel perhaps felt that finally things would again turn in her favor. Unfortunately, however, trouble once more raised its head, this time through a scenario that might have been considered comical were it not so infuriating to Mabel. "The name Mabel Norman(sic)," the *Daily News* reported on September 12th, "linked with Norman W Church, Los Angeles financier, today furnished a sensation when legal papers in the divorce suit of Miss Georgia Withington Church, former Wisconsin girl were filed with the county clerk." In brief, while Mabel was home nursing an abscessed ear that September, word arrived that she was being named in a divorce suit as being the reason for the couple's crumbling marriage.

According to the court papers, Norman Church told his wife Georgia that Mabel would pal around with him while she was healing from a broken collarbone over the summer through "nightgown visits" to his room hospital room. Mabel reportedly shared flowers with Mr. Church, griped with him about the 18th Amendment, engaged in raunchy humor, and even kissed the married man. Suffice to say, Mrs. Church was apparently not amused by her husband's boasts.

At first, Mabel responded that "I do not know anybody by the name given." That, however, was only the beginning. Mabel had clearly had it with the rumors, innuendo, and now wild courthouse claims that had been taking a toll on her reputation for years, and she acted by asking the court if she herself could be part of the trial in order to clear her name. Suffice to say, Mabel wasn't allowed to partake in the trial, as it was ruled the divorce proceedings did not directly concern her. Ultimately, Mr. Church admitted that his tales of an overly friendly Mabel were made up. Indeed, even Mrs. Church apologized for her rash reaction to her husband's wild tales. "Mrs.

Church retracted her charges involving me," Mabel said, "and of course I declined to press libel action."

It's understandable why Mabel at this point simply wanted to take a rest from the chaos that had been enveloping her life. By 1925 she was famous and wealthy beyond measure. She had made a career out of being a movie star, stunt woman, director, producer, advertising spokesperson and model. She had been indirectly involved with two shootings, had gotten her heart broken, had traveled by plane, automobile, train, car, and horse, had developed a drinking problem and was battling tuberculosis. She had been the target of a blackmail attempt and more smears than she probably could even remember.

And she had just turned thirty-two.

Little wonder why learning French, taking college classes, and reading some quality books seemed so appealing to the girl from Staten Island. It was, after all, time to settle down. And, as if to prove, perhaps even to herself, that she was now about to simply start living her life, Mabel finally did what other stars had been doing for years by purchasing herself a Beverly Hills mansion. Indeed, hers was a beautiful Mediterranean styled two story property located on North Camden Drive that remains impressive and stylish in the 21st century.

Yet try as she might to rejuvenate, Mabel couldn't keep from being what she was – a performer. Unfortunately, there weren't outlets for her to perform in anymore. *The Extra Girl* may have proven to have been a surprise hit, but the money and effort that had gone into Mabel's promotional tour and Mack's other methods of salvaging the film's business were simply too much of a burden to attempt again. The verdict was in – the rumors and innuendo had paid off. Mabel was no longer able to be a film star. The working class girl who had the arrogance to become a public figure had finally been removed from her pedestal.

Again, however, Mabel was a performer – and she was determined to perform. The theater, in the guise of producer Al Woods, provided an outlet. "He called me up and asked me to see him at Ambassador Hotel, as he had a play for me on the speaking stage," said Mabel. "We conferred many times, and he said the lead in *A Kiss in the Taxi* was just the thing I'd make a hit in. I told him I was afraid I had no voice, but he said he heard me in Newark when I appeared with *The Extra Girl*, and he was positive I'd make good." Mabel was sold.

"We finally drew up a five-year contract," she said, "I was to get fifteen hundred dollars a week and ten percent of the gross receipts." Even better: "In the summer I was to make pictures for him. There was a sliding scale of salary and percentage increases and an interest in my picture comedies, until I was to be getting eight thousand a week during the last year of the contract." By June, the partnership was reported in the *New York Times.* "She will continue in comedy roles," the article claimed of Mabel, "and will make her first appearance Aug. 27 at the Ritz Theater, New York, in a comedy."

While no doubt exciting, the endeavor would undoubtedly be challenging for Mabel. She had never acted on stage before. What's more, the public had never heard her performing lines. To help herself prepare, Mabel reached out to famous actress Alla Nazimova, who certainly knew her way around a Broadway stage, for guidance preparing for *A Kiss in a Taxi.*

"Even after I signed," Mabel said, "I was worried about my voice, so I went to see Alla Nazimova, one of my dearest friends, in her lovely home on Sunset Boulevard. She had a high wall about her estate and a great swimming pool, and when either of us was blue we'd telephone and I'd call on her and we'd have a fine time swimming and telling each other how good we were, and how misunderstood, until we felt better with ourselves and the world." Mabel subsequently travelled to New York. "I took an apartment for a year and plunged eagerly into rehearsals on the stage of the Julian Eltinge theater," she said. "But fancy my amazement when Woods told me he wasn't going to put me in *A Kiss in the Taxi*, but had given me the lead in *The Little Mouse*. Well, I didn't know a good play from a bad one, and I supposed Woods knew what he was doing."

What Woods certainly did know what that *The Little Mouse* had been performed before, and to less than excellent results. With that being said, the bedroom comedy never had a name as big as Mabel Normand's attached to it. And so, Mabel moved onward, acting in the play as the wife of a man who switches places with another man in order to engage in some extra marital activity. It may have been unlike all of Mabel's previous work, but the particular production of *The Little Mouse* she performed in seems to have been generally innocuous.

The play's run began impressively enough. "Mabel Normand Finds the Road Profitable," wrote the *New York Times*. "With the film's own Mabel Normand as its star, will be seen in Brooklyn during the coming week, nor is it likely to come closer to New York for a considerable period. Neither, for that matter, will a Chicago verdict be courted." Mabel, however, was the main draw for theatergoers, and the critics, though not outright disapproving of her performance, didn't appear to be awed by it, either.

"Mr. Woods," The *Brooklyn Daily Eagle* stated rather snobbishly, "it appears, has eliminated every bit of acting to which Miss Normand might not or could not due justice." The *Eagle* went on to say, a bit more fairly, that "the role remaining for her is hardly enough to give one a line as to her ability. But it can be seen easily that Ms. Normand as yet is not adapted to her new surroundings behind the footlights. Her speaking tones are too subdued, though her voice is pleasant enough."

About Mabel's voice - Stephan Normand claims that William Morris did a voice test of Mabel during the later 20s and had decided her voice was strong enough to appear in the new "talking films" that were taking the cinematic world by storm. All that came after the run of *The Little Mouse*, however. Besides, after getting her feet wet on stage it was clear Mabel was a film actor, not a theater actor. Even if she could hold her own on stage, she couldn't stand out like she did on screen. When all was said and done, live theater was simply not Mabel's strong suit. As *the Expositor* wrote in October: "Either *The Little Mouse*, or Mabel Normand or both failed to live up to expectations and the comedy will be withdrawn after a brief tryout." The partnership with Al Woods subsequently fell apart.

Hal Roach

"I'm working on my second hundred," Hal Roach told Jay Leno when he sat down for a "Tonight Show" interview in 1992 at the age of one hundred. The famous producer passed away before the year was out, decades after the man got his start in silent films. His death was front page news. A product of Elmira, New York, Roach was born in 1892. Like Ford Sterling and Al Wilson, Roach left home as a teenager. Rather than being drawn to the stage, however, Roach drove trucks, and worked as a mule skinner as well as prospector in Alaska.

"It was while working for a construction outfit in the Mojave Desert in 1912," the "Los Angeles Times" wrote, "that the 20-year-old Roach paid a fateful visit to Los Angeles. He discovered that movie extras worked only from 8 to 4 – when the sun was shining – and received car fare and lunch. They also earned $5 a day, which, Roach later recalled 'was a whole lot of money in those days.'" Roach's life was changed forever. Being good on a horse, Roach got his start in show business as an extra playing cowboys.

Roach, however, was intelligent and ambitious, which meant that soon enough he was a director and producer himself. Harold Lloyd, who was a friend, acted in Roach's films. It was a highly successful pairing, as both went on to become enormously successful. By 1919 Roach had a studio known as the "Lot of Fun" in Culver City. And it was there that Roach created one of his greatest endeavors. After watching a polished young girl audition, a bored Roach stepped to a window and noticed a group of children playing outside. "Then it dawned on him," the "Los Angeles Times" wrote, "that audiences might be just as fascinated watching regular kids doing regular things on screen."

Hence the classic children's comedy team "Our Gang" was born. The first short film in the series, now mostly lost, was released in 1922. The last "Our Gang" film Roach was involved with was in 1938, before MGM took sole control of the series. Yet the series' lasting popularity, which is still strong in the 21st century, is certainly an indicator of Roach's ability to create a timeless property. Yet Roach created another great cinematic act, aside from "Our Gang" which has also remained popular into the 21st century. This time, the main characters were middle aged men rather than children.

Stan Laurel and Oliver Hardy had been appearing in Roach films for some time when, in 1926, the producer realized the two would make an effective duo. "With Laurel and Hardy, you had two comedians without a tag line," Roach would say. "Therefore, you did a gag that was funny, you cut to Laurel and you got a laugh with his reaction. Then you cut to Hardy and you got another laugh with his reaction. So on a gag that a normal comedian would only get one laugh, you got three laughs for the same thing."

Another aspect of Laurel and Hardy was their unique delivery and physical differences. Always rather large, Oliver Hardy became physically bigger over time. Stan Laurel, on the other hand, was shorter and rather lean. What's more, Hardy would appear nervous on screen, comically fiddling with his tie, for instance, while Laurel scratched his head or stared ahead blankly (a technique that's been indicated he learned from Mabel). Simply put, they were a goofy duo whose antics and mannerisms were easy to appreciate. They were an odd pairing, to be sure – but that's part of what made them legendary.

Roach led nothing if not a fascinating life. After moving from shorts to features, he took part in the Second World War as a major in the Army Signal Corps. Even though he was fifty years old, he was assigned to active service in London, which was the heart of the Allied war effort. What's more, Roach allowed the Air Force to use his studio for the war effort. It was subsequently referred to as "Fort Roach." Indeed, a young lieutenant stationed there became President of the United States, for Ronald Reagan "spent the war narrating training and propaganda films" at Roach's converted studios.

Aside from being a film and military man, Roach was known for leading an active life. Even in old age, the man went swimming twice a day. Perhaps this had something to do with Roach's ability to remain fresh and move in new directions as time went on. He was, after all, at the head of the pack when he decided to move from producing films to producing television programs once the new medium exploded in popularity after the war had ended.

Roach ended up selling the studio to his son in the mid-fifties. By the late 50's, the studio, which had become part of a failed combine, went bankrupt. It was ultimately torn down...not that Roach was entirely bothered by the course events had taken, although he did admit he regretted "the passing of the studio as a place for the filming of comedies." Ultimately, however, Roach was seen and honored until his death in Bel Air at one hundred years of age as an impressive titan from a bygone era who nonetheless remained positive and spry long after many of those he had worked with had passed on.

One of those individuals happened to be Mabel. And, although their working relationship in the mid-1920s wasn't the smoothest one, it certainly was memorable. What's more, the two made some funny films together. Whatever their differences, Roach saw something in Mabel at a time when most had written her off. Their opposing personalities didn't lead to a long term partnership, but they did lead to some quality work. In a sense, the two, who came from similar backgrounds, were good for each other, at least in a cinematic and business sense. And that, frankly, would prove to be enough.

After The Tempest

Despite what some of her more snobbish critics liked – or tried - to think of Mabel, there was no doubt that she was an intelligent woman. Keenly intelligent. One simply does not accomplish what Mabel did without having at the very least a large degree of street smarts. Mabel didn't even have a high school education, yet she earned untold amounts of fame and money without the help of a husband or mentor. She was also able to hold on to that money without living frugally. As she herself said, she had enough saved in her thirties to live luxuriously without ever having to work again.

On thing Mabel unfortunately could not save was her reputation. The woman who reportedly helped Chaplin when he was about to be fired from Keystone was largely missing from the public consciousness. As was the woman who paid for the medical treatment of a child suffering from tuberculosis. As was the woman who bought her parents a house and got her brother a job as a cameraman after he returned home from the First World War. As was the woman who treated those who worked on the set as equals. As was the woman who helped support who knew how many parentless kids. That person was not embedded in much of the public's mind.

The Mabel much of the public now knew was indeed "madcap." She was the person who showed up late on set, who trashed Mack Sennett's car, who reportedly ingested illicit drugs and got herself involved with violent crimes, who refused to take an important trial seriously and who expected to be forgiven all simply by flashing a cutie pie smile while inspiring young women across the country to be as reckless as she was. The public knew a charming and talented Mabel, yes, but a Mabel who was, it believed, dangerous to herself and to others, as well.

It all was, when looked at objectively, quite unfair. While Mabel could indeed be "madcap," while she could regularly drink to excess, be late for work, trash a car, act up in a courthouse, and rely on her looks and charm to get out of any bind, she was also the woman who was coupled with crimes she didn't commit, who was accused of engaging in illegal narcotics without serious evidence, who helped others in countless ways without making her charity public, who literally took her country, family, friendships and faith seriously, and who – lest it be forgotten – made people forget their personal problems and laugh year in and year out for well over a decade.

Still, while she could be bitter at times, Mabel had one important factor working in her favor – the fact that she was ultimately an eternal optimist. She was a tough New Yorker from the shore who had toiled in a Brooklyn sweatshop when she should have been in school. When all was said and done, Mabel simply wasn't built to whine excessively. It simply doesn't seem to have been her style. And, to be sure, Mabel had good reason to be optimistic in 1926, for her old friend and director Richard Jones was now the Production Supervisor of Hal Roach Studios. Suffice it to say, Jones wanted Mabel to work with Roach.

"My old director in the Sennett studio, Dick Jones, was now with Hal Roach as vice president and supervisor of all productions," Mabel later said. "He signed my new contract. It was for three years ¾ and I was never to weigh more than one hundred and eleven pounds. Since I've never weighed more than a hundred, I kidded Dick quite a bit about this. The contract called for eight two-reel comedies and then eight of feature length."

Yet Jones wasn't the only one to reach out on behalf of Mabel. "It was largely due to Mary's (Mary Pickford's) efforts that Roach sent for me," Mabel said later. She added that friend and fellow star Norma Talmadge also made it a point to help. Like Pickford, Talmadge "knew I belonged on the screen and not on the stage." In an act of profound loyalty, Pickford let it be known quite publicly that she supported her friend. As she wrote in a public announcement:

"Welcome back to the screen, Mabel Normand! Your return makes us all happy for you have the gifts, the training, the

personality and the technique ¾ the one which is so sure that it does not show.

You have that rare thing, that possession above price, Mabel Normand, the charm of personality! Ever since I first saw you on the screen I have tremendously and sincerely admired your gifts and abilities as an artist. These with your kindly heart and mind make you the screen's very own and we all are proud of your splendid work.

This is a wish, thus publicly expressed, for newer and bigger success to you, and it is a wish that everybody that I know sincerely shares.

The best o'luck, Mabel Normand, and again welcome back to the screen."

Mabel was to be part of what the *Los Angeles Times* referred to as the "'All-Star Comedy' series where **Roach** took former stars and tried to turn them into contemporary comedians." No doubt it stung Mabel when she'd reflect on the fact that she had gone from being one of the biggest stars in the world to once again being involved in short films. Yet this was an individual set on acting before a camera. If not, why take a step down the figurative ladder when she had enough money to live like royalty for the rest of her life? Being a film performer, which was still a relatively new profession in the 1920's, was something Mabel felt she was inherently designed to do – and so acting, even in less prestigious films, was something she was drawn to.

And so Mabel made her way to Culver City to make films for Roach. Ever the optimist, she no doubt felt the Roach contract could benefit her career.

Stan Laurel And Oliver Hardy

Whereas most celebrities find fame and fortune at a young age, Stan Laurel and Oliver Hardy had to wait until they were middle aged before they truly attained stardom. It was, no doubt, a long, hard journey for each man. Indeed, it took more than a little time for the two to become a comedic duo. Hardy had been in films for years when he and Laurel became a team. As for Laurel, he too had been in films for years...but he also had been a writer and director. Unlike his large framed American partner, the small Englishman openly embraced numerous aspects of the film industry. Laurel was, in a sense, a jack of all cinematic trades while Hardy was a craftsman. Decades after each man's death they remain perhaps the most famous comedic duo in history.

It was said the two men were never particularly close while working together, but it's also said that Laurel refused to appear on camera after Hardy's death in the 1950s. To be sure, the two comedic giants certainly weren't enemies. They were simply co-workers and – yes – friends who happened to be entirely different people with entirely different interests. But the mutual affection was there. "Deeply appreciated your kind sympathy over the death of my dear Pal," Laurel wrote to his cousin after Hardy's death, "I miss him terribly and feel quite lost – can't realize that he has gone...God Bless him." These words, written in a private correspondence, hardly express the sentiments of a man who had no emotional connection to his longtime partner.

While they were as different in personality as they were in background and outside interests...Stan Laurel and Oliver Hardy were some kind of comedians. The staying power of their work has been incredibly long lasting. "If you don't like Laurel and Hardy, you are no friend of mine," journalist Martin Chilton quotes Star Wars' star Mark Hamill as saying. Such is the lasting popularity of two men who died in the mid-20th century. "They were the perfect pairing. Georgia-born Ollie always has echoes of the old faded southern gentleman about him," Chilton writes, "twiddling his tie as he yearns for order and dignity. He tries without hope to control the chaotic Stan. While Ollie twiddled, Stan fiddled with his hat and hair (singer Harry Nilsson used to do to do an impression of this to make John Lennon laugh) and, for both Stan and Ollie, tranquility is forever elusive."

A product of Ulverston, England, Laurel was born on June 16, 1890, to a family steeped in show business. According to the "Los Angeles Times," Laurel "made his stage debut playing a newsboy at the age of 7. At 15, he toured Europe with a song-and-dance act. At 17, he joined Fred Arno's London Comedians and spent some time as understudy to the troupe's star, Charlie Chaplin." By 1900, Laurel had arrived in America where he eventually made his way into the motion picture business, as did so many others with similar backgrounds.

Hardy, Laurel's eventual partner, was born in Atlanta on the 18th of January 1892. He attended the Georgia Military Academy and the University of Georgia. Although he played college football, Hardy also worked in theater during the summers. After working his way into show business, Hardy found himself in the film industry, starting in Florida and eventually making his way to California, where he landed at Hal Roach's studio in 1918. Laurel, who had been with Roach since around 1917, was fond of directing as well as writing material, and acting, whereas Hardy seems to have seen himself simply as a performer.

Although the two men did appear together in motion pictures, it wasn't until 1927, when Roach decided they would make a good comedic duo, that the actor's careers truly took off. While they were successful in silent films, they became even more so after making the transition to sound. This was somewhat ironic, as many silent stars couldn't cross over into the era of the "Talkies." Laurel and Hardy, however, were actually funnier when viewers could hear their voices.

The two simply took well to the change in technology, to their great benefit.

"We tried not to copy anybody's style," said Laurel. "Nobody lifted gags in my time like they do now. There was more ethics then, hence more creativity." The two also improvised. A lot. "The pair seldom followed their scripts very closely," wrote the "San Francisco Examiner". "They improvised gags as they went along." It was a strategy that worked through hundreds of films, from shorts such as "The Music Box" to features like "Way Out West." By the 1930s, the duo was at its peak. Laurel himself, however, admitted they shouldn't have continued making movies into the 1940s. "Those films were terrible," he admitted. "We quit too late."

Laurel and Hardy made a huge comeback, however, when their films began appearing regularly on television. Suffice to say, their popularity has remained well into the 21st century. The two men never made a huge amount of money, however, receiving a flat fee from Roach. After dropping an alarming amount of weight, Hardy passed in 1957 while Laurel died in 1965. Both men had been married numerous times. As of the early 21st century, Laurel and Hardy remain enormously popular and well known. It has even been argued that the duo might be more popular and appreciated than Chaplin.

Laurel and Hardy never made a movie with Mabel as a duo, but both worked with Mabel separately. Laurel helped write the script for one of Mabel's films for Roach while Hardy appeared in several with Mabel herself. Although they were roughly the same age, Mabel, Laurel, and Hardy almost represent different eras of film making, for as Mabel's filmmaking days were winding down, the comedic team was on the cusp of stardom. There's no doubt, however, that Mabel, the comedienne par excellence of her era, was able to showcase her screen talents in a way that the still learning Laurel and Hardy were able to find quite valuable.

The Final Films

She looked different in the Hal Roach shorts. A bit older, perhaps, but there's clearly more to it that the natural aging process. The legs of this young woman – only in her thirties – looked disturbingly thin at times. Plus, Mabel's face looked somewhat worn. She always had a chameleon quality, seemingly looking full faced one moment, then almost angular the next, but the change in appearance now had nothing to do with makeup or clothing. It was, sadly, a sign of sickness. Yet even with that in mind, there's no denying that Mabel's films for Hal Roach were funny. Different than her work with Keystone, sure, but funny, nonetheless. There's none of the creative strain here that can be found in her work with Goldwyn. There's no denying the Roach films were effective in their own quirky way.

Roach, however, ended up being none too thrilled with having Mabel on his roster, although he certainly admired her considerable talents. "The greatest woman comedienne of all time was Mabel **Normand,"** he said. "She didn't work for me until years after she worked for Sennett." Reflecting on her career, Roach claimed that: "You could put Arbuckle on a motorcycle, and put her sitting behind him, and they would hit a mud puddle, and she would fall off and land in the mud, and the audience would roar. You'd take any other girl, do the same thing, and instead of laughing, the audience would be mad because here was this gorgeous girl falling into a mud puddle. She was the only beautiful girl who could really pull that off. I was a little stuck on her myself, but she did a lot of drinking, and she was taking other things, other than booze, into her dressing room."

Again, the drug rumors. And again, the simple question: Did people see Mabel ingest illegal narcotics like they saw her drink? Up until the 21st century, the answer has been a sound "no," and must remain a sound "no" unless or until legitimate evidence to the contrary is presented. With that being said, the pairing of Roach and Mabel did indeed produce some quality work. Mabel may have been sick – in fact, it seems obvious watching the Roach films that she was - but she could still be funny. Extremely so. Years in the business had made her an expert in subtle comedic expressions. Once more, although she was no longer able to move about like she did in her prime, the Hal Roach Studio's Mabel was able to maneuver her slight frame in comical manners on a regular basis.

Raggedy Rose, released in 1926 and co-written by Laurel, is a perfect example of Mabel's work with Roach. The film is wild. Confusing, too, really, but no matter. Mabel is older here, of course, but still cute – and very lively in the end. The movie, about a poor girl trying to land a wealthy doctor, is almost surreal in parts. While definitely not fitting the bill of being a "standard" Mabel Normand film, it proves to be successful, nonetheless.

The Nickel Hopper, released the same year as *Raggedy* Rose, is a treat in that Mabel shows real range in this one. The woman can ACT, and Mabel's performance here erases any lingering doubt. Her facial expressions – although at times repetitive – really catch the eye. Like most of her later work, *The Nickel Hopper* presents a fleshed-out story rather than a situation. Mabel's work at this point isn't as high energy as it used to be, but she shows different emotions here – including anger and sadness for a few minutes – that once again point to a gift towards drama. Still, this is ultimately a silly story about a music club dancer looking for a better life, and an entertaining one at that. Boris Karloff can be spotted in his film debut here as a shady dancer while Hardy – looking very young – keeps up the fast pace as a wild, hep cat drummer.

Yet it's 1927's *Should Men Walk Home* that's the standout of Mabel's time with Roach. It's very cute and appealing, this film. Hardy is on the screen once again with Mabel, this time engaging in a fantastic scene where a mischievous Mabel keeps him from drinking a glass of punch at a high end party. Mabel doesn't seem to do quite as much physical comedy at this stage of her career, though she runs around a lot as one half of a crime team (Creighton Hale plays her partner) trying to steal a jewel from the man whose mansion the party is being held at. *Should Men Walk Home* is, in fact, pure lighthearted silliness, and – coming as it does at the end of Mabel's film career – acts as a fine, if premature, sendoff.

There were other works for Roach, of course such as *Anything Once!*, also from 1927, and the missing *One Hour Married*, which was actually the last film Mabel made. All in all, however, Mabel's small body of work for Roach was nothing if not successful and enjoyable to watch. She's still funny, Mabel is. In fact, her ability to use other tools in her toolbox, such as her arsenal of subtle facial expressions, helps make her work at Roach stand head and shoulders above her work at Goldwyn. The Mabel who would run wildly across the Southern California landscape while being chased by a maniacal Ford Sterling well over a decade earlier may have been gone, but the Mabel who took her place in the Roach films was still able to show what a comedic master is able to do, even after the passing of time and health.

"I know no reason why I should not have gone ahead and fulfilled my contract with Roach," Mabel would go on to recall, "save for a couple of facts, I got married and I got pneumonia." Even in the later 1920s, Mabel proved she was still able to make news.

Lew Cody

"Do I believe in marriage?" Lew Cody rhetorically asked "Motion Picture Classic" in 1920. "Yes, indeed – for other people. I think it is a beautiful institution. But the human butterfly type – male or female – should be free. They can't rub up against the little troubles of everyday life and keep the gloss on their wings. They make perfect lovers, but impossible husbands and wives." It was a bold statement for the dashing actor, who starred in a film called "The Butterfly Man" that year. Perhaps he even meant it at the time. How ironic, then, that it would be a marriage that Lew Cody would arguably be most remembered for. And a very unusual marriage at that. Whether or not Cody, in his most rational moments, wanted to be the marrying type, it was the marrying type that he eventually proved to be.

"Lew's real name is Louis Cote, and he is of French-Canadian ancestry," said Mabel. "He was born in New England, about 1885. He had been on the stage and in pictures. He was married to Dorothy Dalton, divorced, remarried to her, and again divorced." Sure enough, Cody was born in Waterville, Maine in 1884. As a young man, Cody decided the New England life simply wasn't for him. Nor was the study of medicine he had partaken in. "One afternoon," he recalled, "after a whole day spent reciting poetry at myself, I went to my father and told him that I was going to go on the stage. 'All right!' my father said. 'When are you going?' Of course, that was all wrong. He should have objected violently. But he must have had too keen a sense of drama, himself, to do such a commonplace thing. Instead, he staked me to a wardrobe, and I went to New York and got my start almost at once."

Cody worked in the theater, but it took a while for the man to finally feel settled. "I've been everything in the profession except a clown in a circus," he joked. Finally, Cody ended up on the West Coast, working for famed producer Thomas Ince. He had found his true calling, for through film the man was able to find security and popularity. Although he could pass for a "heavy" and played one very well, Cody didn't want to be seen primarily as a film villain. With that being said, the man ended up working with Keystone and appeared as the menacing main antagonist in "Mickey". Unlike their screen characters, however, Cody and Mabel were indeed good friends.

Sure enough, Cody was an easy man to like, one who could play a crowd, no matter how small. "I'm a great believer in leaving things to chance; that is, little things," he remarked. "I never have a good time when I plan on it very far ahead. I've generally found that the best way for me to enjoy myself is to start out alone feeling grumpy and dull. Pretty soon I am likely to meet some friend who feels very much the same way. 'Where are you going?' he asks 'Nowhere,' I answer. 'Suppose we go together?' he suggests, and the result is one glad time!"

While Cody was certainly a good actor, his reputation seems to have been more firmly grounded in his colorful personality than on his work as a cinematic thespian. Sure enough, his films, with the exception of "Mickey", generally don't stand out as well as stories of the man himself do. Whether rolling through the night with the likes of Arbuckle and Buster Keaton or being connected with any number of well known women, Cody was the quintessential man about town.

"Married twice," the "Los Angeles Times" wrote upon his death, "his first wife being Dorothy Dalton, Cody had many affairs of the heart and once, earlier in his career, acquired the cognomen of 'butterfly man' because of his many conquests which not only made him talked about – important in Hollywood – but also added to the fame which took him to the highest goal of screendom, a star." The perception of Cody as a suave presence is evident in his work, such as his smooth performance in 1933's "By Appointment Only". It might even be argued the man had a quality similar to the one Errol Flynn rode to stardom on, minus Flynn's physicality.

Yet Cody proved to be far more than just a ladies' man. He was second to none as a party host as well as a party guest. His corned beef dinners with friends were famous around the industry. What's more, Cody had a door in his home into which guests carved their names. It remains in the 21st century as a memory of a lively social scene from the past. Perhaps Cody's greatest gift was his ability to show people a good time – something that required talent, much as his acting did. Ultimately, Lew Cody was an entertainer, be it on stage, on screen, or when enjoying himself.

Not that Cody's life was as smooth as his personal presentation was. By the late 20s he was far from in good health. He also had a breakdown in the early 1930s, one which reportedly took some time for him to recuperate from. Cody passed in bed at his North Maple Drive home in Beverly Hills on the last day of May, 1934. True to form, he had been at a party that night, arriving home at around one in the morning the day he passed. The "Los Angeles Times" reported that Cody was forty-seven years of age at the time of his death.

Cody received ample media attention upon his passing, understandable as he had been in the motion picture industry since before the First World War and had been one of the fortunate actors who was able to make the transition from silent films to the "talkies." Although he had been married a total of three times (two of those three to the same woman, as previously noted) Cody ended up perhaps being most remembered for his second marriage, which happened to take Hollywood by storm. They had been friends for years, but few had probably ever expected Mabel and Cody to get married – especially not in the wildly unusual way they did.

Marriage

"On the night of the fifteenth (of September) I was giving a dinner for a number of friends in my Beverly Hills home." With those words, Mabel told Sid Sutherland one of the more colorful stories to be found in her exceedingly colorful life. "At the last minute," she continued, "John Colton, who adapted *Rain* and the *Shanghai Gesture*, phoned he couldn't come. That left an empty chair, and I wondered whom I could call at that hour to occupy it." Mabel decided to call on an old friend who would make a perfect guest for her upcoming dinner party.

"I thought of Lew Cody," she continued. "We had been friends for more than fifteen years, since I first went into pictures while he was playing on the New York stage." In truth, Cody was most certainly the sort of person Mabel would love to have at her gathering. "I never knew anybody with a more priceless sense of humor, and it was on this foundation of mutual laughs that our friendship had continued all these years." Cody proved happy to oblige. "I called him up and explained my predicament," she said, "and he volunteered to come over and fill out my party. Others there that night were Margaret Namara, the opera singer, and her husband, Minert Lord; Charles Ray and his wife, and one or two other couples."

Available evidence suggests it was some party indeed. It clearly was not a simple gathering of friends.

"After midnight the party was going good," Mabel said, "and Lew thought it would be a rare joke to stage an old-time melodrama proposal to me, and I thought it would be a splendid idea if we really got married after a spectacular elopement." The young woman who felt such a deep sense of betrayal at Mack's actions that she broke off their engagement clearly wasn't viewing marriage with the same seriousness at the moment. "Probably the novelty of Lew's magnificently worded proposal appealed to me," she explained. "At any rate, I said all right."

Of course, after midnight it's not easy for even a movie star to run off and get married. Determined to keep the alcoholic endeavor from going by the wayside, however, Mabel, Cody, and the others decided to travel to Ventura County in order for the marriage to be legally performed. The idea and its subsequent follow through were as wild and random as anything to be found in one of Mabel's early Keystone films. Getting an escort from Beverly Hills motorcycle police (Cody was friends with the Chief), the entire party raced eighty miles through the night to Ventura Country. "There we awoke the county recorder, Judge Thomas H. Meilandt," said Mabel, "and he pulled some pants over his pajamas and spoke the ceremony in his living room, his eighteen-year-old daughter, Ruth, acting as one of the witnesses, the rest of his family taking turns at a keyhole to see us made one. I was quite dazed and nervous over this drastic change in my life."

Just what kind of state was the couple in? Cody reportedly couldn't remember his mother's name while Mabel couldn't provide the year of her birth. It was quite the wedding. Perhaps Mabel's nephew Stephen Normand put it best by claiming that the marriage simply was a farce involving two alcoholics.

"Then we returned to Beverly Hills," said Mabel, "and Lew left me at my house while he went on to the Hollywood Bowl, where he was to be master of ceremonies at a feed the Breakfast Club was having." The matter didn't stay under wraps for long. "As he approached the microphone to begin his stuff," Mabel continued, "somebody asked him why he was late, and he casually mentioned that he had just married Mabel Normand, the radio spreading the news to such parts of the world as happened to be tuned in on that wavelength." Cody appears to have then treated the day just as he would any other day. "Later Lew returned to his home on Maple Drive, also in Beverly Hills," Mabel said.

It was most distinctly not, however, just like any other day for Mabel. With sobriety starting to rear its head with the dawn, Mabel realized the enormity of what she had just done. It's said she cried away to her maid after arriving home in Beverly Hills, which she most likely did. Unlike so many of the incidents which led to bad publicity for her, Mabel had no one but herself to blame for her rash decision to marry Cody. There was no way she could play victim this time around, for she had gone against traditional custom, the rules of the religion she practiced, and general common sense. And now the world knew of it. One could only imagine the more vicious members of the media smiling nastily upon learning of the news – for now Mabel herself had provided the image of an unserious person.

Yet Mabel had proven throughout the course of her life that she was not an unserious person, even though she had now shown she was capable of engaging in jaw droppingly unserious behavior. It makes sense then that, once they had come to their senses, both she and Cody wanted a divorce. What both soon realized, however, was that divorce would bring around even more scrutiny and accusations. With neither she nor Cody being the picture of health, the couple decided to remain legally married while continuing to reside in their own homes.

For all intents and purposes, Mabel's stunt with Cody brought about instant and severe regret. Indeed, the whole affair might have brought about a genuine identity crisis for the now 35 year old actress. Could she have actually proven her harshest critics correct? Was she actually the "Madcap Mabel" upright society would shake its head at? Furthermore, what kind of person had she become? Even her previous antics were essentially larks. Her marriage to Cody, however, was something far different. Still, Mabel was never one to allow herself to simply be swept along with the tide.

She had one more surprise up her sleeve.

Sid Sutherland

The wind can be heard blowing through an ominous patch of desert. There is no sign of life. Suddenly, a trumpet can be heard, and we find ourselves watching a German military convoy make its way across the inhospitable landscape. A radio is playing inside one of the armored vehicles – a woman singing in German. A soldier turns off the radio. The ominous sound of battle drums now coincides with the action appearing on the screen. Moments later, two small, Allied jeeps race alongside the convoy and fire away to the accompaniment of fast paced action music. The machine guns rattle away as the fighting rages at a blistering pace. This is the premiere scene of "Rat Patrol", a World War Two adventure show. It will soon become an enormously popular part of 1960s television programing.

The man who helped deliver colorful sounds from the episode into living rooms, however, was no dashing hero of the Second World War. In fact, he was an aging jack of all trades named Sid Sutherland. And at sixty-six years of age, he was the Sound Editor of this high-octane television program. Although notable, this was simply one of the latest in a long line of achievements that made Sutherland one of the more interesting men in a very interesting industry. Born a decade and a half before the United States even entered the First World War, Sutherland tried his hand at one unique endeavor after another throughout the course of his life. Unlike many who refuse to settle for a single line of work, however, Sutherland proved to have been quite successful over the years.

In 1966, the same year "Rat Patrol" premiered on American television, for instance, Sutherland was the Sound Editor for the popular film "The Russians are Coming the Russians Are Coming." Indeed, Sutherland had been a motion picture sound man for over ten years when he worked on both "Rat Patrol," and "The Russians are Coming the Russians are Coming." Programs such as "The

Cisco Kid," and "Bat Masterson" bore Sutherland's mark on them. Sutherland also worked on legendary director Frank Capra's short, "Rendezvous in Space." Yet even before he became known as a sound technician in Hollywood, Sutherland was known as an animator.

Indeed, three full decades before he dove headfirst into the feature film business, Sutherland was employed by the famous Tex Avery as an animator. Throughout his stint as a motion picture cartoonist, Sutherland worked in a team environment, which meant it was hard to distinguish his creations with another member of his team. Still, he was unquestionably an artist who contributed to the design and performances of such characters as Buggs Bunny, Porky Pig, and Daffy Duck. In other words, the man played a considerable role in the production of iconic works of animation. Yet, as if Sutherland's overall body of work wasn't interesting enough, there was also the matter of the scripts for live action films he penned until the 1940s.

Although he's not remembered for having written any "classic" films, there's no doubt that Sutherland was a screenwriter of note. Screenwriting was and remains an extremely challenging craft, after all. Writers as notable as F. Scott Fitzgerald found the form challenging. One of the more difficult aspects of the craft during Sutherland's time was the fact that writers were often teamed up with at least one other writer for a project. It seemed that a script didn't so much belong to the writer(s) as it did to the studio whose production line process gave it birth. Indeed, Sutherland was never credited as the sole screenwriter on any film he wrote that was subsequently produced. There was always at least one other writer credited alongside him. The fact Sutherland was able to succeed and succeed regularly while plying such a frustrating trade obviously said something about the man's abilities as a writer.

Sutherland's talents as a screen scribe, however, aren't particularly surprising when one discovers he was a working journalist before that. Indeed, Sutherland wrote numerous articles of note for "Liberty Magazine." This was no small thing, as "Liberty" was known to employ such luminaries as Fitzgerald, Agatha Christie, and H.L. Mencken. Sutherland, to be sure, was in good company at the publication. Then again, the man himself presented memorable material. This was especially true in the case of a lengthy piece Sutherland wrote about Mabel.

Through this three-part article, Sutherland provided the world with invaluable insight into his subject and friend. As Marilyn Slater stated, "The 'LIBERTY' Magazine article is the nearest thing we have to an autobiography (from Mabel)." Mabel's mindset, way of speaking, and general worldview come to light while reading Sutherland's lengthy piece. Although it's obvious Sutherland is quite fond of his subject, he doesn't appear to have glossed over the more eyebrow raising information she provides. If Mabel was okay telling it, Sutherland no doubt reasoned, there was nothing wrong with printing it.

When he passed in 1968, Sutherland wasn't remembered for penning his brilliant piece on Mabel. There were, of course, other things to remember the man for, such as his work in animation, sound, and screenwriting. Sutherland's lengthy article about Mabel shouldn't go unnoticed, however, as it has given generations insight into a woman who is far too infrequently seen as a real flesh and blood human rather than an eccentric, inaccessible wild child. Unlike other journalists, Sutherland LIKED Mabel. What's more, Sutherland made no secret of his biases. His article didn't pretend to present an objective look at Mabel so much as it did allow her to give her side of the events that filled her very colorful life.

Though he was clearly a jack of all trades in Hollywood, Sutherland should also be noted for his loyalty to a person it had become far too fashionable to condemn or ignore. He was certainly a man with the courage to publicly support a person whose glory days had passed and who had come to unfairly be seen as a scandalous footnote.

The Long Fight

"In January, 1927, I became ill with bronchial trouble," Mabel said to Sutherland, "and in February they took me to the Santa Monica Hospital, where double pneumonia came along to keep me company. I remained there nearly ten weeks and I spent the summer and fall trying to convalesce. It has been a long hard climb, but I think my physicians are persuaded that I am at last on the way to health." Unfortunately, Mabel was never again "on the way to health." Shortly after marrying Cody, she began the final long fight, one that she could not win.

Mabel had put an end to her film making career before heading off to the hospital. "I went back to the studio," she recalled, "but it wasn't long before Dick and I broke our contract by mutual consent. I didn't feel like working, and when one isn't happy one cannot work. At least I can't." Actress Anita Garvin worked with Mabel while Mabel was still with Roach and her memories paint a picture of a woman in clear physical decline. "She was married to Lew Cody," Garvin said of Mabel, "and he was an angel. He would always be standing by on the set for her. She was losing her mind about that time – or having some kind of problems, and he was absolutely wonderful!"

Mabel was indeed having "some kind of problems." Tuberculosis takes away one's energy, making a sufferer quite weak. Fevers (which Stephen Normand notes his aunt suffered from), can also come with the disease, along with coughing up blood and pains in the chest. Couple these symptoms with an advanced alcoholic lifestyle and it's no surprise that Mabel, who had always marched to the tune of her own drummer on set as it was, came across as "losing her mind" while working with Garvin.

"Mabel was hard to work with," Garvin admitted. "She would move her way – which would confuse you if you were working with her. She kept you jumping, you didn't know what to expect." This, at least, sounds like a report on Mabel that could have been given at any time during Mabel's nearly twenty year career. Mabel, after all, was always known as being naturally quirky. According to Garvin, however, matters went beyond mere eccentric behavior.

"One thing I remember which she didn't do perfect," said Garvin "was that she couldn't find her spot. She would get a little wild and not stay within camera range where she was supposed to be, if you know what I mean. But you must realize that this happened in her later days." Sadly, they were indeed Mabel's later days in the film industry. There is always some final wall that even the most determined soul cannot successfully climb by force of will. For Mabel, that wall was tuberculosis, which had been a part of her life since childhood. It had taken her older brother decades earlier, and it would eventually take her.

Yet Mabel was not one to literally lie back and die. She was game for the long fight. "When I do come back physically," she told Sutherland, "I intend to return to the pictures, and I hope to do some lovely things in the modern vogue of comedies. The day of the rough and tumble and slapstick seems to have passed, and I should like to find some genuine fun in the comedies they are writing today. If I am lucky, I hope again to make the world laugh as I once did." Yet Mabel also remained a realist. "But even if I discover some really glorious stories of the kind I want," she added, "I'm afraid that never again will the world find such things to laugh at as it used to find when Charlie Chaplin and Roscoe Arbuckle and Ford Sterling and Charles Murray and I made our comedies together."

Things were different, and Mabel knew it. Times hadn't changed so much as they had accelerated. Movies were finally on the verge of regularly offering audiences synchronized sound. Radio broadcasts covered such events as major boxing matches live. Athletes, literary figures and even gangsters had become celebrities. The cult of youth had gripped the country and would subsequently hold it in that grip for decades. Again, things were different. Still,

Mabel put up a good front. In June, back from the hospital, she and Cody actually had a party at her Beverley Hills home. Grace Kingsley wrote of the occasion for the *Los Angeles Times*:

"You would never know she had been ill," Kingsley wrote of Mabel, "except that she is much thinner than before. But she is as full of mischief and pep as ever. And she has bobbed her hair!" With Cody playing the gracious host, the event appeared to have been a success. "One corner of the big living room was devoted to dancing to the music of the jazz orchestra," wrote Kingsley, "and Mabel took two or three twirls there with Lew, but was too busy with her guests to do much stepping." Still, such an event was clearly a lot for Mable at this point. "She must have grown dreadfully tired," Kingsley continued, "and once we know she slipped away upstairs to lie down for five minutes."

Perhaps not surprisingly, by August Mabel was back at Santa Monica Hospital, though it was said her stay this time was merely a precautionary measure. Her personal doctor, George Dazey, addressed the media. "Following her (Mabel's) attack of pneumonia some months ago," he said, via the *Los Angeles Evening Post-Record*, "we thought it would be best that she remain here for a few days rather than to chance possible recurrence of that malady." Once again, Mabel proved she was a fighter. She even became well enough to travel in the fall to New York to see Cody, who was on the road performing a vaudeville act.

"A husband doesn't exactly know how to take care of himself," Mabel joked upon stopping in Chicago, "when to dress warm and how to keep his wardrobe in order when he's away from home, so I'm going on to see if he's comfortable. Yet Mabel also admitted she hadn't been in the best of health. "I've been very ill," she declared, "but feel that I must take a little trip to see my husband." This was to be no brief trip. In November, Mabel and Cody were in Washington, where Mabel lost a diamond pendant that had been attached to her necklace. Though things seemed serene enough on the surface (the loss of the diamond pendant aside), later that same month rumors swirled that the couple was divorcing, something both Mabel and Cody at first denied.

Indeed, by December, Mabel was back home and telling the media that she and Cody would no longer live in separate residents (something that didn't prove to be true, whatever Mabel and Cody's intent might have been at the time). Yet, matters were clearly strained. In January, Mabel, who had been supposed to travel with Cody to Denver, remained at home, reportedly due to a tooth infection that led to her being hospitalized for several days. Then, in February, word finally broke that Mabel was looking for a divorce.

"I will file suit for divorce right away," she said. "If any scandal develops," she continued, "that is Cody's concern. I have put up with everything as long as I can." Mabel went on to indicate that she was the one who was pulling the weight in the relationship. "I want to be released from an unbearable situation," she was quoted as saying. "I am packing up at this moment. I have paid every expense I had around here since I was married; if there are any bills Lew Cody paid for me I don't know what they are." Mabel then tellingly said: "I have had good detectives working for me."

Difficult times, to be sure...though by April it was reported that the two had settled their differences. Again, with neither in good health, the serious consideration of divorce must have presented a hellish scenario for both, as the press would clearly have had a field day at their expense. By this point it was obvious Mabel's long fight was not only against her declining health; it was also against the consequences of a marriage that had been founded on a lark. With that being said, Mabel reportedly directed a kind of elaborate home movie starring herself to give to Cody while he was away in New York that Christmas before he headed to Europe.

What's more, Mabel continued to put on the best front she could. As Marilyn Slater said: "In 1929 Mabel was ill and had been ill for a long time but she didn't lock herself away in her lovely Beverly Hills home, which she had purchased in 1925; she was still socially active, going to parties, planning vacations, entertaining her friends."

Indeed, on January 20th of that year the *Los Angeles Times* reported that Mabel (along with Una Brown) had hosted a birthday party at Hollywood's Roosevelt Hotel for Doris Deane Arbuckle (Roscoe's second wife). "The ability of Mrs. Brown to make groups happy and the wit and humor of Miss Normand, made the affair one of the most sparkling of the season," wrote the *Times'* Myra Nye. Earlier that same month, however, the *Daily News* wrote that "one bright light in moviedom who, in all likelihood, will never twinkle again is Mabel Normand." The title of the January 6th article? "The Has-Beens Of Hollywood."

It was not the kind of retirement Mabel probably ever imagined – if she had ever imagined retiring at all. Yet there was something to be said about Mabel's staying power. "Mary Pickford was pretty much spent by 1927, when Mabel made her last film" Michael Ventura wrote in *Los Angeles Magazine* decades later. "Pickford lived unhappily for decades longer." A harsh assessment, true, but the point is well taken. The truth was that Mabel's career trajectory was essentially on par with those of her peers. Sterling had toned done his act by the time the sound era came around. Arbuckle, was of course, persona non grata. Sennett went bankrupt. Even Chaplin found himself embroiled in his own self-inflicted scandals starting as early as the 1920's. Feeling hounded by authorities, he eventually went into bitter exile after the Second World War.

Happy endings were not easy to come by for legends of the silent screen. Still, rumors found a way to persist. *The Los Angeles Times*, for instance, reported in late February of 1929 that Mabel was teaming up with Serling and Arbuckle in the creation of a studio the three could run. An interesting project to imagine, but one that couldn't possibly come to fruition. Mabel had money saved, to be sure, but Sterling was the only one of the three who had both his money and his reputation intact at the time. Furthermore, Mabel had other concerns that month.

Indeed, Cody almost found himself in the obituaries in February of 1929, when influenza had put him close to death in New York

City. At the same time, Mabel was struck by the flu back in California. Cody survived the scare, but the situation with Mabel became critical. By March her tuberculosis had advanced to such a degree that her doctor, E.C. Fishbaugh, had to assure the media she was not on the verge of death. What's more, Cody, although back in California, was reportedly now "seriously ill with a nervous breakdown," and was temporarily residing at a San Bernadino area health spa.

By the following month, Mabel's illness had reached an alarming enough state to present the public with the grim truth: Mabel, who had been bed ridden since January, was suffering from tuberculosis with two infected lungs and was being allowed no visitors. Furthermore, due to the seriousness of her condition, Mabel had only been able to leave her room once. She had been reading novels to pass the time. "Plans were being made yesterday," wrote the *Los Angeles Times* on March 20th, "for the removal of Mabel Normand, once a star of the motion picture world to a sanitorium near Los Angeles to aid her in her desperate fight against tuberculosis." Dr. Fishbaugh came across as positive, telling the *Times* that Mabel might well recover provided the treatments that would be given to her at the sanitorium proved helpful. Meanwhile, Cody was still in the San Bernadino area recovering. It was reported that neither he nor Mabel knew how poor the other's condition was.

Frances Pottenger

"No one can say this positively," Dr. Francis M Pottinger told a local California group known as the Pure Air Committee in 1953, "but we suspect," he added, "we have reason to believe this." Pottinger was speaking of the smog which was plaguing greater Los Angeles, something that individuals, himself included, felt might be presenting deadly consequences for some of those who breathed it in. "Many patients of mine have left this area because of air contamination. I know individuals suffering from pulmonary trouble leave here and seem to get better elsewhere." Dr. Francis M Pottinger was a man people listened to, and there was a good reason why.

Pottenger, as the "Los Angeles Times" put it, "was known internationally for his work in the tuberculosis field which he entered after his bride of 1894 developed the ailment, to die from it within a few years." The man combined his determination with his natural intelligence and personal tragedy to fight a disease that at the time was still very much deadly. The matter was clearly very personal to Pottenger. Those who were in his care or who went to him for guidance knew the man viewed his work as more than simply a job.

Born in New Baltimore, Ohio, in 1869, Pottenger went on to have an interest in medicine, studying at Otterbein College as well as the Cincinnati College of Medicine and Surgery. Becoming a doctor, he traveled around the globe to places such as Vienna, Munich, and Berlin to learn of the latest advancements in medicine. The man was an Ohioan, however, and ended up settling down in the suburbs of Cincinnati. Yet less than a year into his practice, Pottenger's wife developed tuberculosis. The development altered the course of Pottenger's entire life. Tubuerculosis was a deadly disease -as it remains in the 21st century – though there had yet to be methods developed to contain the illness at the time.

In order to save his spouse, Pottenger moved with his wife to California in the hope that the temperate climate might improve her condition. They settled in Monrovia, a city less than twenty miles away from Los Angeles, which at the time was not the bustling metropolis it would become. Close to the desert, there was good reason to believe the climate of Monrovia at the time might have at least some kind of input on Pottenger's wife. Unfortunately, the poor woman passed in 1898. Pottenger then took on tuberculosis as if it were a personal enemy, which it literally was.

"In the years that followed," the "Los Angeles Times" wrote, "he participated in many discoveries concerning the disease, developed methods of treatment and worked out important and successful therapy." Yet the man became best known for the Pottenger Sanitorium for Diseases of the Lungs and Throat, which he founded in his hometown of Monrovia in 1903. Located on forty acres of land, the sanitarium started with eleven patients, but eventually was able to house one hundred thirty four.

Pottenger reportedly treated more than one thousand five hundred patients at the fortress he built to battle tuberculosis. The man was dedicated to such a degree that he lived on the campus. And, to his credit, Pottenger's sanitorium was regarded as the premier institution of its kind. Yet Pottenger was also an active member of the Monrovia community. "While he lived in Monrovia, beginning in 1895," the "Daily News-Post" wrote, "Doctor Pottenger was an early City Councilman and was active in civic affairs. He was instrumental in persuading Henry Huntington to bring the Pacific Electric Lines to Monrovia." The obscure matters that are of great importance to some at particular times.

On top of his civic and institutional responsibilities, Pottenger was a prolific author of papers and books. He also worked as a professor and lecturer at the University of Southern California for close to twenty-five years. He was Professor of Medicine Emeritus at the University and was Chairman of the school's Tuberculosis Treatment center, as well.

Pottenger finally retired in 1955 and passed away in 1961 back in his original home state of Ohio. One of his children, Frances Pottenger Jr, was also a doctor as well as a controversial nutritionist. Unlike his son, Pottenger's career was not associated with controversy.

"If I knew this was my last year, or month or day," he had written, "I would be sorry only because it would take me from my family and friends and terminate the possibility of completing many unfinished tasks." The reality was that Pottenger and others helped push tuberculosis further and further into the margins of American society as time moved on. Indeed, the disease affected fewer and fewer people than it previously had during the 1920s and 1930's.

An eventual emphasis on hygiene, nutrition, exercise, and an overall healthy lifestyle had a huge impact on those who might otherwise have been infected by the disease known as T.B. After learning that tuberculosis was not a heredity disease, but rather was spread through the air by those suffering from the disease, the public learned how to keep the bacteria from spreading as much as possible. Then, when antibiotics were found to profoundly help those who had tuberculosis, the illness was no longer the major killer it had been for centuries. Naturally, tuberculosis could still take lives, but the days of its leading to the deaths of one out of every seven people were long gone.

Unfortunately, antibiotics weren't put to use until after the Second World War. That meant that Mabel never had the chance to receive the lifesaving treatment. Tuberculosis cases may have been in decline in 1929, but the disease was still prominent enough to physically destroy someone who had recently been one of the most popular and influential women in the world. Not that Frances Pottenger didn't do everything he could to save Mabel from the illness which plagued her.

Those Going About Their Everyday Lives

"I am a Catholic," Mabel had once said, "but don't hold that against the church." In 1929, Mabel's life was on its journey to a Catholic ending. In the spring it was reported that Cody, now feeling well enough for a trip, was able to meet Mabel in her Beverly Hills home. Neither was well, but it was clearly Mabel's condition that was most concerning. The media had portrayed the meeting as a sign that Mabel's condition had improved – as indeed it perhaps had – but only slightly.

As summer worked its way into autumn it remained obvious that Mabel could no longer stay in her Beverly Hills' mansion if she hoped to significantly improve her health. Matters were grave enough for her to go to Pottenger's Sanitorium, where she would reside in the hope that the esteemed Pottenger and his staff might be able to battle the wave of illness which was now beginning to drown her. Perhaps she could have simply spent her remaining days at home, but Mabel simply wasn't of that nature. If there were an opportunity to push on, then she'd take it. That had been her way since she was a young sweatshop worker in Brooklyn all those years ago.

One has to wonder what went through Mabel's mind during the thirty or so mile ride from Beverly Hills to Monrovia. She had been a fighter her entire life, but it's hard to imagine Mabel not bothering to reflect that she might never see her home again, or many of those who loved her, or those of the film industry entirely. Clearly, one suspects, the still young woman was aware that her chances of survival at this point were far less than those of the people she rode past on the street, those going about their everyday lives while she went about her (perhaps final) defining moments. Still, even in her current situation it's difficult to believe Mabel's mind had gone to an entirely dark place. Comediennes have built in defenses, after all.

What's more, Mabel wouldn't be alone at Pottenger's. Julia Benson, a convent trained nurse and widow, acted as Mabel's personal nurse and companion at the sanitarium. The two had been very close for years for good reason – Benson had lost her husband John to tuberculosis some years earlier. Benson was, in a sense, the perfect person to be with Mabel at Pottinger's. There were three other nurses who watched over Mabel, as well. They read to her, but avoided telling her about the sudden renewed interest in the William Desmond Taylor murder. The last thing Mabel needed at the moment was to have to relive one of her life's great nightmares once again.

"Even Dr. Francis Pottenger," wrote Slater, "shielded Mabel and Julie told the investigators that Mabel had told all she knew of the Taylor case time and time again and had nothing new to relate." For sure, no one was allowed to visit Mabel at the time except for Cody himself. All others, be they friends, relatives, or media, had to be kept away from Pottenger's Sanatorium. And, for the briefest of moments, the treatments at the institution, strategically located where the air was clean and the nights cold, seemed to be having a positive impact on Mabel, with Pottenger himself telling the media that she had shown slight improvement.

Even the smallest of celebrations proved to be brief, however, for by Christmastime Mabel had relapsed. "A relapse following an apparent improvement in the condition of Mabel Normand, one-time luminary of the films," wrote the *Associated Press*, "today created anxiety over her condition, at a sanatorium here, where she is confined for treatment of tuberculosis." The article went on to claim that: "Attending physicians described her state of health as 'serious'.' Some time ago they said it was doubtful if she would recover."

With the end quite near, some found the desire to view Mabel through the lens of her tarnished reputation irresistible. "And now

Mabel Normand is doomed," wrote the *Sunday Mercury and News* almost gleefully. "All hope has been given up by the physicians at the sanitorium in California where she is battling with tuberculosis and the effects of dope. And Madcap Mabel is getting the wish that she has so often expressed to her friends and intimates – that she would die young!" Reports of Mabel regularly expressing a wish to die young are unverified and are almost entirely untrue as well as ridiculous. Mabel was a risk taker to be sure, but wasn't known to have longed for death, much less an early death at that.

With that being said, Mabel proved that the end wasn't as near as some might have thought or had even perhaps wished. In early February, Mabel was given a one-pint blood transfusion in an operation that proved successful. The *New York Times* quoted Pottenger as saying Mabel had "withstood the ordeal very well." This was likely no surprise to those at the sanitorium, for Mabel could still very much be alert while at Pottenger's, at one point writing specifically about one of the doctors treating her.

"Dr. came in," she wrote. "He has wonderful hands. Not beautiful, but full of a strange singular expressiveness. Probably Leonardo Da Vinci had hands like that...Sometimes when he's talking, he will gradually close his fingers into a fist, then suddenly open with a gesture of silent good." So much for the argument that Mabel was an intellectual pretender. Here was an artist, whose trade at least partially required her to be keenly aware of the things and people around her. Rather than think in generalizations, Mabel had the artist's gifts to see in specifics.

None of Mabel's gifts, however, nor Pottenger's treatments, could save her now. By late February it was decided that it was more appropriate to focus primarily on spiritual matters. A priest was called in and Mabel, still conscious, gave her last confession and received the Eucharist. She lost consciousness that evening. At 2:30 on the morning of February 23'd, 1930, Mabel Normand, the Catholic girl from Staten Island, passed away.

Although it certainly wasn't surprising, Mabel's death at the very young age of 37 was indeed newsworthy. Although she had long ago ceased to be the center of public attention, she had remained a well-known figure from the silent era of film which was now all but slipping away. Newspapers wrote of her life and the scandals that had surrounded her. Friends and old acquaintances expressed grief and fond memories of films' first great female comedienne, director, producer, and studio head. Roscoe Arbuckle, upon hearing the news, perhaps spoke for a great many. "My pal's dead!" he said mournfully.

Claude Normand, Mabel's father, had died shortly before his oldest daughter did. Mabel, however, wasn't given the news due to her own fragile state at the time. Her mother, Mary, flew out to California to attend the funeral, then moved into Mabel's Beverly Hill's home. Mabel had left her considerable estate to Mary. It may have surprised some that Mabel, who could certainly be reckless in life at times, was sound with her money. Not only had she handled her fortune so that she, then her mother, could live well, but she had also provided considerable sums to those in need, orphans in particular. Charity was more than an occasional kind act for Mabel. Indeed, as records indicated after she had passed, charitable giving had been a full-fledged part of her life.

Not that that the star had wanted such things to be known. This most public of figures had certainly had a private side, which is perhaps why the numerous scandals she survived took such a toll on her. Years' old scandals certainly didn't keep those Mabel had worked with away from her funeral, however. D.W. Griffith, Mack Sennett, Charlie Chaplin, Samuel Goldwyn, and Douglas Fairbanks were among the pall bearers. Mary Pickford, always loyal, was there, as was old friend Marie Dressler.

And, of course, Cody was there. He reportedly not only insisted that Mabel's fortune go to her mother but had also admitted an uncomfortable truth to the Catholic Church - that his marriage to Mabel had never been consummated, subsequently making the marriage null and void in the Church's eyes. That, no doubt coupled with Mabel's last confession hours before losing consciousness and passing, allowed her to receive a Catholic funeral – which, of course, was something she had wanted. Thus, after Father Michael Mullins performed the funeral service at Beverly Hill's Church of the Good Shepherd, Mabel's parish, her body was taken to Calvary Cemetery in East Los Angeles, where it was laid to rest in the mausoleum.

Much had been accomplished in a very short life.

Epilogue

We see her once more, in costume, walking through a desolate terrain, her pigeon-toed step making her appear comical yet determined. She walks on and on it seems. Wherever she is heading, it appears to be taking her some time to arrive there. What's more, no one is around as she continues on her trek. We feel uneasy for her, frightened even. And yet she keeps going forward, quickly and without pause. For all we know, she may well be in danger.

Yet she is clearly not afraid. Onward she travels, a singular figure in a dry landscape, controlling our thoughts and emotions. Just what is she telling us about herself as she pushes onward, completely at ease, it seems, in this menacing setting? What is she telling us about ourselves as we worry for her? She provides no answer. She simply covers ground, her pace almost a natural trot, as she heads to her intended destination, to a place we have yet to know.

The End

Notes

Staten Island

1. "Biography." *Mabel Normand Estate.* https://mabelenormand.com/about-mabel/legend/
2. Drenier, Nigel, host. "All About Aunt Mabel." *Modern Times Podcast*, episode 10, Nigel Drenier, 5 Sept. 2015. https://www.youtube.com/watch?v=SwPF7OoQ15s&t=17s
3. Sidney Sutherland. "Madcap Mabel Normand." *Liberty Magazine*, 6 Sep 1930.
4. Chandler Sprague. "Mabel Normand's Own Life Story!" *Los Angeles Examiner,* Feb 1924.
5. "Achievements in Public Health, 1900-1999: Healthier Mothers and Babies." *Centers for Disease Control and Prevention,* 01 Oct. 1999, https://www.cdc.gov/mmwr/preview/mmwrhtml/mm4838a2.htm
6. "Tuberculosis (TB)." *Centers for Disease Control and Prevention,* https://www.cdc.gov/tb/topic/basics/signsandsymptoms.htm

Max Linder

1. Pamela Hutchinson. "Fame at last – was this the world's first film star?" *The Guardian*, 22 Nov. 2019, https://www.theguardian.com/film/2019/nov/22/fame-at-last-was-this-the-worlds-first-film-star
2. *The Skater's Debut.* Directed by Louis S. Gasnier. Performance by Max Linder. 1906.

From Sweatshop To Studio

1. Amanda. "Behind the Scenes of the Butterick Building." *Village Preservation*, 09 Sept. 13, https://www.

villagepreservation.org/2013/09/04/behind-the-seams-of-the-butterick-building/
2. Michael Schuman. "History of child Labor in the United States – part 1: little children working." *US Bureau of Labor Statistics,* Jan 2017, https://www.bls.gov/opub/mlr/2017/article/history-of-child-labor-in-the-united-states-part-1.htm
3. Drenier, Nigel, host. "All About Aunt Mabel." *Modern Times Podcast*, episode 10, Nigel Drenier, 5 Sept. 2015. https://www.youtube.com/watch?v=SwPF7OoQ15s&t=17s

Flickering Images On A Screen

1. Michael Aronson. *Nickelodeon City: Pittsburgh at the Movies, 1905-1929*. University of Pittsburgh Press, 2008.
2. William Paul. *When Movies Were Theater: Architecture, Exhibition, and the Evolution of American Film.* Columbia University Press, 2016.
3. "A Very Short History of Cinema." *Science and Media Museum*, 18 June 2020. https://www.scienceandmediamuseum.org.uk/objects-and-stories/very-short-history-of-cinema

A Face To Be Found Everywhere

1. Chandler Sprague. "Mabel Normand's Own Life Story!" *Los Angeles Examiner,* Feb 1924.
2. Sidney Sutherland. "Madcap Mabel Normand." *Liberty Magazine*, 6 Sep 1930.

D. W. Griffith

1. Kenneth S Lynn. "The Torment of DW Griffith." *American Scholar*, vol 59, issue 2, 3 Jan 1990, pp. 255-264.
2. Kelly Brown. "Florence Lawrence." *Women Film Pioneers Project,* https://wfpp.columbia.edu/pioneer/ccp-florence-lawrence/

3. Linda Arvidson. *When the Movies Were Young.* E.P. Dutton & Company, 1925.
4. *The Birth of a Nation.* Directed by D.W. Griffith, Performances by Lillian Gish, Mae Marsh, and Frank E. Woods, David W. Griffith Corp., 1915.
5. *Intolerance.* Directed by D.W. Griffith, Performances by Lillian Gish, Robert Harron, and Mae Marsh, David W. Griffith Corp., Wark Producing Corp., 1916.

"Great Big Brown Eyes, And Eyelashes Two Inches Long"

1. Chandler Sprague. "Mabel Normand's Own Life Story!" *Los Angeles Examiner,* Feb 1924.
2. Sidney Sutherland. "Madcap Mabel Normand." *Liberty Magazine*, 6 Sep 1930.
3. Mary Pickford. "Mary Pickford's Daily Talk Chatty Letters From Photoplay Favorite Mabel Normand, Who Played Villlanesses." *Long Beach Press*, 8 Sept 1916, p. 8.

Mack Sennett

1. Chandler Sprague. "Mabel Normand's Own Life Story!" *Los Angeles Examiner,* Feb 1924.
2. Mack Sennett and Cameron Shipp. *The King of Comedy.* iUniverse, 1954.
3. Linda Arvidson. *When the Movies Were Young.* E.P. Dutton & Company, 1925.

Starting from Scratch

1. Chandler Sprague. "Mabel Normand's Own Life Story!" *Los Angeles Examiner,* Feb 1924.
2. Lida Livingston. "Ford Sterling Seen Victor Against Illness." *Los Angeles Evening News,* 4 Aug 1939, p. 9.

3. Linda Arvidson. *When the Movies Were Young,* E.P. Dutton & Company, 1925.
4. Drenier, Nigel, host. "All About Aunt Mabel." *Modern Times Podcast*, episode 10, Nigel Drenier, Sept. 2015. https://www.youtube.com/watch?v=SwPF7OoQ15s&t=17s

John Bunny

1. Wes D. Gehring. *"John Bunny: America's First Important Film Comedian." Literature/Film Quarterly,* 1995. PP 120-124.
2. "A Brief History of the Vitagraph Studios - A short Film from Tony Susnick." YouTube, uploaded by Tony Susnick, 12 Oct. 2014, https://www.youtube.com/watch?v=FiOXH7LqgL4

"Troublesome Secretaries"

1. *Wilful Peggy.* Directed by D.W. Griffith. Performances by Mary Pickford, Clara T. Bracy, and Henry. B. Walthall, American Mutoscope and Biograph, 1910.
2. Sidney Sutherland. "Madcap Mabel Normand." *Liberty Magazine*, 6 Sep 1930.
3. *Troublesome Secretaries.* Directed by Ralph Ince. Performances by John Bunny, Ralph Ince, Mabel Normand, and Alec B. Francis, Vitagraph Company of America, 1911.
4. *Betty Becomes a Maid.* Performances by Mabel Normand, Evangeline Blaisdell, and James Morrison, Vitagraph Company of America, 1911.
5. *The Subduing of Mrs. Nag.* Directed by George D Baker. Performances by John Bunny, Flora Finch, and Mabel Normand, Vitagraph Company of America, 1911.
6. Sidney Sutherland. "Madcap Mabel Normand." *Liberty Magazine*, 6 Sep 1930.
7. Mack Sennett and Cameron Shipp. *The King of Comedy.* iUniverse, 1954.

8. Drenier, Nigel, host. "All About Aunt Mabel." *Modern Times Podcast*, episode 10, Nigel Drenier, 5 Sept. 2015. https://www.youtube.com/watch?v=SwPF7OoQ15s&t=17s

Fred Mace

1. "Fred Mace Dies Suddenly." *The New York Times,* 22 Feb 1917, p. 11.
2. "Fred Mace to Be Buried in East." *Los Angeles Evening Express,* 22 Feb 1917, p. 2.
3. *The New York Times,* Mar 1907.
4. Craig Owens. "Fred Mace – Photos and Quotes." *Bizarre Los Angeles,* 8 May 2018, https://bizarrela.com/2018/05/fred-mace-photos-quotes/
5. *The Diving Girl.* Directed by Mack Sennett, Performances by Mabel Normand, Fred Mace, and William J. Butler, Biograph Company, 1911.
6. *A Dash Through the Clouds.* Directed by Mack Sennett. Performed by Mabel Normand, Fred Mace, and Phillip Orlin Parmelee, Biograph Company, 1912.

"A Determined And Unrepentant Comedienne"

1. *Saved From Himself.* Directed by D.W. Griffith. Performances by Mabel Normand, Joseph Graybill, William J. Butler, and Charles Hill Mailes, Biograph Company, 1911.
2. *The Eternal Mother.* Directed by D.W. Griffith, Performances by Blanche Sweet, Mabel Normand, Edwin August, and Charles Hill Mailes, Biograph Company, 1912.
3. *A Squaw's Love.* Directed by D.W. Griffith. Performances by Mabel Normand, Dark Cloud, and Alfred Paget, Biograph Company, 1911.
4. Chandler Sprague. "Mabel Normand's Own Life Story!" *Los Angeles Examiner,* Feb 1924.

Ford Sterling

1. Wendy Warwick White. *Ford Sterling: The Life and Films,* McFarland, 2007.
2. *Keystone Hotel.* Directed by Ralph Staub. Performances by Ford Sterling, Chester Conklin, and Ben Turpin, The Vitaphone Corporation, Warner Bros. Pictures, 1935.
3. Hubbard Keavy. "Ford Sterling Back, Broke But Still Gay." *Sioux City Journal,* 28 April 1935, p. 4.
4. *Barney Oldfield's Race for A Life.* Directed by Mack Sennett, Performances by Mabel Normand, Ford Sterling, Barney Oldfield, and Mack Sennett, Keystone Film Company, 1913.
5. "(1/2) Ford Sterling – marked." YouTube, uploaded by Jayne Osborne, 19 Nov 2012. https://www.youtube.com/watch?v=zF2ipyKtCfA
6. "(2/2) Ford Sterling inurnment niche is finally marked!" YouTube, uploaded by Jayne Osborne, 19 Nov 2012. https://www.youtube.com/watch?v=TDS0i1j3kwY

"The Diving Girl"

1. Mack Sennett and Cameron Shipp. *The King of Comedy.* iUniverse, 1954.
2. *The Diving Girl.* Directed by Mack Sennett, Performances by Mabel Normand, Fred Mace, and William J. Butler, Biograph Company, 1911.
3. *Her Awakening.* Directed by D.W. Griffith. Performances by Mabel Normand, Kate Bruce, and Harry Hyde, Biograph Company, 1911.
4. Sidney Sutherland. "Madcap Mabel Normand." *Liberty Magazine*, 6 Sep 1930.
5. Adam Kessell. *Internet Movie Database. https://www.imdb.com/name/nm0450254/*

Thomas Edison

1. Mack Sennett and Cameron Shipp. *The King of Comedy.* iUniverse, 1954.
2. "Decline of the Edison Company." *Library of Congress,* https://www.loc.gov/collections/edison-company-motion-pictures-and-sound-recordings/articles-and-essays/history-of-edison-motion-pictures/decline-of-the-edison-company/
3. "How Thomas Edison (Accidentally) Created Hollywood." YouTube, uploaded by Business Casual, Feb 1, 2019, https://www.youtube.com/watch?v=24AH2d6sGmA

California

1. Mack Sennett and Cameron Shipp. *The King of Comedy.* iUniverse, 1954.
2. Sidney Sutherland. "Madcap Mabel Normand." *Liberty Magazine*, 13 Sep 1930.
3. Chandler Sprague. "Mabel Normand's Own Life Story!" *Los Angeles Examiner,* Feb 1924.
4. Slater, Marilyn. *Looking for Mabel Normand.* (Retrieved 2022/2023). https://www.looking-for-mabel-normand.com/marilyn.htm

Roscoe Arbuckle

1. Stuart Oderman. *Roscoe "Fatty" Arbuckle: A Biography of the Silent Film Comedian, 1887-1933,* McFarland, 2005.
2. "Roscoe Arbuckle." *Britannica,* https://www.britannica.com/biography/Roscoe-Arbuckle
3. I.S. Mowis. "Minta Durfee Biography." *Internet Movie Database.* https://www.imdb.com/name/nm0244030/bio/?ref_=nm_ov_bio_sm
4. Gilbert King. "The Skinny on the Fatty Arbuckle Trial." *Smithsonian Magazine,* 8 Nov 2011. https://www.

smithsonianmag.com/history/the-skinny-on-the-fatty-arbuckle-trial-131228859/

5. Jennifer Rosenberg. "The 'Fatty' Arbuckle Scandal." *ThoughtCo.,* 21 July 2019. https://www.thoughtco.com/fatty-arbuckle-scandal-1779625

A Comedy Of Irreverence

1. Mack Sennett and Cameron Shipp. *The King of Comedy.* iUniverse, 1954.
2. *The Brave Hunter.* Directed by Mack Sennett. Performances by Mabel Normand, Mack Sennett, and Dell Henderson, Biograph Company, 1912.
3. *The Tragedy of a Dress Suit.* Directed by Mack Sennett. Performances by Mabel Normand, Ford Sterling, and Dell Henderson, Biograph Company, 1912.
4. *Mabel's Stratagem.* Directed by Mack Sennett. Performances by Mabel Normand, Fred Mace, and Alice Davenport, Keystone Film Company, 1912.
5. *A Dash Through the Clouds.* Directed by Mack Sennett. Performed by Mabel Normand, Fred Mace, and Phillip Orlin Parmelee, Biograph Company, 1912.
6. *Tomboy Bessie.* Directed by Mack Sennett. Performances by Mabel Normand, and Mack Sennett, Biograph Company, 1912.
7. Drenier, Nigel, host. "All About Aunt Mabel." *Modern Times Podcast*, episode 10, Nigel Drenier, Sept. 2015. https://www.youtube.com/watch?v=SwPF7OoQ15s&t=17s
8. Phillip Orlin Parmelee. *Internet Movie Database.* https://www.imdb.com/name/nm0663095/?ref_=tt_cl_t_3
9. Slater, Marilyn. *Looking for Mabel Normand.* https://www.looking-for-mabel-normand.com/marilyn.htm (Retrieved 2022/2023).

Barney Oldfield

1. Michael Kernan. "Wow! A mile a minute!" *Smithsonian,* vol.1, no.2, May 1998.
2. *Barney Oldfield's Race for A Life.* Directed by Mack Sennett. Performances by Mabel Normand, Ford Sterling, Mack Sennett, and Barney Oldfield, Keystone Film Company, 1913.

Insanity Can Be Fun

1. *The Speed Kings.* Directed by Wilfred Lucas. Performances by Mabel Normand, Ford Sterling, Roscoe Arbuckle, Earl Cooper, and Teddy Tetzlaff, Keystone Film Company, 1913.
2. Keystone Cops. *IMDB.* https://www.imdb.com/name/nm0465957/
3. *A Muddy Romance.* Directed by Mack Sennett. Performances by Mabel Normand, Ford Sterling, Charles Inslee, and Minta Durfee, Keystone Film Company, 1913.
4. *Barney Oldfield's Race for A Life.* Directed by Mack Sennett. Performances by Mabel Normand, Ford Sterling, Mack Sennett, and Barney Oldfield, Keystone Film Company, 1913.

Minta Durfee

1. Minta Durfee Interviewed By Stephen Normand and Don Schneider, 1974. https://www.angelfire.com/mn/hp/minta2.html
2. I.S. Mowis. "Minda Durfee Biography." *Internet Movie Database.* https://www.imdb.com/name/nm0244030/bio/?ref_=nm_ov_bio_sm
3. *A Quiet Little Wedding.* Directed by Wilfred Lucas. Performances by Minta Durfee, Roscoe Arbuckle, and Chales Inslee, Keystone Film Company, 1913.
4. *Portnoy's Complaint.* Directed by Ernest Lehman, performances by Richard Benjamin, Karen Black, and Minta Durfee, Chenault Productions, Warner Bros. Pictures, 1972.

5. *A Muddy Romance.* Directed by Mack Sennett. Performances by Mabel Normand, Ford Sterling, Charles Inslee, and Minta Durfee, Keystone Film Company, 1913.
6. Evelyn Wells. "Minta Talks Hats, 'Fatty' Laughs at Reporter's Jokes, As Trial Nears; Relatives Stand By Accused Comedian." *Des Moines Tribune,* 28 September 1921, p.9.
7. Universal Service. "Mrs. Arbuckle Gets Divorce From Erstwhile Famous 'Fatty.' *Pomona Progress Bulletin,* 1 January 1924. P. 1.
8. "Minta Arbuckle Forgets Vow To 'Stick By' Fatty." *Pomona Progress Bulletin*, 1 Jan 1924, p.3.

Moving Behind The Camera

1. *Barney Oldfield's Race for A Life.* Directed by Mack Sennett. Performances by Mabel Normand, Ford Sterling, Mack Sennett, and Barney Oldfield, Keystone Film Company, 1913.
2. *Mabel's Dramatic Career.* Directed by Mack Sennett. Performed by Mabel Normand, Mack Sennett, Roscoe Arbuckle, and Ford Sterling, Keystone Film Company, 1913.
3. "They Really Have Voices." *Lost Angeles Times, 15* Feb 1913, p. 19.
4. W.A. Cory Secretary. "San Francisco Exhibitor's Ball." *The Moving Picture World,* April-June 1913, p. 1010.
5. *The Motion Picture World.* Dec 1913.
6. "Mabel Normand Only Woman Director in the World." *The Marysville Appeal,* 17 May 1914. P. 6.
7. Drenier, Nigel, host. "All About Aunt Mabel." *Modern Times Podcast*, episode 10, Nigel Drenier, Sept. 2015. https://www.youtube.com/watch?v=SwPF7OoQ15s&t=17s
8. Women in the Labor force." *Infoplease,* 5 Aug 2020. https://www.infoplease.com/business/labor/women-labor-force

9. "Mabel's Firsts." *Mabel Normand Estate.* https://mabelenormand.com/about-mabel/mabels-firsts/
10. Brent E. Walker. *Mack Sennett's Fun Factory: a history and filmography of his studios and his Keystone and Mack Sennett Comedies, with biographies of players and personnel.* McFarland and CO. Inc., 2010.
11. Mabel Normand. *Internet Movie Database.* https://www.imdb.com/name/nm0635667/
12. *Won In a Cupboard.* Directed by Mabel Normand. Performances by Mabel Normand, Charles Inslee, Alice Davenport, Charles Avery, Keystone Film Company, 1914.

Charlie Chaplin

1. *Modern Times.* Directed by Charlie Chaplin. Performances by Charlie Chaplin, Paulette Goddard, Charles Chaplin Productions, United Artists, 1936.
2. Charlie Chaplin. *My Autobiography.* Simon and Schuster, 1964.
3. Vijay Prashad. "The Political Life And Cinema Of Comrade Charlie Chaplin." *The Wire,* 29 Jul 2017, https://thewire.in/external-affairs/charlie-chaplin-communism
4. Charlie Chaplin, and Lisa Stein Haven. *A Comedian Sees the World.* University of Missouri, 2014.
5. *A Countess from Hong Kong.* Directed by Charlie Chaplin. Performances by Marlon Brando, Sophia Lorren, and Sydney Chaplin. Universal Pictures, Charlie Chaplin Productions, 1967.
6. *City Lights.* Directed by Charlie Chaplin. Performances by Charlie Chaplin, Virginia Cherill, and Harry Myers, Charlie Chaplin Productions, United Artists, 1931.
7. *The Kid.* Directed by Charlie Chaplin. Performances by Charlie Chaplin, Edna Purveance, and Jackie Coogan, Charlie Chaplin Productions, 1931.

8. *The Great Dictator.* Directed by Charlie Chaplin. Performances by Charlie Chaplin, and Claudette Goddard, Roy Export Company Establishment, United Artists, 1940.
9. Sidney Sutherland. "Madcap Mabel Normand." *Liberty Magazine*, 13 Sep 1930.

Also Known As Muriel Fortescue

1. "Mabel Normand Only Woman Director in the World." *The Marysville Appeal,* 17 May 1914. P. 6.
2. *Lyons Daily News.* 11 Mar 1914.
3. *The Sea Nymph.* Directed by Mack Sennett. Performed by Mabel Normand, Mack Sennett, and Ford Sterling. Keystone Film Company, 1912.
4. Al G. Waddell. "Big Bakersfield Races Will be Held Today." *The Los Angeles Times,* 22 April 1914. P. 26.
5. *Perth Sunday Times,* 5 May 1914.
6. "MOVIE ACTTRESS, 20 YEARS OLD, IS HER OWN MANAGER: Miss Mabel Normand Dares Death Cheerfully and Often in Order to Provide Thrills for Patrons on Film Dramatic Productions." *The Sunday Oregonian,* 25 Jan 1914.
7. *Mable's Blunder.* Directed by Mabel Normand. Performances by Mabel Normand, Harry McCoy, and Charley Chase, Keystone Film Company, 1914.
8. *Those Country Kids.* Directed by Roscoe Arbuckle. Performances by Mabel Normand, Roscoe Arbuckle and Al St. John, Keystone Film Company, 1914.
9. Drenier, Nigel, host. "All About Aunt Mabel." *Modern Times Podcast*, episode 10, Nigel Drenier, Sept. 2015. https://www.youtube.com/watch?v=SwPF7OoQ15s&t=17s
10. Charlie Chaplin. *My Autobiography.* Simon and Schuster, 1964.

11. *Mabel's Strange Predicament.* Directed by Mabel Normand. Performances by Mabel Normand, Charlie Chaplin, Alice Davenport, and Chester Conklin, Keystone Film Company, 1914.
12. *Mabel at the Wheel.* Directed By Mabel Normand, Performances by Mabel Normand, Charlie Chaplin, and Harry McCoy, Keystone Film Company, 1914.

Marie Dressler

1. *Dinner at Eight.* Directed by George Cukor. Performances by Marie Dressler, John Barrymore, and Wallace Berry. Metro-Goldwyn-Mayer, 1933.
2. Hedda Hopper. "Marie Dressler, Mary Garden, Intrigue Hedda." *The Spokesman Review*, 17 Jan, 1953, p.9.
3. Barbara Garrick. "The Dressler Story," *Marie Dressler Foundation*, 1997.
4. *Time Magazine.* 7 Aug 1933.
5. Tony Fontana. Marie Dressler. *Internet Movie Database. https://www.imdb.com/name/nm0237597/bio/?ref_=nm_ov_bio_sm*
6. "Tillies Nightmare." *Playbill.* https://playbill.com/production/tillies-nightmarebroadway-herald-square-theatre-1910
7. *Tillie's Punctured Romance.* Directed by Mack Sennett. Performances by Marie Dressler, Mabel Normand, and Charlie Chaplin. Keystone Film Company, 1914.
8. *Min and Bill.* Directed by George W. Hill. Performances by Marie Dressler, Dorothy Johnson, and Wallace Berry. Metro-Goldwyn-Mayer, 1930.

The First Feature Length Comedy

1. Ventura, Michael. "Funny Lady." *Los Angeles Magazine*, 1 June 2009, pp. 62-64.

2. McCarthy, Jay. "Eyes on the pies: how Mabel Normand, Chaplin's mentor, changed cinema." The Guardian, 7 Sept. 2018. https://www.theguardian.com/film/2018/sep/07/eyes-on-the-pies-how-mabel-normand-chaplins-mentor-changed-cinema
3. Slater, Marilyn. *Looking for Mabel Normand.* https://www.looking-for-mabel-normand.com/marilyn.htm (Retrieved 2022/2023).
4. *Mabel's Busy Day.* Directed by Mack Sennett. Performances by Mabel Normand, Charlie Chaplin, and Chester Conklin, Keystone Film Company, 1914.
5. *His Trysting Place.* Directed by Charlie Chaplin. Performances by Mabel Normand, Charlie Chaplin, and Mack Swain, Keystone Film Company, 1914.
6. *Mabel at the Wheel.* Directed By Mabel Normand, Performances by Mabel Normand, Charlie Chaplin, and Harry McCoy, Keystone Film Company, 1914.
7. Sidney Sutherland. "Madcap Mabel Normand." *Liberty Magazine*, 20 Sep 1930.
8. Chandler Sprague. "Mabel Normand's Own Life Story!" *Los Angeles Examiner,* Feb 1924.
9. Charlie Chaplin. *My Autobiography.* Simon and Schuster, 1964.
10. *Tillie's Punctured Romance.* Directed by Mack Sennett. Performances by Marie Dressler, Mabel Normand, and Charlie Chaplin. Keystone Film Company, 1914.
11. "Where Picture Features Flourish." *The Reading Times,* 22 Mar 1915, p. 4.
12. "At The Theaters." *The Fresno Morning Republican,* 21 Mar 1915, p. 19.
13. "Big Comedy Film Opens At Modesto Theater Sunday." *Modesto Morning Herald,* 3 Mar 1915, p.3

14. "Tillies Punctured Romance." *The Daily Times,* 15 June 1915, p. 8.
15. "The World's Champion Comedy." *The Daily Times,* 15 June 1915, p. 9.

Franz Ferdinand

1. "Assassination of Archduke Franz Ferdinand: Topics in Chronicling America." *Library of Congress,* https://guides.loc.gov/chronicling-america-assassination-franz-ferdinand
2. Leslie Midkiff DeBauche. *Reel Patriotism: The Movies and World War*, University of Wisconsin Press. 1997.

"Queen of the Movies"

1. Slater, Marilyn. *Looking for Mabel Normand,* https://looking-for-mabel.webs.com/reprintarchive.htm#87649157 (Retrieved 2022/2023).
2. Slater, Marilyn, *Looking for Mabel Normand,* https://looking-for-mabel.webs.com/10otherhomesofmabe.htm (Retrieved 2022/2023).
3. *Mabel and Fatty and the Law.* Directed by Roscoe Arbuckle. Performances by Mabel Normand, Roscoe Arbuckle, and Minta Durfee, Mack Sennett Comedies, 1915.
4. *Mabel and Fatty's Married Life.* Directed by Roscoe Arbuckle. Performed by Mabel Normand, Roscoe Arbuckle, and *Dan* Albert, Keystone Film Company, 1915.
5. *Fatty and Mabel at the San Diego Exposition.* Directed by Roscoe Arbuckle. Performances by Mabel Normand, and Roscoe Arbuckle, Keystone Film Company, 1915.
6. *Mabel and Fatty Viewing the World Fair at San Francisco.* Directed by Mabel Normand, and Roscoe Arbuckle. Performances by Mabel Normand, and Roscoe Arbuckle. Keystone Film Company, 1915.

7. Slater, Marilyn. *Looking for Mabel Normand,* https://looking-for-mabel.webs.com/burbankvisittomabel.htm (Retrieved 2022/2023).
8. Grace Kingsley. *Photoplay,* 1915.
9. Karnick, Kristine Brunovska. "MABEL NORMAND: NEW WOMAN IN THE FLAPPER AGE." *Hysterical!: Women in American Comedy.* edited by Linda Mizejewski, and Victoria Sturtevant. University of Texas Press, 2017.
10. Drenier, Nigel, host. "All About Aunt Mabel." *Modern Times Podcast*, episode 10, Nigel Drenier, Sept. 2015. https://www.youtube.com/watch?v=SwPF7OoQ15s&t=17s

Mae Busch

1. "Mae Busch, Broke, Tells Own Story of 'Going Hollywood' Toll." *The San Francisco Examiner*, 13 Feb 1929, p. 21.
2. Marilyn Slater. *Looking for Mabel Normand,* https://looking-for-mabel.webs.com/maebusch.htm (Retrieved 2022/2023).
3. *Germ Magazine,* 23, Dec 2014, https://germmagazine.com/day-342-2014/
4. *Unaccustomed As We Are.* Directed by Hal Roach, and Lewis R. Foster, Performances by Stan Larel, Oliver Hardy, and Mae Busch. Hal Roach Studios, 1929.
5. *Ladies Man.* Directed by William D. Russell. Performances by Eddie Bracken, Cass Daley, and Mae Busch, Paramount Pictures, 1947.
6. "BARREN!" Mae Busch. *Daily News*, 21 Sep 1924. P. 124.

Beyond The Breaking Point

1. Charlie Chaplin. *My Autobiography.* Simon and Schuster, 1964.
2. Drenier, Nigel, host. "All About Aunt Mabel." *Modern Times Podcast*, episode 10, Nigel Drenier, Sept. 2015. https://www.youtube.com/watch?v=SwPF7OoQ15s&t=17s

3. Minta Durfee Interviewed By Stephen Normand and Don Schneider, 1974. https://www.angelfire.com/mn/hp/minta2.html
4. Anne Helen Peterson. "Hollywood's Bathing Beauties." *Lapham's Quarterly,* 13 Aug 2013. https://www.laphamsquarterly.org/roundtable/hollywoods-bathing-beauties#:~:text=For%20every%20Megan%20Fox%2C%20you,of%20the%20oversaturated%20laugh%20market
5. *Settled At the Seaside.* Directed by Frank Griffin. Performances by Charley Chase and Mae Busch. Keystone Film Company, 1915.

Vincent Chiappa

1. "Noted Italian Churchman Here All Next Week." *Bakersfield Morning Echo,* 30 April 1926, p. 3.
2. *Our Sunday Visitor.* 8 Mar 1929, p.3.
3. "The Catholic Mission In Anaconda." *The Anaconda Standard,* 28 Mar 1910, p. 2.
4. Reverend Vincent Chiappa, S.J. "The Catholic Church." *The Anaconda Standard,* 28 Mar 1910, p. 3.
5. "Ten Day Mission Opens At Saint Patrick's Church, Rev. Father Vincent Chiappa Will Have Charge." *The San Francisco Call and Post,* 6 Dec 1911, p.10
6. "Coming Events." *The Whitefish Pilot,* 2 Feb 1911, p.8.
7. "St. Thomas Indian Chapel." *The Tidings,* 24 December 1924, pp. 9-10
8. Herbert Howe. "Hollywood's Hall of Fame: Mabel Normand" *New Movie Magazine,* https://www.silentera.com/taylorology/issues/Taylor88.txt

Mabel Normand Studio

1. "Mabel Normand's Condition Improves." *Los Angeles Times,* 20 Sept 15, P. 5

2. "Film Flashes." *The Baltimore Sun,* 7 Nov 1915. P.39
3. *The Fresno Morning Republican,* 12 Dec 1915, pp.26-27.
4. "Keystone Company Builds $500,000 Film Factory for Mabel Normand." *The Tacoma Times,* 11 Sep 1915, p. 7
5. Dana Stevens. "Why Women In Hollywood Had More Power In 1916 Than They Do Now." Slate, 29 Jan 2022, https://slate.com/culture/2022/01/charlie-chaplin-buster-keaton-mabel-normand-female-directors.html
6. Aaron Barlow, editor. *Star Power: The Impact of Branded Celebrity.* Praeger, 2014.

Minnie Devereaux

1. "Indian Woman Tells History." *Mack Sennett Weekly,* vol. 1, 1917.
2. *A Dash Through the Clouds.* Directed by Mack Sennett. Performed by Mabel Normand, Fred Mace, and Phillip Orlin Parmelee, Biograph Company, 1912.
3. Robert E. Hayes. "Frontier Dr. A Man of Many Achievements." *Deadwood Magazine*, Jan/Feb 1999.
4. Christopher Klein. "What Happened At The Wounded Knee Massacre?" *History,* 13 May 2022. https://www.history.com/news/wounded-knee-massacre-facts
5. N, Evans. Photo

Mickey

1. Pearl Gaddis. *Motion Picture Magazine,* Dec 1916.
2. "Flickerings from Filmland." *Chicago Tribune,* 29 May 1916, p. 14.
3. "Sennett to Manage Mabel Normand." *Chicago Tribune,* 10 Jan 1917, p.12.
4. "Mabel Quits Screen For Year To Create Masterpiece." *The Butte Miner,* 22 April 1917. p. 41.

5. "Mabel Quits Screen For Year To Create Masterpiece." *The Santa Fe New Mexican,* 27 April 1917. p. 2.
6. Aaron Barlow, editor. *Star Power: The Impact of Branded Celebrity.* Praeger, 2014.
7. *Mickey.* Directed by F. Richard Jones, and Mabel Normand. Performances by Mabel Normand, Lew Cody, and Minta Durfee. Mabel Normand Feature Film Company, 1918.
8. "Accused of Attempt To Blackmail Screen Star." *The Los Angeles Times,* 26 Aug 1916, p. 11.
9. "Doctor Raymond A. Swett Arrested, Mabel Normand His Accuser." *The Los Angeles Examiner,* 25, Aug 1916.
10. "Chance To Fleece Actress." *Los Angeles Evening Herald,* 25 Aug 1916.
11. "Blackmailer's Given Freedom." *The Los Angeles Times,* 26 Aug. 1916.
12. Sidney Sutherland. "Madcap Mabel Normand." *Liberty Magazine*, 20 Sep 1930.
13. Drenier, Nigel, host. "All About Aunt Mabel." *Modern Times Podcast*, episode 10, Nigel Drenier, Sept. 2015. https://www.youtube.com/watch?v=SwPF7OoQ15s&t=17s

Samuel Goldwyn

1. Samuel Goldwyn. *Behind the Screen.* George H. Doran Company, 1923.
2. David E. Smith. "Samuel Goldwyn Biography." *Internet Movie Database.* https://www.imdb.com/name/nm0326418/bio/?ref_=nm_ov_bio_sm
3. "1890 Fast Facts." *United States Census Bureau,* 12 Dec 2022. https://www.census.gov/history/www/through_the_decades/fast_facts/1890_fast_facts.html
4. *The Squaw Man.* Directed by Cecil B. Demille. Performances by Warner Baxter and Lupe Velez, Metro-Goldwyn-Mayer Corp, 1931.

5. Chuck Frownfelter. "Scholar's Spotlight: Sameul Goldwyn." *Cinema Scholars,* 12 Oct 2022, https://cinemascholars.com/scholars-spotlight-samuel-goldwyn/
6. *Porgy And Bess.* Directed by Otto Preminger. Performances by Sidney Poitier, Dorothy Dandridge, and Samm Davis Junior, Samuel Goldwyn Productions, Inc., 1959.
7. *Guys and Dolls.* Directed by Joseph L. Mankiewicz. Performances by Marlon Brando, Jean Simmons, and Frank Sinatra. Metro-Goldwyn-Mayer Corp.; Samuel Goldwyn Productions, Inc., 1955.
8. *The Best Years of Our Lives.* Directed by William Wyler. Performances by Fredrick March, Julie Andrews, and Myrna Loy. Samuel Goldwyn Productions, and RKO Radio Pictures, 1946.
9. *The Secret Life of Walter Mitty.* Directed by Normand Z. Mcleod. Performances by Danny Kaye, and Virginia Mayo, Samuel Goldwyn Productions, Inc., 1947.

A Thousand Dollars A Week

1. "The Strange Death Of The Mabel Normand Feature Film Co." *THEKEYSTONEGIRLBLOGS,* 8 Aug 2017, https://thekeystonegirlblogs.wordpress.com/2017/08/08/the-strange-death-of-the-mabel-normand-feature-film-co/
2. Minta Durfee Interviewed By Stephen Normand and Don Schneider, 1974. https://www.angelfire.com/mn/hp/minta2.html
3. Drenier, Nigel, host. "All About Aunt Mabel." *Modern Times Podcast*, episode 10, Nigel Drenier, Sept. 2015. https://www.youtube.com/watch?v=SwPF7OoQ15s&t=17s
4. Meher Tatna. "Forgotten Hollywood: Mabel Normand." *Golden Globe Awards,* 15 April 2021, https://www.goldenglobes.com/articles/forgotten-hollywood-mabel-normand

5. Mark Lynn Anderson. *Twilight of the Idols : Hollywood and the Human Sciences in 1920s America.* University of California Press, 2011.
6. Slater, Marilyn. *Looking for Mabel Normand,* https://looking-for-mabel.webs.com/reprintarchive.htm#87649157 (Retrieved 2022/2023).
7. Aaron Barlow, editor. *Star Power: The Impact of Branded Celebrity.* Praeger, 2014.
8. Linda Mizejewski, and Victoria Sturtevant. *Hysterical! : Women in American Comedy.* Vol. First edition, University of Texas Press, 2017.
9. "Mabel Normand In Goldwyn Pictures." *Calgary Herald,* 10 Nov 1917, p.9.

Edith Wilson

1. Judith L. Weaver. "Edith Bolling Wilson as First Lady: A Study in the Power of Personality, 1919-1920" *Presidential Studies Quarterly,* vol 15, Winter 1985, pp. 51-76.
2. Allida Black. "Edith Bolling Galt Wilson." *The White House, https://www.whitehouse.gov/about-the-white-house/first-families/edith-bolling-galt-wilson/*
3. "Mrs. Wilson Dies; Widow Of President." *The Hartford Courant,* 29 Dec 1961, p.4.
4. Betty Boyd Caroli. "*First Ladies.*" *Oxford University Press,* 1995.
5. Edith Bolling. *My Memoir,* Bobbs-Merrill Company, 1939.
6. "Woodrow Wilson's Widow, Edith Wilson Dies; WWI First Lady." *The Springfield News-Leader,* 29 Dec 1961, p. 1.

"Dark, Windy Days and Chocolate Cake"

1. Norbert Lusk. "The Girl On The Cover." *Picture Page Magazine,* Feb 1918.

2. "Curious About Mabel Normand? Well - ." *Pittsburgh Daily Post,* 17 Mar 1918, p. 16
3. David Raymond. "Mabel Normand Dotes On: Storms, Chocolate Cake, Vampires." *The Winnipeg Tribune,* 30 Mar 1918, p. 30.
4. "Mabel Normand Picks Own Play." *The Muscatine Journal,* 19 April 1918, p. 3.
5. "Helpless Mabel Normand." *The Tampa Times,* 12 Mar 1918, p.13.
6. "Mabel Normand's Dread Is Anything German." *The Winnipeg Tribune,* 15 June 1918. P. 32.
7. Drenier, Nigel, host. "All About Aunt Mabel." *Modern Times Podcast*, episode 10, Nigel Drenier, Sept. 2015. https://www.youtube.com/watch?v=SwPF7OoQ15s&t=17s
8. "'Joan of Plattsburg' With Mabel Normand At The Textile Hall." *The Greenville News,* 14 July 1918, p. 16.
9. Aaron Barlow, editor. *Star Power: The Impact of Branded Celebrity.* Praeger, 2014.

Alexei Nikolaevich Romanov

1. "Why Czar Nicholas II and the Romanovs Were Murdered." *History,* https://www.history.com/news/romanov-family-murder-execution-reasons
2. Drenier, Nigel, host. "All About Aunt Mabel." *Modern Times Podcast*, episode 10, Nigel Drenier, Sept. 2015. https://www.youtube.com/watch?v=SwPF7OoQ15s&t=17s

Hollywood Pioneer

1. "Mickey: The Forgotten Blockbuster." *FilmsRanked,* 12 Dec 2021, https://www.filmsranked.com/mickey-the-forgotten-blockbuster/

2. Drenier, Nigel, host. “All About Aunt Mabel.” *Modern Times Podcast*, episode 10, Nigel Drenier, Sept. 2015. https://www.youtube.com/watch?v=SwPF7OoQ15s&t=17s
3. Sidney Sutherland. “Madcap Mabel Normand.” *Liberty Magazine*, 20 Sep 1930.
4. *Springfield News-Sun,* 29 Jun 1919, p.48.
5. “’Mickey’ Wins Commendation Of Movie Reformers.” *Lansing State Journal*, 29 Mar 1919, p. 8.
6. Sidney Sutherland. “Madcap Mabel Normand.” *Liberty Magazine*, 20 Sep 1930.
7. *Mickey.* Directed by F. Richard Jones, and Mabel Normand. Performances by Mabel Normand, Lew Cody, and Minta Durfee. Mabel Normand Feature Film Company, 1918.

F. Richard Jones

1. Chandler Sprague. “Mabel Normand’s Own Life Story!” *Los Angeles Examiner,* 9 Mar 1924.
2. Harry Carr. “Dick Jones Hollywood Anomaly.” *The Los Angeles Times,* 21 Dec 1930, p. 35.
3. “F. Richard Jones Biography.” *Internet Movie Database,* https://www.imdb.com/name/nm0428059/bio/?ref_=nm_ov_bio_sm
4. Jones, Ada, and Murray, Billy. “When Francis Dances With Me.” *Victor,* 1921. https://www.loc.gov/item/jukebox-41933/
5. “Irene Lenz Leaps To Death.” *Fallon County Times,* 22 Nov 1962, p. A5.

Back To Mack (Professionally)

1. Chandler Sprague. “Mabel Normand’s Own Life Story!” *Los Angeles Examiner,* 16 Mar 1924.
2. “Mabel Normand Inspiration Says George Loane Tucker.” *The Edmonton Bulletin,* 16 Mar 1918, p.11

3. "Mabel Normand Pancakes." *The Baltimore Sun,* 23 June 1918, p. 31.
4. "Mabel Normand Creates Chief Costume." *Calgary Herald,* 4 July 1918, p. 10.
5. "Obliging Herself." *The New Britain Herald,* 2 Aug 1918, p.6.
6. *Albany Evening Journal*. "A Movie Kiss." *The New Britain Herald*, 2 Aug 1918, p. 6.
7. "Mabel Normand's Gowns." *The New Britain Herald*, 2 Aug 1918, p. 6.
8. *What Happened to Rosa?* Directed by Victor Schertzinger. Performances by Mabel Normand, and Doris Pawn, Goldwyn Pictures Corp., 1920.
9. Anne Helen Peterson. "Hollywood's Bathing Beauties." *Lapham's Quarterly,* 13 Aug 2013. https://www.laphamsquarterly.org/roundtable/hollywoods-bathing-beauties#:~:text=For%20every%20Megan%20Fox%2C%20you,of%20the%20oversaturated%20laugh%20market
10. *Joan of Plattsburg*. Directed by William Humphrey and George Loane Tucker. Performances by Mabel Normand, William Fredric, and Robert Elliott, Goldwyn Pictures Corporation, 1918.
11. *Jinx*. Directed by Victor Schertzinger. Performed by Mabel Normand, and Florence Carpenter. Goldwyn Pictures Corporation, 1919.
12. Anthony Anderson. *The Los Angeles Times,* 27 May 1918, p. 16.
13. *The Floor Below.* Directed by Clarence G. Badger. Performances by Mabel Normand, and Tom Moore, Goldwyn Pictures Corporation, 1918.
14. *Variety*, 11 Feb 1921.

Virginia Rappe

1. Jennifer Rosenberg. “The ‘Fatty’ Arbuckle Scandal.” *ThoughtCo.,* 21 July 2019. https://www.thoughtco.com/fatty-arbuckle-scandal-1779625
2. Gilbert King. “The Skinny on the Fatty Arbuckle Trial.” *Smithsonian Magazine,* 8 Nov 2011. https://www.smithsonianmag.com/history/the-skinny-on-the-fatty-arbuckle-trial-131228859/
3. Clemence Michallon. “Who was Virginia Rappe? The true story of the rising career and shocking death of a 1920s star – and the Fatty Arbuckle trial.” *The Independent,* 9 Sep 2020.

Molly O’

1. *The Victoria Daily Times,* 6 June 1919, p. 13.
2. *Molly O’.* Directed by F. Richard Jones. Performances by Mabel Normand, Anna Hernandez, and George Nichols, Mack Sennett--Mabel Normand Productions, 1921.
3. Marilyn Slater. *Looking for Mabel Normand,* https://looking-for-mabel.webs.com/maebusch.htm (Retrieved 2022/2023).
4. “Cinderella Of The Screen.” *The Tacoma Daily Ledger,* 4 Dec 1921. P. 51.
5. *Suzanna.* Directed by F. Richard Jones. Performances by Mabel Normand, and George Nichols, Mack Sennett Productions, 1923.

William Desmond Taylor

1. Bruce Long. *William Desmond Taylor: A Dossier,* Rowman & Littlefield Publishers, Inc., 1991.
2. “How I Became A Photoplayer.” *Motion Picture,* Jan 1915. P. 78.
3. Anthony Slide. (1991). Introduction. *William Desmond Taylor: A Dossier,* by Bruce Long, Rowman & Littlefield Publishers, Inc., 1991.

4. "Press Film Star For Taylor Clew [sic]." *The New York Times,* 7 Feb 1922 P. 5.

"Under A Terrible Nervous Strain"

1. Chandler Sprague. "Mabel Normand's Own Life Story!" *Los Angeles Examiner.* 16 Mar 1924.
2. "Actress Expresses Anxiety to Recover Jesting Letters," *Los Angeles Examiner,* 6 Feb 1922.
3. "Press Film Star For Taylor Clew." *The New York Times,* 7 Feb 1922, p.1
4. *Los Angeles Times*, February 6, 1922.
5. "Never Any Love Affair: So Says Mabel Normand." *Los Angeles Record*, 3 Feb 1922.
6. "Assures Her Parents. Mabel Normand Tells Them Police Have Exonerated Her." *The New York Times,* 14 Feb 1922, p. 19.

William Randolph Hearst

1. *Citizen Kane.* Directed by Orson Welles. Performances by Orson Welles, and Joseph Cotton, RKO Radio Pictures, and Mercury Pictures, 1941.
2. David Nasaw. *The Chief: The Life of William Randolph Hearst,* Mariner Books, 2001.
3. "Mr. Hearst saw the insurrection then occurring …", *The New York Times,* (n.d.).
4. *The Perils of Pauline.* Directed by Louis J. Gasnier, and Donald MacKenzie. Performances by Pearl White, and Crane Wilbur, Pathe Freres. 1914.
5. "William Randolph Hearst." *Hearst Castle*, https://hearstcastle.org/history-behind-hearst-castle/historic-people/profiles/william-randolph-hearst/
6. Orrin Konheim. "Who Really Wrote 'Citizen Kane'? Why Was There Controversy Over The Screenwriting Credit?" *The Take,*

https://the-take.com/read/who-really-wrote-citizen-kane-why-was-there-controversy-over-the-screenwriting-credit

Media Assault

1. "'Never Loved Him!' Says Mabel Normand 'On Word Of Honor.'" *San Francisco Bulletin,* 7 Feb 1922, p. 11.
2. Linton Wells. "'Never Any Love Affair'" So Says Mabel Normand. *Los Angeles Record,* 3 Feb 1922.
3. Marilyn Slater. *Looking for Mabel Normand,* Marilyn Slater. *Looking for Mabel Normand,* https://looking-for-mabel.webs.com (Retrieved 2022/2023).
4. Edward Doherty. *New York News*, 5 Feb 1922.
5. Wallace Smith. *Chicago American,* 8 Feb 1922.
6. Mark Lynn Anderson. *Twilight of the Idols: Hollywood and the Human Sciences in 1920s America*. University of California Press, 2011.

William H. Hays

1. Eric Gardner. "The Czar of Hollywood." *Indianapolis Monthly.*
2. William Grimes. "There Will Be Scandal: An Oil Stain on the Jazz Age." *The New York Times,* 13 Feb 2008.
3. "Willian H. Hays". *The Los Angeles Times,* from *The Associated Press,* 8 Mar 1954, https://projects.latimes.com/hollywood/star-walk/will-h-hays/index.html#:~:text=Will%20H.,censorship%20with%20the%20Hays%20Code.
4. "Hollywood Censored: The Production Code." Culture Shock. *Public Broadcasting Service (P.B.S.),* https://www.pbs.org/wgbh/cultureshock/beyond/hollywood.html

Europe

1. Mack Sennett and Cameron Shipp. *The King of Comedy.* iUniverse, 1954.

2. Drenier, Nigel, host. "All About Aunt Mabel." *Modern Times Podcast*, episode 10, Nigel Drenier, Sept. 2015. https://www.youtube.com/watch?v=SwPF7OoQ15s&t=17s
3. "Film Stars To Go Abroad." *The New York Times,* 16 Mar 1922.
4. Marilyn Slater. *Looking for Mabel Normand,* Marilyn Slater. *Looking for Mabel Normand,* https://looking-for-mabel.webs.com (Retrieved 2022/2023).
5. "Mabel Normand Leaves Quietly On The Aquitania." *The Evening World,* 13 Jun 1922, p. 2.
6. "Youth and Moonlight and – Paris." *Photoplay,* December 1922, p. 35.
7. "Between Reels." *Wichita Eagle,* 11 Mar 1923, p. 28.
8. "Betrothed? Nay Blithely Chips Mabel – Again, Nay." *Daily News,* 1 Mar, 1923, p. 17.

Edna Purviance

1. "Edna Purviance, Once Chaplin Film Star, Dies." *Los Angeles Times,* 16 Jan 1958, p. 39.
2. "Edna Purviance Charlie Chaplin's Leading Lady." *A Journey To Paradise...,* https://www.ednapurviance.org/index.html
3. *The Tramp.* Directed by Charlie Chaplin. Performances by Charlie Chaplin, and Lloyd Bacon, The Essanay Film Manufacturing Company, 1915.
4. *The Kid.* Directed by Charlie Chaplin. Performances by Charlie Chaplin, Edna Purviance, and Jackie Coogan, Charlie Chaplin Productions, 1921.
5. *The Idle Class.* Directed by Charlie Chaplin. Performances by Charlie Chaplin, and Edna Purviance, Charles Chaplin Productions, 1921.
6. *A Woman of Paris.* Directed by Charlie Chaplin. Performances by Edna Purviance, and Clarence Gelbert. Charles Chaplin Productions, 1923.

7. Hazel Simpson Naylor. "Little Miss Happiness." *Motion Picture Magazine,* April 1918, p. 75.

The Extra Girl

1. Sidney Sutherland. "Madcap Mabel Normand." *Liberty Magazine*, 4 Oct 1930.
2. *Suzanna.* Directed by F. Richard Jones. Performances by Mabel Normand, and George Nichols, Mack Sennett Comedies, 1923.

Courtland Dines

1. "Denver Assault Rich Mill Owner Assaulted By Prominent Lawyer." *Elbert County Tribune,* 02 Aug 1906, p. 5.
2. Tyson Swinney Dines. Biography. *Find a Grave,* https://www.findagrave.com/memorial/99983605/tyson-swinney-dines
3. Leola Allard. "Bath Parties Of Gay Set In 'Beach Club' Revealed." *The San Francisco Examiner,* 3 Jan 1924, p. 2.
4. "Dines Record is Unsavory." *The Grand Island Independent,* 4 Jan 1924, p. 2.

Another Shooting

1. *The Extra Girl.* Directed by F. Richard Jones. Performances by Mabel Normand, Richard Graves, and George Nichols, Mack Sennett Comedies, 1923.
2. Drenier, Nigel, host. "All About Aunt Mabel." *Modern Times Podcast*, episode 10, Nigel Drenier, Sept. 2015. https://www.youtube.com/watch?v=SwPF7OoQ15s&t=17s
3. Sidney Sutherland. "Madcap Mabel Normand." *Liberty Magazine*, 4 Oct 1930.
4. "TWO MOVIE STARS SEE C.S. DINES SHOT." *The New York Times,* 2 Jan 1924, p.1.
5. "MABEL NORMAN, EDNA PURVIANCE QUIZZED IN L.A. SHOOTING." *The Sane Francisco Examiner,* 2 Jan 1924, p.1.

6. "FILM STARS ON GRILL." *The Cincinnati Post,* 2 Jan 1924, p.1.
7. "COURTLAND DINES BETTER.; Mabel Normand Is Also Reported to Be 'Doing Nicely.'" *The New York Times,* 6 Jan 1924, p. 128.

Asa Keyes

1. "Asa Keyes Succumbs To Stroke." *The Los Angeles Times, 19 Oct 1934, pp. 1 & 3.*
2. Marilyn Slater. "Asa Keyes," 2012.
3. Bruce Long. *William Desmond Taylor: A Dossier,* Rowman & Littlefield Publishers, Inc., 1991.
4. "DISTRICT ATTORNEY KEYES IS ACCUSED!" *The Los Angeles Times,* 01 Nov 1928, p. 1.
5. "Asa Keyes, Former Los Angeles Prosecutor, Dies Of Stroke." *Nevada State Journal,* 19 Oct 1934, p. 2.
6. Roger M. Grace. "Perspectives." *Metropolitan News-Enterprise,* 13 Nov 2007, http://www.metnews.com/articles/2007/perspectives111307.htm
7. "Keyes Had Brilliant Record As Prosecutor." *Fort Worth Star-Telegram,* 19 Oct 1934, p. 2.

Rumors Thrive

1. "Operation On Mabel Normand." *Daily News,* 4 Jan 1924, p. 3.
2. Sidney Sutherland. "Madcap Mabel Normand." *Liberty Magazine*, 11 Oct 1930
3. Aaron Barlow, editor. *Star Power: The Impact of Branded Celebrity.* Praeger, 2014.
4. Fulton Oursler. "Give Mabel Normand A Chance!" *Movie Weekly,* 2 Feb 1924.
5. "Theaters of State Ban Discredited Film Stars." *The Hartford Courant,* 9 Jan 1924, p. 1.

6. Sidney Sutherland. "Madcap Mabel Normand." *Liberty Magazine*, 11 Oct 1930.

Mary Pickford

1. Sidney Sutherland. "Madcap Mabel Normand." *Liberty Magazine*, 11 Oct 1930.
2. Mary Pickford. "New Year's Eve On The Train." *The Lima Times-Democrat*, 03 Jan 1916, p. 9.
3. Drenier, Nigel, host. "All About Aunt Mabel." *Modern Times Podcast*, episode 10, Nigel Drenier, Sept. 2015. https://www.youtube.com/watch?v=SwPF7OoQ15s&t=17s
4. "About May Pickford." *Mary Pickford Foundation.* https://marypickford.org/about-mary/
5. "Mary Pickford, 'America's Sweetheart,' Dies At 86." *The San Francisco Examiner*, 30 May 1979, p. 22.

The Performance Of A Lifetime

1. *The Extra Girl*. Directed by F. Richard Jones. Performances by Mabel Normand, Richard Graves, and George Nichols, Mack Sennett Comedies, 1923.
2. William Thomas Sherman. *MABLE NORMAND A Sourcebook Of Her Life And Films. 7th Ed.,* Gun Jones Publishing, 2006, https://www.angelfire.com/mn/hp/MNSB7.pdf
3. "Calls Mabel Normand To The Greer Trial." *The New York Times,* 17 Apr 1924. p. 9.
4. "Dines Absent as Shooting Is Told," *The Oakland Tribune,* 17 Jun 1924, p.1.
5. "Miss Normand Upsets Court by 'Wise Cracks.'" *Los Angeles Times,* 17 Jun 1924, p.1.
6. "Dines Story Told Be Mabel." *Los Angeles Times,* 17 Jun 1924, p. 21 (Part Two, Page 1).

Al Woods

1. *Chicago Tribune,* 15 Apr 1951.
2. *The Ottawa Citizen,* 30 Mar 1907.
3. *New-York Tribune.* 25 Sep 1909.
4. "Music And Drama," *Vancouver Daily World,* 24 Oct 1908, p. 26.
5. *Chicago Tribune,* 25 Apr 1951.
6. *The Kingston Whig Standard,* 1951.
7. "Woods To Plead Today For His 'Demi Virgin.'" *Daily News,* 21 Nov 1921, p. 7.
8. Sidney Skolsky. "SAMUEL HOFFENSTEIN'S CREATION." *Times Square Tintypes,* Ives Washburn, 1932 via https://cladriteradio.com/times-square-tintypes-a-h-woods/
9. "What The Public Wants." *The Kingston Whig-Standard,* 05 May 1951, p. 4.

"The Little Mouse"

1. *Daily News,* 12 Sep 1924.
2. "Denial is Voiced By Normand." *Los Angeles Times*, 13 Sep 1924.
3. Sidney Sutherland. "Madcap Mabel Normand." *Liberty Magazine*, 11 Oct 1930.
4. William Thomas Sherman. *MABLE NORMAND A Sourcebook Of Her Life And Films. 7th Ed.,* Gun Jones Publishing, 2006, https://www.angelfire.com/mn/hp/MNSB7.pdf
5. *The Extra Girl*. Directed by F. Richard Jones. Performances by Mabel Normand, Richard Graves, and George Nichols, Mack Sennett Comedies, 1923.
6. "She will continue in comedy roles…" *New York Times,* 10 June 1925.
7. "Gossip Of The Rialto." *The New York Times,* 13 Sep 1925, p. 205.

8. Mabel Normand Seen As Star At Tellers." *The Brooklyn Daily Eagle,* 15 Sep 1925, p.12
9. Drenier, Nigel, host. "All About Aunt Mabel." *Modern Times Podcast*, episode 10, Nigel Drenier, Sept. 2015. https://www.youtube.com/watch?v=SwPF7OoQ15s&t=17s
10. "Plays And Players." *The Expositor,* 16 Oct 1925, p. 12.

Hal Roach

1. "Jay Leno chats to 100 year old Laurel & Hardy Producer Hal Roach - 1992." *YouTube,* Uploaded by the Laurel and Hardy Forum, 2014, https://www.youtube.com/watch?v=ap-eBNB0ieM&t=9s
2. "ROACH: Movie Pioneer, Comedy King, Dies at 100." *The Los Angeles Times,* 03 Nov 1992, p. 380.
3. "The Roach MGM Talkies." *The Lucky Corner,* 3 Jan 2005, http://theluckycorner.com/

After The Tempest

1. Drenier, Nigel, host. "All About Aunt Mabel." *Modern Times Podcast*, episode 10, Nigel Drenier, Sept. 2015. https://www.youtube.com/watch?v=SwPF7OoQ15s&t=17s
2. Sidney Sutherland. "Madcap Mabel Normand." *Liberty Magazine*, 11 Oct 1930.
3. Mary Pickford. April 1926
4. *Los Angeles Times,* (n.d.).

Stan Laurel And Oliver Hardy

1. Jeremy Armstrong. "Stan Laurel's heartbreak at Oliver Hardy's death revealed in letters up for auction." *The Mirror,* 9 Sep 2015.
2. Martin Chilton. "Laurel and Hardy: Two angels of our time." *The Independent,* 04 Jan 2019, *https://www.independent.co.uk/*

arts-entertainment/films/features/laurel-and-hardy-stan-and-ollie-film-steve-coogan-john-c-reilly-london-film-festival-a8580421.html

3. Art Berman. "Film Comedian Stan Laurel, 74, Dies at Home." *The Los Angeles Times,* 24 Feb 1965, p. 1.
4. "Oliver Hardy, Film Comedy Star, Dies." *The San Francisco Examiner*, 08 Aug 1957, p.9

The Final Films

1. Hal Roach. "The greatest woman comedienne of all time," (n.d.).
2. *Raggedy Rose.* Directed by Richard Wallace. Performances by Mabel Normand and Jimmy Finlayson, Hal Roach Studios, 1926.
3. *The Nickel Hopper.* Directed by F. Richard Jones. Performances by Mabel Normand, Boris Karloff, and Oliver Hardy. Hal Roach Studios, 1926.
4. *Should Men Walk Home?* Directed by Leo McCarey. Performances by Mabel Normand, Oliver Hardy, and Creighton Hale, Hal Roach Studios, 1927.
5. *Anything Once!* Directed by Richard Jones. Performances by Mabel Normand, and Jimmy Finlayson, Hal Roach Studios, 1927.
6. *One Hour Married.* Directed by Jerome Strong. Performances by Mabel Normand, Creighton Hale, and Jimmy Finlayson, Hal Roach Studios, 1927.
7. Sidney Sutherland. "Madcap Mabel Normand." *Liberty Magazine*, 11 Oct 1930.

Lew Cody

1. Elizabeth Peltret. "Lewis Cody, H. V." *Motion Picture Magazine,* Feb 1920, p. 19.

2. Sidney Sutherland. "Madcap Mabel Normand." *Liberty Magazine*, 11 Oct 1930.
3. "Lew Cody Dies While Sleeping." *The Los Angeles Times,* 1 June 1934, p. 2.

Marriage

1. Sidney Sutherland. "Madcap Mabel Normand." *Liberty Magazine*, 11 Oct 1930.

Sydney Sutherland

1. "The Chase of Fire Raid." *Rat Patrol*. Tom Gries, season 1, episode 1, Mirisch Rich Productions, and Tom Gries Productions, 12 Sep 1966.
2. *The Russians are Coming the Russians are Coming*. Directed by Norman Jewison. Performances by Carl Reiner, Eva Marie Saint, and Alan Arkin, The Mirisch Corporation, 25 May 1966.
3. *The Cisco Kid.* ZIF Television Programs.
4. *Bat Masterson.* ZIF Television Programs.
5. *Rendezvous In Space.* Directed by Frank Capra. Performances by Marcia McBroom, Mel Blanc, and Jim Backus, Frank Capra Productions, 10 Sep 1964.
6. "Bob Clampett's 'A Tale Of Two Kitties' 1942." *Cartoon Research,* 29 APR 2015, https://cartoonresearch.com/index.php/bob-clampetts-a-tale-of-two-kitties-1942/
7. Sidney Sutherland. "Madcap Mabel Normand." *Liberty Magazine*, 1930.
8. "The LIBERTY Magazine article is the nearest thing…", Marilyn Slater, n.d.

The Long Fight

1. Sidney Sutherland. "Madcap Mabel Normand." *Liberty Magazine*, 11 Oct 1930.

2. Anita Garvin. "Interview with Anita Garvin." Interviewed by William Thomas Sherman, *Mabel Normand A Source Book to Her Life and Films Vol 7),* Guy Jones Publishing, 2006, pp. 435-437. https://www.angelfire.com/mn/hp/MNSB7.pdf
3. Drenier, Nigel, host. "All About Aunt Mabel." *Modern Times Podcast*, episode 10, Nigel Drenier, Sept. 2015. https://www.youtube.com/watch?v=SwPF7OoQ15s&t=17s
4. Grace Kingsley, *Los Angeles Times,* 1927.
5. "Mabel Normand Not in Danger." *Los Angeles Evening Post-Record,* 03 Aug 1927, p.1.
6. "Movie Star Here." *Chicago Tribune,* 9 Oct 1927, p. 17.
7. "Lew and Mabel To Join Houses." *Los Angeles Record,* 2 Dec 1927.
8. George Shaffer. "Mabel Normand Announces She Will Sue Cody." *Chicago Tribune,* 26 Feb 1928. P. 7.
9. "In 1929 Mabel was ill…", Marilyn Slater, (n.d.).
10. Myra Nye. "Honor Doris Deane Arbuckle." *The Los Angeles Times*, 20 Jan 1929, p. 60.
11. "The Has-Beens Of Hollywood." *Daily News,* 6 Jan 1929.
12. Michael Ventura "Funny Lady." *Los Angeles Magazine*, 1 June 2009, pp. 62-64.
13. "A Three Star Constellation." *Los Angeles Times,* 24 Feb 1929. p. 55.
14. Peggy Ballard. "Keeping Tragedy From Film Mates." *Los Angeles Evening Post-Record,* 19 Mar 1929. P. 1.
15. "Actress' Condition Grave." *The Los Angeles Times,* 20 Mar 1929, p. 23

Frances Pottenger

1. "Physician Tells of Evidence That Smog Shortens Lives." *The Los Angeles Times,* 13 Oct 1953, p. 31.

2. "Doctor Pottenger, Tuberculosis Expert, Dies." *The Los Angeles Times,* 11 Jun 1961 p. 73.
3. Jim Wigton. "The Pottenger Sanatorium." *The Monrovia Patch,* 18 June 2011, https://patch.com/california/monrovia/the-pottenger-sanatorium
4. "F.M. Pottenger, Famed TB Specialist, Dies." *Daily News-Post,* 12 Jun 1961, pp. 1-2.

Those Going About Their Everyday Lives

1. Herbert Howe. "Hollywood's Hall of Fame: Mabel Normand" *New Movie Magazine,* https://www.silentera.com/taylorology/issues/Taylor88.txt
2. "Even Dr. Francis Pottenger shielded Mabel…," Marilyn Slater, n.d.
3. "Ill Actress Worse." *The Philadelphia Inquirer,* 19 Dec 1929, p.2
4. "Mabel Normand Dying." *Sunday Mercury,* 12 Jan 1930, p. 6.
5. "MABEL NORMAND VERY ILL." *The New York Times, 7 Feb 1930*, p. 16.
6. Ventura, Michael. "Funny Lady." *Los Angeles Magazine*, 1 June 2009, pp. 62-64.
7. Kingsley, Grace. "Romping Through Hollywood." *The Los Angeles Times,* 06 Apr 1930, p. 103.
8. "Biography." *Mabel Normand Estate.* https://mabelenormand.com/about-mabel/legend/

Vodafone WiFiCall
18:22
28%
1 of 2
Brown Brothers

T-Mobile
10:27 PM
68%
Search in WISHED ON...
About
Discussion
Photos
File
MOTION.PICTURE.
JANUARY
MAGAZINE
25 cts
Mabel Normand

A MABEL
NORMAND
WEEKEND

FEATURE FILM CO.
MABEL NORMAND

-30-

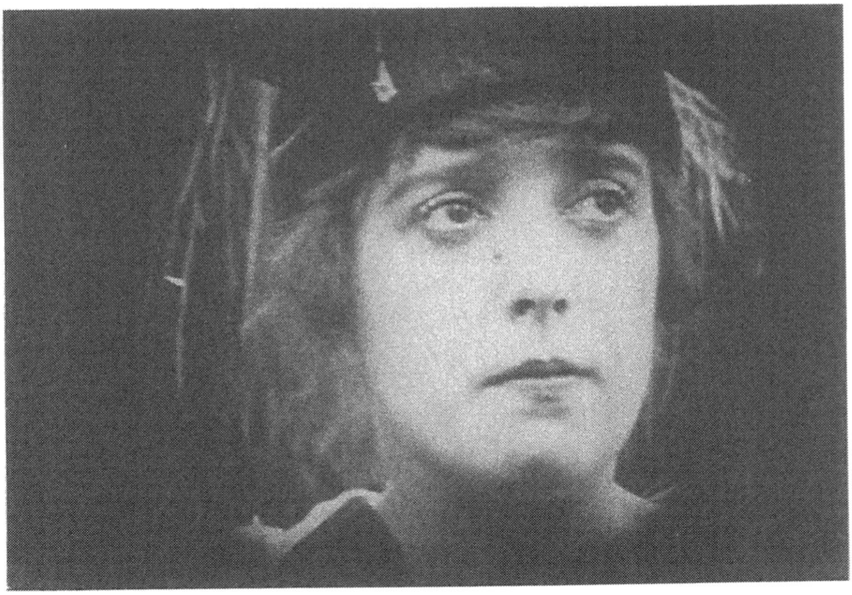

ERZBERGER ASSASSINATED; SHOT 12 TIMES

Photograph © by E. O. Hoppe

MABEL NORMAND

Mabel Normand has returned from her latest European holiday. Whenever Mabel seeks a vacation, she books passage on the first steamer for Paris. She has returned this time to begin work immediately upon a new Mack Sennett production which will follow the release of "Suzanne"

Picture Show

A wonderful face!
Mabel Normand is the most liberally imitated comedienne in the world-but do you know of one actress who can even remotely approach her?
'Pinto' reveals her in a thousand entrancing moods.
SAMUEL GOLDWYN PRESENTS
MABEL NORMAND
PINTO
WRITTEN AND DIRECTED BY VICTOR SCHERTZINGER
GOLDWYN PICTVRES CORPORATION

Made in the USA
Columbia, SC
29 October 2024

45229588R00174